Kathy Griffin's
Celebrity Run-Ins

Also by Kathy Griffin

Official Book Club Selection

(A Memoir According to Kathy Griffin)

Kathy Griffin's
Celebrity Run-Ins

{ My A-Z Index }

KATHY GRIFFIN

FLATIRON
BOOKS
NEW YORK

KATHY GRIFFIN'S CELEBRITY RUN-INS. Copyright © 2016 by Kathy Griffin. All rights reserved. Printed in the United States of America. For information, address Flatiron Books, 175 Fifth Avenue, New York, N.Y. 10010.

www.flatironbooks.com

Designed by James Sinclair

The Library of Congress Cataloging-in-Publication Data is available upon request.

ISBN 978-1-250-13432-5 (Target Edition)

Our books may be purchased in bulk for promotional, educational, or business use. Please contact your local bookseller or the Macmillan Corporate and Premium Sales Department at 1-800-221-7945, extension 5442, or by e-mail at MacmillanSpecialMarkets@macmillan.com.

Target Edition: November 2016

10 9 8 7 6 5 4 3 2 1

I proudly dedicate this book to Lil Wayne, Drake, Nicki Minaj, Tyga, Birdman, DJ Khaled, Rich Homie Quan, Celine Dion, Young Thug, and everyone in my Cash Money Records family.

"Cash money for life."

Kathy Griffin's
Celebrity Run-Ins

Can't get enough?

Exclusive bonus material for Target readers is

included at the end of the book!

Dear Lucky Reader:

— OR —

Dear Famous Person Who Is Wildly Scanning This Book to See If You Are Mentioned:

Are you prepared to have your mind blown?

My purpose in writing this book is not only to make you laugh, but also to share with you some of my intimate moments with icons and celebrities in situations where I had to pinch myself and ask, *Is this really happening?* Some of these stories are jaw-droppers, while others are touching. Some of Hollywood's most intriguing personal relationships happen authentically and by chance; others are the result of my adorable and charming "chase and pursue" philosophy. The stories I tell are up close and personal, and hopefully you will be as riveted reading about them as I was when I lived them.

It's been several years since my last book, which became a #1 *New York Times* bestseller, so I've been waiting for a *sign*. I'm not a religious person, but one night that sign came to me when I was watching . . . *Straight Outta Compton* from my hotel room at the Trump International Hotel & Tower in New York City. Just take that all in.

While watching the film, I turned to my boyfriend, Randy, and casually said, "Most people probably don't know that I know four of the people portrayed in this film." I met Tupac Shakur backstage at a taping of a sketch television show I was working on, where I watched him struggle to read. That was astonishing to me! Dr. Dre directed me in the music video for Eminem's "The Real Slim Shady." I made out with Snoop Dogg as part of a sketch when I hosted the Billboard Music Awards. Oh, and I have cuddled with Suge Knight. Cuddled. Do I have your attention yet?

The reason I mention the Trump International Hotel & Tower is that it may surprise many of my longtime and loyal fans that I have not only met four people portrayed in *Straight Outta Compton* but that I actually know Donald Trump as well. (Unfortunately, I have met him several times.) One time, I shared the backseat of a golf cart with Liza Minnelli, and the driver was none other than the Donald. Are you getting the idea?

This book is a total departure for me, part spoof of an old-fashioned dictionary and part shocking tidbits I have never uttered publicly. I will give you an A to Z HUMOROUS and PERSONAL encyclopedia of my unique encounters with people that you know I know as well as people you couldn't have imagined your Kathy Griffin would ever know. I have officially turned into that person who has pretty much met EVERYBODY!

A word about my use of quotation marks in this book. While my encounters with the glorious personalities described in this book are very real, or surreal as the case may be, I did not tape or transcribe any conversations. So the use of quotation marks does not mean that I am quoting anyone verbatim, and instead it means that I am giving you the gist of the dialogue to the best of my recollection.

You'll find names from the worlds of music (Britney Spears spanked me!), TV (I'm the only person who doesn't love Jon Hamm), movies (what's Jack Nicholson like at a dinner party?), sports (I put the beast in Beast Mode!), dogs (I love dogs), politics (Speaker Nancy Pelosi had my back at a party), and even author Salman Rushdie (don't worry, that story includes Cher). You know me as someone who has built a career telling personal and long-form stories about a range of topics from my own up-close and personal run-ins with the famous and the infamous and, of course, have seen me on television sharing the stage and screen with just about everyone you've ever heard of. So many that I had to take some of them from the index in my brain and pass them on to you lucky bastards.

Can you handle it?

Kathy Griffin

ALLEN, WOODY

Director, Writer, Actor

I was seated next to him at a small dinner party in November of 2014.

First impressions: He's quite feeble in person. He mumbles. Obviously, as he has been so swirled in controversy, I had my eyes on him the whole evening. The two takeaways are as follows: First, 95 percent of my time spent near him that evening was shockingly boring. And second, he said a couple of things that were genuinely shocking.

Prior to the dinner, I expressed my discomfort regarding how to handle myself in Allen's presence. Let's just say that while professionally I'm a fan, personally . . . I believe Mia, Dylan, and Ronan. Get it? I knew you would.

When he walked in with his wife Soon-Yi, he announced, "I'm Woody, and this is my child bride!"

Hmmm, okay, okay, that was a pretty upfront opening joke, I thought. I do love a great opener from a comic. Maybe he'll have a sense of humor about everything in his life and be as candid about it as he was with that entrance line.

We all sat down, and the bitter truth was that his child bride remark would be his opening and closing joke. I had questions about his career, like his use of stand-up comedians in various roles (Louis CK, Andrew Dice Clay, Lily Tomlin). I asked him, "What was it like directing stand-up comics as opposed to traditional actors?" He seemed perplexed by this question. I mentioned that Louis CK was great in *Blue Jas-*

mine, and it was as if he had just been reminded that Louis CK was in *Blue Jasmine*. I wouldn't stop, throwing the rod and reel and trying to hook him with any of twenty different topics related to his incredible body of work and all the brilliant people he's worked with, but he sounded more engaged talking about his soup or chicken pot pie, neither of which were particularly funny or interesting. How was I going to get anything insightful out of this living legend?

He did describe a typical day to me as essentially getting up, eating, writing, and falling asleep before the end of a Knicks game on television. Reality shows were a no-go as a topic. "Smart" television didn't work. (Supposedly friends with Liev Schreiber, he said he'd never seen a single *Ray Donovan*.) At the end of my rope, I decided to give up on my fishing expedition and just pretend HE was completely up on MY act regarding pop culture and celebrities and ask him about things he surely had no clue about. At least I was going to make it fun on my end.

I turned to him: "So, Woody, you obviously asked to be seated next to me to gossip about everything going on with Kylie Jenner and Miley Cyrus these days." I was ready to let fly with another name when he responded after a beat that he'd seen every episode of *Hannah Montana*. Yeah. I'll let that sink in a bit. Every episode . . . of *Hannah Montana* on the Disney Channel. Not only that, he continued by expressing concern about what had happened to Miley regarding her "current rebellious phase." Yeah. Pick your jaw up off the floor and let that nestle somewhere uncomfortably in your stomach. As I was trying to digest this information—Woody's seen every episode of *Hannah Montana*—the conversation actually morphed into current events. By the time I'd fully recovered from the unexpected Miley bombshell, the dinner was coming to a close. Yes, I know Woody Allen went on to cast Miley in an Amazon series.

At the end, get ready, Woody said to me with what seemed to be complete sincerity, "And now I have to watch my friend Bill Cosby get railroaded by the media."

ABRAMS, J. J.
Professional Nerd, Needs a Hit

Okay, all you straight male geeks and straight boyfriends/ husbands secretly leafing through this in the bookstore or sneaking a peek while your better half (because she's a fan of mine) is out of the room: guess what? I'm onto you. I put Your Precious J. J. Abrams in here so I could talk to you directly. Put your robot toys away and turn off your damn Ashley Madison browsing and wise up! Now to your good stuff: Your Precious J. J. was my student at the LA impro- visational theater the Groundlings before anyone knew who he was. We even used to double-date, and no, that doesn't mean Your Precious J. J. got anywhere near my girl parts. It meant we were the third wheels in trying to get his buddy Greg Grunberg to find true love with my friend Nancy Dye. That connection never happened, but since J. J. went on to marry someone named Katie, which is pretty much the same as Kathy, it's obvious he's still in love with me. (Deal with it.)

The best thing about knowing J. J. back in the day—before he became a screenwriting wunderkind in his twenties, and then his brain and talent became clouded with meaningless shit happening in space—was that he used to work for his

TV producer dad, Gerald W. Abrams, at his company Phoe-nix Entertainment Group as the phone girl. That's right, *the phone girl*.

I'd call him there just to bust his balls. *Ring ring.* "Phoe-nix."

"It's Kath. I'll take a coffee, black, two cubes. Have it on my desk in five. Do you have a tight dress on today?"

I called him "Junior Ger," even though he wasn't—techni-cally speaking—a junior. I even call him "Junior Ger" to this day, even though he's insanely wealthy and influential and a big deal with galaxy-worshiping losers like you. I consider it my duty to give him shit about his big movie-directing jobs. (In December of 2015, I referred to his "new Star Trek" movie, and he wrote back, "It's Star WARS!!!!" Isn't that cute?)

I also regularly chastise him for not making movies for Lifetime, since they're actually about important topics like suburban sexting and Christmas weddings. Stop almost-vomiting and get this: he's so super nice to me, *anyway*, that he routinely sends me e-mails saying he hopes I'm doing well, to give his love to my mom, Maggie, and after my last New Year's telecast, wrote the sweetest note in which he said, "Man, nobody can carry four and a half hours of live like you." That means he's watching *me* on New Year's and not wasting his time with a movie about some dumb shoot-out on a planet made of lucite or whatever. No, I haven't seen *Star Trek: The Fierce Awakens* yet—yeah, I know, it's not the title, but I'm sure it's good. J. J. was always talented, but *When Friendship Kills* good? I just don't know if he has the chops for Lifetime just yet.

ALLEY, KIRSTIE

Actress, Scientologist, Fluctuator

I've known Kirstie a while. She even cast me on her TV Land show, playing myself, and we had fun. But I'll always cherish the moment we shared backstage at the *Today Show*.

She had, yet again, secured another contract with Jenny Craig and had lost fifty pounds. So she was skinny Kirstie once more. (Not my favorite Kirstie, by the way, if anyone cares.) We were in the wings together—I was scheduled to go on after her—and whenever she sees me, she calls me "Kathygriffin!" She talks fast. This time she decided to play the nervous celeb.

"What are you gonna say about me NOW, Kathygriffin! God only KNOWS what you're gonna put in your comedy routine NOW, Kathygriffin!"

So I sat next to her, and when she pulled out her iPhone, I noticed that it had a big spiderweb of cracks. I said, "Well, your cracked iPhone isn't helping. My God, you're Kirstie Alley. You can afford to have one of your assistants or martians from your religion get you a new iPhone before Matt Lauer sees it. Because guess what the first sign of crazy is? A CRACKED IPHONE." Admit it, whenever you see a friend with a cracked iPhone, you instinctively think, *Hmm, everything okay at home?*

She immediately began yammering, "Ooooh, why did I let Kathygriffin see my cracked iPhone! Grrrr!" So she turned it on, and the first thing I see is the weather app showing the temperature in fricking Clearwater, Florida, for the next seven days (in case you didn't know, Clearwater is the hub of Scientology). Not the weather where she lives, mind you, but where her nutty religion operates.

I said, "Wow, you're in deep, babe. You have to know the weather in Clearwater on your cracked iPhone every minute? If you don't, do you clean toilets for a month?" Kirstie watched my lips move, but I'm pretty sure she doesn't pay attention to anything I say anymore, period. She had an exasperated look on her face and may have uttered a slight sigh of despair, but she was in game mode for her interview. I got the impression she neither had the time nor the inclination for any lengthy banter with me at that moment. Get 'em when they're vulnerable.

I don't censor myself around the likes of a Sci-Ti like Kirstie Alley anymore. What's the point, really? She just guffaws along with it now. (When you're in a cult that makes you do manual labor for a week or whatever to atone, what Kathy Griffin has to say is seriously not your biggest issue.)

ANDERSON, PAMELA
Baywatch Babe, Platinum Canadian

Many people assume that celebrities all know each other, and there's a slight truth there in that two famous people who've never met but who obviously know about the other because they're famous can oftentimes jump right into a familiar-sounding rapport. In my case, when I'm presented with the chance to talk to a celebrity, I do what I call "pulling a Pam." No, not that, you perverts. It comes from this:

One night, at a fund-raiser hosted by VH1 at the trendy (now closed) Hollywood eatery Geisha House, I was looking for a place to sit and noticed Pam Anderson and Kid Rock in a booth. It must have been the one happy day in their tabloid-covered, tumultuous relationship. Remember, they did get married on a yacht, and Pam was in a bikini, wearing a sailor cap. I'm not sure if Kid Rock was wearing Confederate flag boxers or briefs. Anyway, there they were, and I said to myself, *Oh, Pam's here; I'll go sit with them!* I squeezed in next to her and said, "Pam?!"

She said, "Oh, hi, Kathy. Good to see you!"

We hugged.

She said, "Do you know Bob?"

I said, "Of course! Hi, Bob!"

Kid Rock looked at me and muttered, "Hey, Kathy."

We had a perfectly pleasant evening, and as I went home, I thought, *Wait a minute, I've never met her or Bob!* In my twisted mind, I had taken the fact that Pam and I share a business manager as a form of knowing her. Well, I knew her about as well as *you* know Pam Anderson, and you certainly wouldn't walk up to her and say, "Pam?!" (What do I know? Maybe you would.) I was unconsciously playing a form of that celebrities-know-each-other game. I'd closed some formality in my head—we share a CPA, we're pals!—so I could just go, "Hi, Pam! Hi, Bob!" I mean, I didn't know Kid Rock went by "Bob." (His name is Robert James Ritchie, which would not have been nearly as effective opening the rap megahit "Bawitdaba.") But since nothing bad happened—Pam and Bob didn't kick me out of that booth—I now think "pulling a Pam" is a perfectly reasonable way to insert myself into the orbit of a famous person I want to meet. Let's play this hand out: *"Barack?!" "Your Holiness?!" "Malala?!* Great to see you again!"

BALDWIN, ALEC
Actor, Intellectual, Joshua Rush from Knots Landing

I have so much gratitude for *Hollywood Squares* I can't even quantify it. Don't be hatin' on that show. How else are you guaranteed to meet eight celebrities a week? Whoopi Goldberg was the center square for a lot of the tapings I did, because the center square is reserved for the biggest star. One time I did it, though, Alec was the center square, and when I met him, he initiated what I now call the A-List Celebrity Preemptive Strike.

The nine of us were backstage, waiting to be introduced so we could walk out and climb the rickety ladder into our box. I felt as if it were the same ladder Paul Lynde may have vomited on decades earlier. But I digress.

Suddenly, Alec pulled me aside. It's already disarming enough when a gorgeous guy grabs you and whispers in your ear. But then he said in that delicious baritone of his, "I think you are both one of the *sexiest* ladies out there and one of the *funniest*. You got me." He laid it on thick. Well, of course I melted like butter. But then I realized, *Hey! He thinks by saying that I won't turn anything he does into material!* So I pulled myself together and said, "Thanks, but . . . you're still in the act."

Now, when I see him, he practically noogies me. We make

no pretense about it. I go, "Baldy! What's up?"

He says something like, "Hey, the corner's missing a hooker—you're late!" He doesn't even try to be a seductive gentleman. He's like, "Honey, how much you make? What's the market price for between the legs?" It's all horrible, but he's so funny about it, and so crazy smart, and such a good actor, I can't be offended. It's certainly not lost on me that he's probably given that exact come-on to countless women for various reasons. In my case, he was a good-looking actor trying to use his charm to score some points and hopefully keep me from skewering him. Instead, he gave me the phrase "the Alec Baldwin Preemptive Strike." Take that, Situation Room.

BARRYMORE, DREW
Actress, Barrymore

This is one of the examples I often give about how I walk the line between deepening a friendship with a celebrity or not. Several years ago during the years of *My Life on the D-List*, out of the blue, I got a call from Drew's gay assistant (who must have gotten my number from the Gay Phone Book), letting me know that Drew was having a theme party and I was invited. It was at her home, which I remember thinking was surprising: I was being invited to an A-lister's house. But she was apparently a fan or at least didn't loathe me, so I was excited. Excited but apprehensive. After all, it would be packed with stars, possibly from my act, and if I were to go to her party, whatever happened there wouldn't stay there.

This was, if I remember correctly, an '80s prom theme, and

I vowed to wear as little as possible that was theme-oriented. I probably had on a cardboard tiara. Areas were cordoned off to prevent snoopers like me, which was a bummer because I wanted a tour. Anyway, the celebrities were indeed there, including Parker Posey, Molly Shannon, Eva Mendes, too many to remember. Courtney Love was there with her "prom date," the famous photographer David LaChapelle. It made me not want to leave, I can tell you that.

Well, eventually Drew came up to me and said, "Oh, I'm so glad you came."

I said, "I'm surprised you're letting me loose around all these celebrities!"

She said, "Look, we should have dinner. I love you! This is a big party, but I have these eight-person dinner parties, and I'd love for you to come. We hate all the same people!"

I said, "Yes, but I actually say their names on television."

Drew gave a quick giggle and turned and waved to Parker Posey. She was in full-on hostess mode. While I appreciated her declaration that we hated all the same people, I actually hear that a lot from celebrities. What they don't realize is due to my stand-up comedy disorder, when I am dishing the dirt with someone, whether it be my mom, Maggie, or Drew Barrymore, my brain processes everything we talk about as being potential material for my act. It's just how my brain works.

Now when I run into her, she's still super friendly, but I never got that dinner invite, and I think we'd both agree it was the best outcome for both of us.

———

BEATTY, WARREN
Shampoo, Rinse & Repeat

I've been invited to birthday parties, and I've been invited to *birthday parties!* At Jane Fonda's epic seventy-fifth birthday, I knew it was going to be wall-to-wall legends, so I hoped and prayed my table would be well stocked with screen legends. At catered parties like these, in which you can choose where to sit, I like to go for the one near the buffet table. That way, I basically have a ringside seat because, hey, everyone has to eat at some point.

And then Barbra Streisand walked in. For me, even in this room filled with celebrities, Barbra Streisand's presence alone conjures three thoughts immediately: she is unapproachable, she's royalty to me, and yet, when I looked at her, she is a real person. And I almost fainted when she sat her real person ass down at my table. Gasp! Eva Longoria, who I've known for years and who has also seen me in action, was seated next to me, and she gave me a look she likes to give in social situations in which she's worried about my behavior—a serious stare that says, "Behave, it's Streisand." I just said to Eva, "I know, I know."

Catherine Keener was also at our table, so the three of us started up some easy chatting, and what do you know, Streisand threw out a "Hello." Now that that gate had been opened, I darted in. Look, it's not like I taped this conversation or something; just know that what follows is to the best of my recollection.

"Look, Barbra," I said. "Here's the thing. I know you want to sing 'People' and 'Happy Days Are Here Again' and 'Papa, Can You Hear Me?' but how about if we all just get the night *off* for once. I know you only show up at these parties if you can sing for free, and then you make us wait, and then we have to resort to begging and reassuring you that you'll be just fine without the band, but for God's sake, honey, gimme a minute before we have to get you up on this cocktail table so you can start your *Funny Girl* medley."

And then I paused.

And then fear set in.

Eva morphed her warning face into a much more threatening "You're going to die" look. But Streisand burst out laughing. "Oh, sh-uah [in full Streisand Brooklyn accent], you know me!"

I turned to Eva, my eyes and triumphant smile saying, *Problem?*

Then Warren Beatty strolled up looking like the movie star that he is. I couldn't resist acting like I knew him by simply saying, "Beatty!?! Hello there!"

He was wearing jeans and a shirt as if he had just stepped off of the set of *Shampoo*, albeit thirty years later but just as gorgeous, still rocking the feathered hair. He asked, "What's going on at this table?"

"Well," I said, "Barbra's rehashing that story about how you always claim to have hooked up with her in the back of a car."

Beatty took the bait. "I thought we did."

Barbra started shaking her head. "Warren, I'm not going to have this fight with you again. We nev-ah hooked up."

"Noooo, Barbra, I think we did," Beatty said. "I think we were coming back from that little club in the Catskills . . ."

I realized these two have probably known each other since the early '60s. He's going waaaaay back, and he's bringing up details like it all happened yesterday.

"I think there was a time when you got a little handsy in the backseat," he said, and Streisand's casually eating, adding little "No, Warren"s.

Then fricking Sean Penn appeared, and I said, "Penn?!?!? Warren's bragging about his conquests. When are you going to start rattling off your list?"

"Well, I'm not going to start with my ex-wife," he said.

"That was your fuckup," I agreed, and he chuckled.

In all seriousness, though, the rapport between Beatty and Streisand was absolutely adorable, with him trying to start a rumor that he'd banged her—because that would only make him look good—and her gently beating back his insistent remarks like an expert fencer. And Penn's presence officially made us "the cool table" for a brief shining moment. It might have been Jane's birthday party, but all I kept thinking was *Happy birthday to me!*

BYNES, AMANDA
Actress, Person of Interest

In 2005, my friend Lance Bass produced a movie called *Love Wrecked*, a cute romantic comedy in which he asked me to take a small role. The movie's big get was Amanda Bynes, who at the time was trying to break out of the tween TV world and into features that would allow her to grow up and be a sexy twentysomething. I remember Lance saying her bikini-clad screen test went well and that she "was all grown up now." (I did not get a screen test in a bikini, incidentally, though I asked for one forty-two days in a row.)

The movie also starred Jonathan Bennett, Chris Carmack (then on *The O.C.*), and Jamie-Lynn Sigler (riding high from *The Sopranos*) and was directed by Randal Kleiser (*Grease*, *The Blue Lagoon*). We were going to be spending three weeks in the beachy Dominican Republic—the movie took place mostly at a resort—and Lance promised a good time. Knowing his social director skills, I trusted him, and it was indeed fun. Jamie-Lynn was put up in a great pad, so her place became the gathering house.

I remember once sitting in that house's master bedroom, in front of an old-fashioned vanity mirror, and Amanda and Jamie-Lynn stormed in, all high energy and cute, and started asking about face-lifts and plastic surgery. Feeling a little like a den mother, I said something along the lines of how it was okay to get a little work now and then, but that neither of them had the facial structure that would ever require serious face work. I remember them dancing around the house afterward, saying, "Kathy Griffin says we don't need face work! Kathy Griffin says we don't need face work! And she knows all about that!" It's good to be the king.

Amanda's parents and sister were there, and they all stayed in an incredible house with a housekeeper, a chef, and a pool. We only ever really hung out there maybe twice. But what I recall is that Amanda was the consummate young professional, working long days and being all business.

The thing that struck me about her had to do with a local village puppy she took in for the duration of the shoot. I went over to her house one day, and she introduced me to a six- to eight-week-old puppy. "Have you met Peanut Butter?"

I said, "Uh, no. How did you get a dog into the country? Aren't there quarantine laws?"

She explained that Peanut Butter was a stray, and she seemed happy to have an adorable puppy staying with her.

I said, "Great." Hey, dogs are wonderful to have around and have been known to calm many a stressed-out actor at the end of a long day.

Amanda kept Peanut Butter at her rented mansion while she shot all day, and I remember how attentive Amanda and her family were toward the dog. It was all about Peanut Butter. Then, after my last day on the movie, I said good-bye to Amanda and asked, "So how are you going to get Peanut Butter from the Dominican Republic to your house in Hollywood?"

She told me she was leaving Peanut Butter there. Hmmm.

"Well, who's going to take care of that eight-week-old puppy?" I asked.

She told me she had left Peanut Butter with the housekeeper.

I should have said something to broaden her animal sympathies a bit. Maybe something like, "Amanda, what do you think is really going to happen to Peanut Butter? Do you really think the temporary housekeeping hired for a movie is going to continue nurturing Peanut Butter for the rest of his life? Don't you think that dog's maybe headed straight for a puppy mill?" When I brought this up to her in a softer way, it didn't seem as if this question had occurred to her. That was a little bit of a red flag for me, that you could love and care for and feed and bond with a puppy for weeks and then just leave it behind for the housekeeper, which, let's be real, probably wasn't going to continue living in that fancy house. So yeah, at the time: a fun girl, hard worker, and talented actress, but dog rescuers might need to put her on a watch list in Santo Domingo. As for Peanut Butter, his whereabouts are unknown.

CHER
Singer, Actress, Cher

"You're going to get a call from Cher."

That was Rosie O'Donnell's phone call to me. Just a few days prior, Rosie had taken me backstage at Caesars in Las Vegas to meet the one-of-a-kind superstar. When you meet someone who is not only one of the most famous people on the

planet, but also famous in part for the way he or she looks and presents himself or herself, you tend to give that person the once-over. That's right. Little freckly, pale Kathleen Mary Griffin from Forest Park, Illinois, is standing next to Cher. And she did not disappoint.

Cher was in her full "Just Like Jesse James" getup: blond wig, Navajo belt, and a puffy shirt. Believe it or not, when I meet a star of this magnitude, sometimes I am not the obnoxious trouble starter that you may think I would be. On this night, I was happy to sit back and observe. We sat on a cozy sectional backstage in her dressing room. I was impressed by how quickly Cher was able to go from "show mode" into "real person mode."

I know you are laughing at the idea that I just called Cher a real person. But damn it, she was relaxed, laughing, and eager to chat about politics, touring, and a little showbiz gossip on the side. There's something I'm gonna call the "Cher Factor," not to be confused with anything resembling the Fox News Bill O'Reilly show, as Cher would hate that, which means you really can't forget that it's Cher when you are in her presence. It was a great way to meet Cher and spend some time with her. But now she was going to call?

"Oh God. Did I say something?" I asked Rosie.

She said no, that Cher wanted my number because she wanted to get together. "Just remember, no matter what, she's always fucking Cher." Many years into my friendship with Cher, I can tell you that Rosie was right in the BEST possible way.

Sure enough, my phone rings, and someone was calling me doing a really good Cher impression. "Kathleen? This is Cher."

To which I responded, "Um, yeah, hi, Cher. This is awkward. I'm too famous for you to call my cell phone directly. Would you mind having your assistant call my agent first?"

She laughed, and a friendship was born.

The first time Cher invited me to hang out with her and watch a movie at her house—I'm sorry, her castle—she instituted the signature Cher policy: "Okay so, if you come over to mah howse, it's a no-makeup-and-sweatpants kind of night.

I don't feel like getting all done up tonight even though Ahm fuckin' Cher!" (You must read this while keeping my Cher impression voice in your head.) To be friends with her is to know she is going to proclaim "I'm fucking Cher" several times in one sit-down.

Ever since that first phone call, I've always been cognizant of wanting to make her giggle. I believe I responded with "Well, I'm Kathy fucking Griffin, and I'll come over in my sweatpants, fine. I just don't want you to lose your shit when you see me arrive in my very expensive and paid-off Maserati."

Without missing a beat—and this is one of my favorite things to do with Cher; she returns the volley every time—she said, "Oh, okay, I'll alert the staff. There's a crazy bitch named Kathleen coming over." Cher calls me by my baptismal name.

Look, there's so much I can tell you about Cher, and I know you want to hear everything, but let's just get to my arrival into her bedroom. I can hear her now, "Bitch, you did NOT just tell people you were taking them to mah bedroom. Kathleeeeeen!" Let's turn back time, shall we?

There I am holding a gift bag in one hand and my phone in the other. I was left to wander her Cher Vatican compound, yelling, "Cher? Cher? Where are you?" at the top of my lungs. "It's me, Dorothy, I'm here to see *The Wizard of Oz*."

All of a sudden, I hear, "Kathleen, is that yew? I'm up here."

I walked up the stairs and was blinded by the reflection bouncing off her Academy Award and Golden Globe Award on the shelf outside her bedroom door. "I'm coming," I said. "I just didn't want the Oscar to hit me on the head on the way in."

I heard a "A-huh, ay-heh, uh-hah!" Cher's laugh is delicious. It's a little bit of a combination of a hacking cough and involuntary exhalations of joy.

I walked into her bedroom suite, which is her sanctuary and is also larger than most people's homes, and saw Cher in sweatpants and no makeup. Guess who is still very beautiful without makeup, has the body of a twenty-five-year-old, and loves a casual pair of sweatpants with a matching bedazzled lime-green hoodie?

Fuckin' Cher.

The first thing I noticed was her hair. It's real, thick, long black hair that is parted and halfway down her back. I said, "Nice wig. Very natural."

Her response: "This isn't a wig. My wigs are way better than this."

What? Her real hair is Cher Hair! And that's not the only thing that's real. She's real. Dare I say . . . normal? As normal as you can be when you are Cher calling C-SPAN at 3:00 in the morning as "Cher from Malibu."

I brought her a regift that night. You know, when someone gives you something, you leave it wrapped, give it to someone else, and tell them you bought it. I said, "Here. This is a regift. I don't even know what it is, but it's probably nice."

She said, "What's a regift?"

I laughed and asked her, "How did you survive all these years without my expert celebrity guidance?"

She responded with an "Ahm fuckin' Cher!"

Another time, Cher invited me over to (try to) watch a movie again. By the way, you can watch a movie with practically anybody, but I'll be honest, if I'm alone with Cher, I wanna talk! By now, Cher had become a Twitter darling, and that meant pictures were on the table. In response to our followers, we decided to live tweet our visit. You're welcome,

America and Indonesia. This was going to be a case of blonde leading the blonde, or for our purposes, the blind leading the dark lady. We may not be IT experts, but we knew this wasn't going to be a makeup-free night after all.

I said, "Our fans demand glitter right now! Do you happen to have any?"

Cher responded, "Yew know where to fihnd eht!"

Cher was referring to her bathroom. *Bathroom* is the wrong word—second bedroom with a sink in it. That's how big it is. I ran down the hall past the walk-in closet and attacked her makeup department. Yes, I use the word *department*, because hers rivals Sephora. I pull out one drawer, and it's *hundreds* of pairs of eyelashes in various sizes. I yell to Cher, "Do we want natural or full drag?"

At the same time, we both responded.

Cher: "Natural!"

Me: "Full drag!"

Perfect. I pulled out the drawer below the eyelashes as well as the drawer below that. I yelled, "Slight shimmer or full glitter?"

Once again we responded in unison.

Cher: "Shimmer!"

Me: "Full glitter!"

I reentered her room with two arms full of gay. Sorry, two arms full of LGBTQIAs.

I dumped the makeup on her nightstand and said, "Have you ever applied what's called 'theatrical makeup' before?"

"Jesus, Kathleen, you emptied mah sparkle drawer!"

"Don't worry, I've already tweeted to the world that you have something called a 'sparkle drawer.'"

"Yer ridiculous," Cher replied. "The light is better if yer laying down."

I blurted back, "I wanna look like a gypsy, a tramp, *and* a thief."

As Cher was doing my makeup, we alternated between giving each other crap for no reason and Cher dropping pearls of wisdom in her inimitable style. Stuff like, "No matter how old I get, I still feel twenty-one." That's always stuck with me because I feel the same way. We talked humor, politics, history, people we know in common, men (and when men are boys), what it's like to be a woman in show business, and a woman of a certain age in show business who is still fighting the good fight.

After Cher finished my makeup by proclaiming, "Okay, Kathleen, you're very sparkly," I replied, "Your turn!"

Cher rebuffed, "I'll do mah own. I'm not letting yew do mah makeup."

I said, "Fine. But gimme the full *Moonstruck*."

Once the final lash was applied, I raided her closet. She said jokingly, "Don't steal anything, bitch."

I said, "Just a couple of furs and two pairs of shoes, that's all."

We live-tweeted our photo shoot from her bedroom. She even let me wear her original fur vest from the "I Got You Babe" days with Sonny! Of course, the conversation went back to that era, and she said that whenever she hears a ghostly creak in the house, she'll go, "Oh, Sonny's here."

After hours of modeling, friendship, and fabulousness, I headed for the door to say good night. Cher had one more pearl of wisdom for me before I left. "Remember, Kathleen, no matter how old you get, your boyfriends can never be older than thirty-five." Words I live by.

Sometimes I reach out to Cher if I have said something in the press that will get me in trouble or let her know that I've done something once again that's "too far." She'll text back, "KEEPING Your COOL isn't your most fabulous attribute . . . BLOWING IT . . . IS."

By the way, we have never gotten to the movie. I kind of hope we never do.

COLFER, CHRIS
Actor, Author, Hope for Gay Mankind

Chris Colfer is so wonderfully talented, deserving of his Golden Globe Award and Emmy nominations for *Glee*, and I love that he's a bestselling author, too. But he and I share something that I especially cherish, which is we love people over eighty.

When he was a guest on my talk show, and I asked him if he could be on with anybody else, whom would he choose, he said, "Angela Lansbury." He openly mourned the loss of Elaine Stritch. This kid respects the greats and knows his classics—he's working on a frickin' Noël Coward biopic, for Chrissakes. I wasn't surprised, then, to show up at his house for a backyard pajama party movie screening, decorated with outdoor couches and a popcorn machine, and see octogenarian *Nebraska* star June Squibb wrapped up in a blanket.

"Hi, June!"

"Hi, Kathy!"

The movie that night was the memorable '80s campy wet dream, *Mommie Dearest*, with Faye Dunaway chomping everything in sight as legendary Hollywood diva Joan Crawford. Chris had indicated that talking to the screen and editorial comments were encouraged. I saw Jane Lynch there, so I walked up and said, "Jane, let's be the Greek chorus. These kids don't know what they're in for, so let's show them how it's done."

Jane and I had a blast yelling out *Mystery Science Theater*–style jokes. When it was over, Chris came up to us and with absolutely no irony in his voice said, "Can you believe that when this film came out, it got a Razzie?" (Razzies, or the Golden Raspberry Awards, are the notorious prizes given out each year for the worst films, and *Mommie Dearest* pretty much swept in 1981.) Jane and I looked at each other, then realized he wasn't kidding.

"Well, yeah, I can believe it," I said. "Because it's *terrible*."

Chris was having none of it. "I mean, is Faye Dunaway not *amazing*?"

Jane and I could not stop laughing, but you have to love Chris's enthusiasm, misguided as it was. He's probably hosted *Glitter* soirées where all his young pop culture–obsessed friends openly bemoaned it not having won a dozen Academy Awards. Incidentally, Chris is so charming, he probably could have gotten Faye to come and huddle with June. Then he would have had at least one more in his corner defending that hot mess of a movie.

COLLINS, JACKIE
Author, Confidante, Panther

I miss my friend Jackie. I just loved her. We became close after she appeared on *My Life on the D-List*, and the clincher was after I'd just gone through a horrible breakup and she

magnanimously agreed to give this sobbing redhead girl some time at her home. She became that kind of friend.

That day, she told me, "You can't have your heart broken by *one man*—darling, there's a man for every occasion! There's not a void that can't be filled with one or more. Don't feel you ever have to fall in love with just one person again. Fall in love with two, or three, or four people! Have boyfriends for different occasions. You could have a traveling boyfriend!"

Whether we were sitting one-on-one in her backyard or out on the town at Craig's restaurant, Jackie was always in full hair and makeup. She really did live the drama of her characters and was the real deal that way.

She was also my world-traveling friend. One night, I had a show in Melbourne, Australia, and she happened to be on a book tour. So, she came to my show, and we had dinner and laughed the night away down under. (Wait, I don't mean it like that, although I would if I were a genuine Santangelo.) Another time, my boyfriend and I went to Hawaii for Christmas. Coincidentally, Jac Jac rented a gorgeous house on the beach with her kids and grandkids just down the shore from the hotel we were staying in. I thought I might see her once during the vacation, if I was lucky. Well, she basically ended up adopting my boyfriend and me. I think we went to Jackie's house four times that week. Swimming, laughing, gossiping, and she was always the first to whip out her cell phone camera and start taking pictures or video at will. I had no idea that Jackie had been battling breast cancer for years at that point. I'm so glad she posted those photos on her social media. And of course, I have several more of my own.

One time, when I hosted a dinner party at my house that included Jackie, Sidney and Joanna Poitier, and Suzanne Somers, I marveled at how they all had known each other for so long. I even turned to Jackie and said, "How do you all originally know each other, since I'm obviously the new one in the group?"

Without hesitation, Jackie said, "Oh, darling, it was the '70s. We all know each other from three-ways."

Everyone at the table laughed, including the globally renowned trumpeter Chris Botti. Who, by the way, looked back at me after that comment as if to say, "Are they being for real?" When I saw how long Jackie's friendships with people were, it gave me a secret thrill, because I wanted to believe she and I would have a relationship that deep and lasting.

And we did, right up to the very end.

COOPER, ANDERSON
Newsman, Partner, Catalog Model

I know you want to hear what really happens off camera and during the camera breaks with your beloved Anderson Cooper on CNN New Year's Eve during our LIVE broadcast. I call it CNN's Kathy Griffin's "Soon-to-Be Emmy Nominated for Best Variety Special . . . with Special Guest Anderson Vanderbilt" Special.

Nothing made me prouder than when Anderson was asked about doing *New Year's Eve Live* with me and his response was, "I sweat more with Kathy Griffin than I do when under fire in Jalalabad." Feel free to look up any of our greatest hits moments online, but keep reading and feel free to tweet him @andersoncooper to confirm what you are about to read here.

I met Anderson in 2001 when he was a guest, not once but twice, on my MTV ahead-of-its-time series *Kathy's So-Called Reality*, and we have been friends ever since. In those days, I had my mom and dad as regulars on the series. When Anderson showed up, he didn't even have his full silver-fox gray hair yet. He was shy and sweet and especially respectful to my mom and dad, so I instantly fell in love with him. My mother was nervous to even talk to him because she is such a fan of Anderson's mother, living legend Gloria Vanderbilt. I admit I didn't know he was a Vanderbilt the day I met him, but don't worry, I have reminded him of it every day since. Yes, yes, he is Anderson Cooper, newsman extraordinaire.

He's the guy you expect to see on location in a war zone, in the tsunami, rescuing a child in Haiti after the earthquake. The real deal. Once a year, purely for your amusement, I'm pretty much the Hannibal Lecter to his Clarice Starling. You know, in a good way. They did love each other.

Anyhoo, back to New Year's Eve, it's all about the trickery. For the 2015/2016 show, my objective was to wear this Vanderbilt-Cooper down to the nub. You should know that Anderson has the NYPD pat me down before I'm allowed to get on the riser with him. I hope this is not because one year I innocently handcuffed myself to him and threw the key below into the crowd of five hundred thousand people. I also hope it's not because one year I wanted to make it rain with $5,000 in singles, which the producers and the police said would cause a riot. I am far too much of an artist to be

bothered with these details.

I put a ton of prep work into the New Year's Eve broadcast. Anderson finds this hilarious. On air, he's admitted that he just shows up on the platform and hopes to survive. I actually think about our show all year long. I am plotting right now.

My plan couldn't have worked out better for the 2015/2016 four-

and-a-half-hour live broadcast. First off, rather than sharing a room at the Marriott with Anderson as we did the previous year, I insisted on getting a different room to hang out in, just to be a diva and to see if Anderson even cared.

There's no entourage with Anderson—it's one of the things I love about him. I've caught him just sitting around and reading Nietzsche.

I got a jump start on messing with his mind; knowing he was in the next room wondering what was going on, I purposely waited in my own room. I swear I would have stayed there until about thirty seconds before going on air. Sure enough, a production assistant came to me and said, "Anderson's just alone in the other room."

"Good. Is he crying?" I asked.

Ten minutes later: "Um, Anderson wants to know if he can come over."

When I finally allowed him in my hotel boudoir—this is maybe half an hour before we're going on the air live—he said, "Are we good? Are we cool? What's going on? We have to catch up."

Naturally, we had a fast and furious gossip session, I made him call my mom, Maggie, and say hi, I teased him about how challenging his life is, and reminded him to never forget he's a Vanderbilt. He grabbed his hair nervously. I could tell we were getting into the groove. Then I said, "I don't think it's a big secret at this point, but I'm going to do something on air."

And he said defeatedly, "Yeah, I figured."

"All I'm asking is that you just laugh. It won't hurt you in any way. It's silly, and if you laugh, you'll look like a hero. Are you in?"

"Yes, of course! You know I'm in!" he said.

Then I said, "Fine, just don't embarrass me." See how I like to flip it on him?

For our big live-on-air walk from the hotel to the platform, which CNN had never done before, I had planned to wear a big, heavy winter coat, then whip it off and walk through Times Square in boots, a bikini, and body paint. I was proud of that moment, especially because I think Anderson—who naturally got embarrassed—thought, *Okay, that's her surprise. Whew.* Hardly.

I had managed to sneak past the NYPD pat-down a couple of plastic spoons from the hotel room for a little something later. At the point in the broadcast when I felt like I had gotten Anderson to a nice and comfortable place, I simply asked him to close his eyes, put these two plastic spoons over his eyes, and trust me for ten seconds. AND HE DID! I couldn't believe it either. I then took a small can of the darkest, JLo, *Dancing with the Stars*, shimmery tanning spray out of my bra and sprayed his gorgeous face. He took the plastic spoons off of his eyes (even I am not such an asshole that I would want to blind him) and looked into the small monitor in front of us where we can see ourselves and had a reaction that was so genuine. It was epic. He just kept saying "Wow" and "Jesus." Mission accomplished! I also got a little bit of the dark spray tanner in his silver hair, which he himself has called "the moneymaker." The most important thing is I got *the giggle.* That's why you watch; that's why I do it. I won't stop until I get you your giggle.

During the commercial break, my curiosity got the best of me. I wanted to remind him once a Vanderbilt, always a Vanderbilt. I said to him, "Are you mad at me? You can tell me. We're friends. Did I make you mad?"

He assured me he was not one bit mad, and I love him for that. But I had to push it. I said, "Well, now that I know you're not mad, I have to ask you . . . and I know we are coming back LIVE in thirty seconds . . . but what were you thinking? When you had your eyes closed and you knew I was spraying you with something and you had covered your eyes with spoons. What possibly could have been going on in your mind?"

To which he answered, "I thought you were hydrating me with Evian spritzer."

Now that is some Vanderbilt shit right there.

COWELL, SIMON
Music Impresario, Prickly Brit

Who didn't fall in love with Simon Cowell when he un-wrapped those brutally helpful critiques on *American Idol*? (Well, Clay Aiken, probably, for one. BTW, who knew Clay Aiken was using *AI* as a springboard to becoming a future politician? A politician, I might add, who ran for Congress as an openly gay Democrat who chose to distance himself from both Barack Obama and Hillary Clinton. How'd that work out for you, Clay?)

Back to you, Simon. When you watched *American Idol*, you practically tapped your watch waiting for Paula Abdul and Randy Jackson to finish so Simon could tell it like it is. Thankfully, I've had many encounters with him, and every time I see him, I make sure I get private time.

When we both were on set together for a daylong non-*Idol* television shoot, the show sent every one of its stars to the same eating area so they could sit together during lunch. I took him aside and said, "You and I are eating alone, sir!" In just thirty minutes, I found him to be smart, honest, funny, and, dare I say, inspiring. I point this out because often I'm asked about certain celebrities with a certain tone as if to say, "Oh, that person is mean," or "You met so-and-so. How do they sleep at night?" These celebrities are the types of people who often turn out to be surprisingly generous, serious, and kind. Simon will let me bust his balls, but he can give it back, too. We speak the same language. The accent almost puts a rosy tint on any insult he tosses off. He's said to me things like, "Good to see you. Hideous color dress." And "What a pleasant surprise. Boyfriend still lacking a high school diploma?" And I just love it. But he's also been like the TV Simon Cowell to me, too, when he's in advice-giving mode.

One time, I had just gotten in trouble for something, and I was simultaneously up for a gig, so I was worrying about repercussions, and I sought his counsel. He said, "Here's the thing, Kathy. What's unique about you, and what's going to keep you unique, is that you never hold back. And you must never hold back, ever. No matter how much you get banned from talk shows"—he knew that about me—"and no matter how much a studio head is mad at you"—as Steven Spielberg was for a year, which I wrote about in *Official Book Club Selection*—"you should only ever take jobs where you can be 100 percent yourself. I never want to see you watered down in any way. That's the thing I want you to keep doing. Keep being fearless, and don't worry about being in trouble, because the people who are successful are always in trouble."

What I loved about what he said was that it wasn't the blind "You get 'em, girl, say what you want" support you get from a friend. It was advice with context from a kingmaker who knows something about why people succeed and why others don't. And he ended his advice with this: "The last thing you should be is just anybody." And then he went off to count his money. I can't prove this, but I think I saw thousands of Krugerrands flying out of his ass as he walked away.

CRANSTON, BRYAN
TV Dad, TV Drug Dealer, Unaware Source of
Lasting Personal Embarrassment

The year was 2008. It was my third year in a row as an Emmy nominee for *My Life on the D-List*, the year after I won it for the first time, and I was feeling pretty good the night of the ceremony. Being a "previous Emmy winner" will do that for you. I recommend winning one.

I was in my seat, and I looked across the aisle and who do I see but Bryan Cranston. I've known Bryan since he played the dad on *Malcolm in the Middle*. As long as I've known Bryan, he's been respected and known as a hardworking actor's actor who people are always pulling for. Only he's now bald and wearing a ridiculous hat. He looks pretty skinny, and I think, *Oooh, boy, he has let himself go-o-o-o-o.* As in, clearly this guy has not worked in a long while. I felt terrible. If he's sick, that's one thing, but did he go through all that *Malcolm* money so quickly he can't even afford a frickin' toupee? Ouch. (You have no idea where my mind was going.) Is he living in Jane Kaczmarek's spare room? Will I see him at the Laugh Factory soup kitchen next? Did the Emmys look at him and think, *We have to give him a pity ticket?* I started thinking about what I should say to a colleague who's clearly on the skids and, frankly, looking awful. Or can you say anything? I could go over and hug him, I guess, although I'll be honest, I didn't want my on-top-of-the-world vibe to make him feel bad. I ran through an approach in my head: "Hey . . . hey there . . . Bryan? It's Kath. Good ole Kath. Can I give you my number? Look, I know things didn't pan out, but . . . I'm a friend. You call me. Because friends are there for you in the *down times*, all right? And just remember, you were the dad in *Malcolm in the Middle*. The dad! No one can take that away from you. Those reruns will always be there! Don't hide from that!" If I'm being honest, I thought, he probably turned down a spin-off. Got lazy. That's what separates us Emmy winners from the one-and-done Cranstons. Hard work. It's sad. It's probably a baby daddy sitch. He's going to cry in my arms, isn't he? It's a designer gown, so I'll have to get a hanky from Lea Michele and lay it across my shoulder first, but that's what you do *for the down and out*. We're not heartless.

Anyway, I won another Emmy that night and left without getting a chance to say anything. Is he okay? Anyone??? I now know I was the ONLY person in that room who didn't know that Bryan Cranston was in the intense process of playing the iconic role of Walter White. ALL RIGHT, ALL RIGHT, believe it or not, at that time, I hadn't heard of the groundbreaking, multi-award-winning, globally watched series *Breaking Bad*, and I had not seen a single episode. Understand, I make a living watching crappy TV. I don't always have time to get to the good stuff. I know I'm backpedaling here, but cut me some slack. I get it, HE IS THE DANGER!

CRYSTAL, BILLY
Oscar Host, Comedy Legend, Harry

Back in the 1990s when I was relatively unknown, I had a talent manager at a hotshot management house that also handled Billy Crystal. That means this esteemed management company at the time represented the very known (Crystal) and the very unknown (me).

One day I was at their offices and had to use the restroom, and my manager asked, "Do you want to use the Billy bathroom?" I didn't know what he was talking about, and he said, "We have a bathroom in the office that's just for Billy Crystal."

I believe my answer was, "Hell yeah!"

I was led to a private lavatory just off one of the partners' offices, accessible only with a key. It was relatively small but beautiful and pristine, as if it had just been built yesterday and never entered. Using it, I felt extra clean and special. I don't remember if I went number one or two . . . but I can tell you this, I was a hell of a lot funnier after that bathroom visit.

Not that long afterward, I was in Aspen at the U.S. Comedy Arts Festival, because at the time, festivals were easier to book than regular gigs, and at one point, I walked into an elevator, and who should be in this tiny motorized enclosure but the great Billy Crystal and the equally great Bob Costas. (I believe Bob was moderating a panel Billy was on.) Now, Billy, he's a super talent, a movie star, and a beloved comedian, and he's succeeded at everything, but let's just say Billy isn't the most approachable star in the world. And yet, sometimes even he has to deal with sharing a six-foot-by-six-foot hydraulic-operated moving machine, a.k.a. an elevator. And there he was now, arms folded, looking forward, and before I could even say anything—because I'm usually first—I hear Bob Costas, who I'd never met, say, "Hi, Kathy!" Well, that was super charming and encouraging, because while it's one thing not to be able to read a room it's another thing not to be able to read an elevator.

I said hello to Costas, and then I took on the frost coming from the northwest corner. "Billy! I took a shit in your bathroom!" Naturally, I expected the entire elevator to erupt in laughter. Nothing. No reaction. Billy Crystal is seriously acting as if what I'd just said didn't happen. Bob, meanwhile, burst out laughing—because it's outrageous, out of context, and the last thing you'd expect to hear, for all you who need explanation (like Billy)—and said, "What are you talking about?"

"Bob, you didn't know that Billy's got his own frickin' private bathroom at our manager's office? It's gorgeous!" I turned to Billy. "I was there the other day, Billy . . ." and just continued as if the *When Harry Met Sally* star were actively participating in the conversation instead of looking straight ahead and ignoring me. "You know, Billy, I'm not making the big bucks like you, but I had to use the restroom like anybody else, because when you gotta go, you gotta go . . ."

I was so bad at reading this elevator as well as thinking I was being hilarious, I did everything just short of saying to Billy, "Am I right? Or am I right?" while raising my hand up for a high five that would never be returned by his hand. We've got a couple of floors to go, still, and Bob—bless him— is trying to make it work, because facilitating conversation is his skill set, and he's saying, "Billy, did you know this? Tell me more, Kathy."

"Well, Bob, you get a key . . ." And off I went. And it was as if Bob thought this unknown, obnoxious comic was an equal to the funniest person on the planet. Billy, meanwhile, was still in character as the Guy Who Thinks Only Bob Costas Is On the Elevator with Him. When the doors opened, we all exited as if nothing unusual had happened.

Now "Chilly Elevator Billy" was not at all the Billy Crystal I encountered years later when I filmed a cameo for the Jason Segel *Muppets* movie (a cameo that, regrettably, was left on the cutting room floor, but that's a story for another time). I got to spend the day with Billy and Ricky Gervais, and there was a lot of downtime because setting up the Muppets takes a while. Billy couldn't have been nicer: shooting the breeze, talking comedy, and allowing me to take a selfie with him. And wouldn't you know it, every time that I've seen Billy since then, he has been incredibly gracious and friendly. There's no way he'd have remembered *When Billy Met Kathy*. For me, it was more like *When Kathy Met Bob*.

CYRUS, MILEY
Singer, Human Wrecking Ball

Did you know I could have been on *Hannah Montana*? One of the executive producers was a guy I knew from *Suddenly Susan* days, and he came up to me once and said, "We want to write a really juicy episode for you!" It was a giant show at the time, and I was thrilled. Then on national TV when I won my first Emmy, I said, "Suck it, Jesus. This award is my God now," and all of a sudden it was, "Um, don't expect the call." Well, screw you! It was worth it! All I can say is post-*Hannah* Miley would have gotten that same response when she was going through her "rebellious phase" if she'd had to go back in time and appear on her own show. That is tortured logic, I know, but I don't care.

Miley officially made it into my act with that stripper-pole-while-partying-in-the-USA performance at the Teen Choice Awards, which I saw up close as a guest and nominee that year. One time, I crashed a pre-performance prayer circle of hers backstage at VH1's *Divas Live*.

We have a history. We did a Rock the Vote campaign together in 2012, and my publicist shrewdly engineered the schedule so that Miley and I would cross paths at our shoots. This would be real face-to-face time with someone I'd called every name in the book in my act. Miley had just cut her hair short and dyed it blond, so I decided to break the ice by making a Susan Powter joke, referencing a self-empowerment icon who first became popular when Miley was just born. So naturally I got this response from the ever-energized, raspy-voiced teen star: "Whooz

Soozan POW-ter? Whooz ZAT? Hey, it's ME, MILE-y!" (She always announces herself.) I told her Susan Powter was a lady who'd been wronged by a man and had gotten revenge by getting fit, becoming a motivational speaker, and stopping the insanity.

"She got a haircut like yours," I said.

"THAT sounds really KEWL!"

She was really sweet and spunky, bragging about the ring Liam had given her the first time around, if you know what I'm saying. I wanted to say, "You're way too young to get married to that fucking stiff," but I didn't. I was on good behavior, keeping the teasing to a modest level. Better still, I can probably say I saved our photo shoot when it became patently clear that Miley's see-through top was making every picture unusable. That's right, Kathy Griffin: Miley Cyrus Savior.

At one point, I just had to say out loud, "Um, Miley, honey, no one else is going to tell you this, but none of these pictures are going anywhere because we can all see your nipples. So either put on an effing jog bra or accept that these photos will never get out."

Miley lifts her top and starts doing a shimmy. "Wouldn't you be PROWD of THEEZ if you had 'em?" (That's how you get me to fall in love with you.)

We got the pictures eventually, which was great, and honestly, Miley was super nice the whole time. Then she said the thing that I really thought I was going to avoid. "So, this WHOLE TIME, you've just been making JOKES about me?"

Look around. Shrug shoulders. "Yeah."

"All those things you say about me, you're just trying to make people LAFF?"

"Yeah."

"All right, we're KEWL."

We've been kewl ever since. When I met Hannah and she was still from Montana, frankly, she just wasn't very interesting to me. I have since come to respect her tremendously. I have seen her sing LIVE several times. She has a great voice in an industry filled with contemporaries that don't really have the chops. I think she's a smart, creative nutjob. One time, she squeezed my butt on a red carpet in front of several photographers. That's what friends do, right? I'm KEWL with that.

DICAPRIO, LEONARDO
Actor, Activist, Man Slut

When you have the opportunity to call Leonardo DiCaprio a man whore, you take it.

At the Directors Guild of America Awards in 2016, I had the distinct honor of presenting an award, and let me tell you, that's some Oscar-level shit when it comes to stars. I've never had an encounter with Leo in any way, much less seen him across a room. But there he was at a nearby table, with what appeared to be four bodyguards or handlers, and glued to his damn phone. I decided to use my tablemate Lily Tomlin as my winglesbian. When he walked by us to go backstage to get ready to present an award, I stood up and said, "Don't be a douche bag, Leo. Get off your fucking phone and say hi to the great Lily Tomlin!" He either didn't hear me or chose to ignore me. You decide. I repeated it until he finally turned his head, pulled his precious phone away, and kindly said hello to Lily. (He really is gorgeous, by the way.)

Since I now had his attention, I said again, "Jesus, Leo, don't be such a douche bag."

He walked away and with an adorable smile said, "I *am* a douche bag."

Touché, Leo.

But agreeing with me only makes me stronger.

Lily then foolishly asked me to accompany her to the ladies' room. In the backstage hallway, we saw Leo with two of his handlers practicing his speech. I very loudly said for his benefit, "I swear to God if I see that fucking asshole Leo DiCaprio I'm going to give him a smack in the face." He did manage to look up for a second with an expression of, shall we say, irritation mixed with bewilderment. But I wasn't done yet.

You know those movie scenes in restrooms when the timing of a stall door flying open is everything? Well, I emerged from one of the stalls at just the exact moment the women's room door was opened and Leo was walking past. I flipped him the bird and screamed, "Leo, you pervert!"

I was saving the best for last. When my moment at the podium came, and all eyes were on me to give the great commercial director Joe Pytka his career achievement award, I couldn't resist busting Leo's balls, because he was pretty much directly in front of me. I kept stopping my presentation to yell at him to get off his phone and stop swiping Tinder, lovingly referring to him as a man whore. He finally looked up at me with those baby blues and with both hands gave me the "bring it" signal. I continued to let him have it about his damn phone, reminding him that all the women you always see on his boat will gladly wait for him. He took it well, like a champ. He's a brilliant actor, which is why he makes a great target. I just wish he'd stop calling me. It's getting uncomfortable. He's a little old for me.

———

DICKINSON, ANGIE
Ring-a-Ding-Ding Ringer, Police Woman

Those of you who are old enough might remember Angie Dickinson's memorable ad campaign for California avocados. Her fantastic gams took up most of the billboard as she lay on her side in a white one-piece, the caption underneath reading, "Would this body lie to you?" It made absolutely no sense regarding avocados but probably sold a lot of them.

For the longest time, that ad was what sprang to my mind when her name was mentioned—not her movies, or *Police Woman*, or the heartbreaking struggles she went through raising her autistic daughter . . . until I met her. Then something else about Angie replaced her visual appeal in my consciousness.

I had booked an appearance on the Bravo series *Celebrity Poker Showdown*, which was a reality game show hit in the mid-2000s. Playing at my table were Penn Jillette, Jeff Gordon, Ron Livingston, and the still-smokin' hot Angie Dickinson. What's funny about me being on competition shows is that I really do try to win. Instead of approaching it like a chance to have fun, I practiced playing poker around the clock in the time leading up to the taping in Las Vegas. It was a dumb waste of time, really, but in those weeks of prep, I talked to male friends who played in regular poker games, and one of them said something interesting: "You need to be afraid of Angie Dickinson at that table." I was surprised. The sexy movie star? Not card magician Penn Jillette? Or a die-hard competitor like stock car racer Jeff Gordon? Or a bro actor like Ron Livingston? He said, "Think about it. All those nights with the Rat Pack. All those times when she was probably the only girl in the suite and how much frickin' poker those guys played. I'll bet she's played countless hours with Frank and Dino. If that's not a master's class, I don't know what is."

He was right. She was a frightening poker player and kicked ass. I even said to her right before taping, "You're the one to watch, right? Did you play with those guys in Vegas back in the day?" Angie's always been a sweetheart to me, but she replied, without any emotion, "Every night." Chills went down my spine, as if I'd met a mob boss. Angie Dickinson has more poker experience than Phil Hellmuth! No more avocados and gams when I think of Angie. It's a stone-cold, honey-haired killer staring down some quivering weekend warrior across a table and turning his meager bluff into an excuse to take him for everything he has.

DOG, BEETHOVEN THE

The Shaggy Diva, My Costar

I appeared in a *Beethoven* movie, and if you think I mean the composer, you really don't know what kinds of movies get made nowadays.

This was the fifth movie in the *eight-film* franchise starring the trouble-causing Saint Bernard, and the last one to be any good. How do I know that? Because they put me on the DVD cover even though I had maybe three lines. We didn't even have Judge Reinhold, who had starred in the third and fourth movies.

Anyway, that doesn't matter, because from what I saw on the set the days I shot, the loveable and full-figured pooch got more star treatment than Jennifer Lawrence in *The Hunger Games*. It was hilarious. That particular day in Los Angeles was a scorcher, and the way it worked on set was that Beethoven would shoot for forty-five seconds at most, then the director would yell, "CLEAR! CLEAR THE SET!" and then the Beethoven wranglers ran up to him because he needed to look perfect all the time. If you didn't know, Saint Bernards are titanic droolers, and frankly, it's their nature; so one guy was on drool towel duty, because the director would routinely yell out, "I don't want *one frame of film* with that drool! NOT ONE FRAME!" Another member of this doggie pit crew was the wet towel guy, for when BTD needed to be cooled down. ("What's his temperature, damn it?") Another wrangler was on brush patrol ("Let's go, people. Those ears don't brush themselves!"), and four others were needed to walk him into a shady part of the Universal backlot between takes so he could rest up and gather his motivation for the next scene ("Everyone! Please, out of his eye line!"). No disrespect, BTD, but we're not talking a genius dog here. This wasn't some specially trained canine who could do tricks. I've worked with those. They can bark three times at a signal, tilt their head on cue, play cutesy, whatever. This was a big, dopey dog who drooled like a spigot, took craps the size of Montana, and panted louder than a broken air-conditioning unit in Nakatomi Plaza. That was his "acting." Then again, Saint Bernards were bred to rescue people in the Alps. Beethoven probably took one look at that blazing Southern California sun and thought, *This is BS.*

Of course, I wanted to pet him. But honestly, he was treated so royally I thought I'd get thrown down by the wranglers if I went near him. I didn't know the protocol for actor dogs. But someone said, "Sure, you can pet him." I did, and I was slathered in saliva, and then it was "CLEAN UP GRIFFIN! CLEAN UP GRIFFIN! How's Beethoven? How's his temperature, and more importantly, how's his mood?"

I can only imagine this is what Francis Coppola had to deal with on *Apocalypse Now* with Brando. Coppola has to have the same stories.

EFRON, ZAC
Actor, High School Graduate, Twelve-Pack

Sometimes in the excitement of any pre-Hollywood red carpet arrivals process, I need to give myself a project. And by project, I mean any new and exciting way I can think of to turn this event into potential material for my explosive, award-winning, and ever-changing comedy act. (Go to KathyGriffin.com for tickets.)

The quest to get pictures with celebrities—or simply to extend my lingering on the red carpet in the glare of the media—is a never-ending strategy of cajoling, cleverness, and outright deceit. One night attending the 2011 People's Choice Awards (as a nominee, I might add!), I made it my mission to get super hot guys to let me touch their hair. Oh, why do I have to be the one that keeps coming up with these genius ideas that make celebrities fall in love with me even more?

I needed a ruse, though, so I came up with a crazy story that a fancy art gallery had asked me to contribute to a very high-profile exhibit. I saw the twenty-three-year-old Zac Efron coming toward me, and he was in a perfectly tailored suit and looked gorgeous. He was even sporting a new haircut, short and buzzed. Someone like that—at the height of fame, wanted by every girl—is a snapshot catch, but I needed to be careful with the approach. So I started with a simple, "Hi, Zac!"

To him, I'm basically an old lady he probably feels he needs to be respectful to, so he said, "Hey."

I told him, "I'm a nominee tonight. You look great."

Sticking with the Boy Scout patter, he said, "Oh, hey, you do, too."

I said, "I'm doing this art project where I'm supposed to get silly pictures of me petting the heads of handsome guys. Can I pet your hair?" Beat.

He said, "Yeah."

The picture was perfect: Zac even gave it this regal, poised touch by looking upward. I knew that my Twitter feed would go bananas, especially from boys who like boys.

I continued my reign of terror (I mean, hilarious comedy hijinks for no one other than myself) on *True Blood* star Alexander Skarsgård, too, who is at least ten feet taller than I am. I asked him. He was aloof. Typical fanger. I said, "I just finished Zac." He didn't even say yes or no. His hands were in his pockets the whole time. I just reached up and touched it, said, "Thanks, Eric Northman!" and moved along.

Zac Efron owes me more than a muffin basket. I truly believe the mere gesture of Ms. Kathy Griffin gently touching his hair (and yes, there are pictures online to prove it) was the night he truly became a man. Yes, I made it possible for Troy Bolton to become the ripped, shirtless hot guy who barely remembers high school.

EMANUEL, RAHM
Chicago Mayor, Ex-White House Chief of Staff, Scary Guy

A Washington reporter friend of mine invited me as her plus one to a Washington, D.C., event called the Radio & Television Correspondents' Association Dinner, which Vice President Joe Biden hosted. It's not nearly as star-studded as the White House Correspondents' Dinner, but the room was filled with hundreds of Washington, D.C., figures. To me, though, it looked as if everyone went to both events, because you saw all the same people. There's always a comedian hosting, and the vibe is loose and satirical.

I was seated at then Republican Massachusetts senator Scott Brown's table. Brown, who had just taken the late Ted Kennedy's seat earlier that year, pulled the Alec Baldwin Preemptive Strike with me, saying about the comedian who was hosting, "I bet this guy's funny, but I wish you were performing."

Not fazed by the compliment, nor dazzled by his good looks, but remembering how he was referred to by detractors, I said, "It's Ken, is it? Or Mr. Doll? Anyway, you should really be happy I'm not up there, because I'm going to give a performance at this table that'll rival anything onstage."

My reporter pal looked nervous, as if she were thinking, *Oh God, I'm representing my global media outlet.* I bragged to the table about how I, too, was a legitimate journalist based on my hard-hitting New Year's Eve coverage on CNN with Anderson Cooper. I gave Scott Brown so much shit I was practically writing my act that night.

I noticed that at a nearby table, Obama senior advisor Valerie Jarrett was sitting next to Fox News chairman Roger Ailes. I couldn't resist. I'd met Valerie once before, so I was going to use her as my inroad to confront Ailes. Bold as brass, I went up and said, "Hi, Valerie. Kathy Griffin! Remember me?"

"Of course! That story made me cool to my teenage daughter!" (The short version: at a women's conference, Katie Couric and I banged on Valerie's hotel room door in our pajamas. Katie wanted an interview. I was just kidding around. It's all Katie's fault.)

"Why don't you tell me about your friend sitting next to you?" I asked.

"Kathy, this is Roger Ailes," Valerie said.

"Hi, Rog."

"Hello," he said.

I said, "How's everything going over at the propaganda machine?"

And then, like an awakened guard dog, a nearby Rahm Emanuel got up and stood right behind me as Valerie said, "Oh, Kathy, you're so funny. I know what you're doing. You're being a troublemaker!"

Roger Ailes started in on me. "I remember when you used to do *Fox & Friends*."

I shot back with, "And I remember when your 'show' had cooking segments and Richard Simmons and me doing jumping jacks, and Steve Doocy was the *weather guy*, and Brian Kilmeade was the *sports guy*. It wasn't you calling the dogs to war every five seconds. Way to go, *Rog.*"

At this point, Valerie tried to escape because I was going at Ailes hard. But then I felt these firm hands on my shoulders as Rahm Emanuel himself pivoted me from the table, walked me away, and said, *"We are not doing this now!"* He struck me as a man who was obviously in a position of power in that room at that moment. I got the impression that he was a seasoned pro at encounters like this that would include the president's advisors. To this day, I can't tell you if Rahm Emmanuel is a prick or just a guy doing his job. It happened so fast I barely had a chance to get out a "Hey, Rahm, tell Ari I said hi! I'm a star client!!!"

ESTEFAN, GLORIA
Cuban Diplomat, Diva Para Siempre

Gloria Estefan keeps trying to improve me. She thinks I'm going to change. She is like the hot girlfriend who thinks that her boyfriend, Kathy Griffin, will change. Ladies and gay men: people don't change. Here are some photos that prove my point.

In this pic, Glo is putting me in the doghouse because of my rather free-spirited hair-don't. I think secretly she wishes I would just learn how to scrunch my hair properly in the way she has been doing for decades to her own.

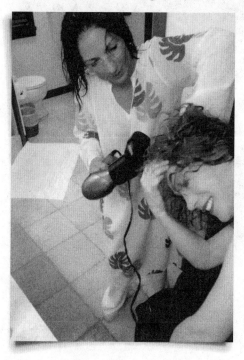

She was even willing to do it in a muumuu in her own home in Florida.

And here she is that same night at a fancy dinner party in Miami, still trying to get it right.

Gloria Estefan, in addition to being arguably one of the rulers of all things Latina, has been an incredibly generous friend to me. One time when I was on tour in Miami, she let me stay in one of her homes on Star Island. You heard me. One of her homes. Not a guesthouse. Not a spare room. She was in the kitchen, and I, of course, was on a mission to embarrass her and make her regret her decision to let me stay at ONE OF HER HOMES. I decided to try to make her laugh by dancing around the dock area without my pesky bikini top. That's right. I was very proud of myself running around the dock of her property with just my bikini bottoms on, white titties flapping in the air, flailing my arms and yelling, "LOOK AT ME! LOOK AT ME! I'm getting on my feet and making it happen! The rhythm got me! The rhythm got me!"

To which she dryly shouted out the window, "You know, the paparazzi are stationed across the bay with long lenses all the time!"

Like I care!

A few days later, my first and last genuine candid paparazzi shot surfaced online and in all the weekly rags—topless, pale, wiry hair, and makeup-free. Trust me when I say this was not a staged photo. I was just trying to make my friend laugh while she was trying to be a friend and save me from myself. Gloria, don't worry—someday, I'll change. Everyone does.

FERRELL, WILL
Actor, Former Student of Mine (Yep)

You may not know this, but my day job for several years was teaching improv classes at the famed Groundlings improv theater group in Los Angeles, of which I was a long-standing company member. Prior to being on *Saturday Night Live*, Will was my student. Both he and Cheri Oteri were my students. So yes, I was there when they invented the cheerleaders and was fully aware that they were geniuses in the making.

The thing people don't know is that when I was his teacher, before he was famous, he and his brother lived in his mother's basement. You know, like *Silence of the Lambs*? You can imagine how much I enjoyed teasing him long after he became a star. "Hey, how are you and your brother doing in the basement? Do you have your own bed now? Your movies seem to be doing well, so I would think you would."

The other thing about Will is that he's what I affectionately call "lost to fame." Let me give you an example. One year, I was a red carpet correspondent for the E! channel, and when Will walked onto the carpet, I could not get his attention. He was surrounded by publicists, security, and the like, and everybody wanted a piece of him. He was at the height of the *Anchorman* frenzy. Good God, straight guys love that movie. I innocently shouted his name. He and his posse blew by. They probably didn't hear me. Okay, maybe they heard me and had to move on. Was he being purposely rude? I doubt it. I used to take it personally, but he's just so out of the stratosphere now with his career that I just don't think it even occurs to him to say hello to his old pal Kathy. He probably has to meet a million people every time he goes to an event like the Emmys. There's no vibe from him about it, either. And it doesn't bother me one bit. He was always a funny, nice guy, but there are some rocket ships to stardom you just don't see coming, and Will—sweet, hairy, suburban Will—was one of them.

FONDA, JANE
Movie Star, Works Out, Personal Chef

Jane Fonda made me the worst quesadilla of my life. And I was never so happy to eat it.

Of course, I've always wanted to get to know the great Jane Fonda. I mean, what a life! A true feminist, a wildly talented star of stage and screen, a survivor and victor.

I initially reached out to Jane through Lily Tomlin in 2010. Lily was a guest in an episode of *My Life on the D-List* where she and I called Jane on speakerphone. Once I had her contact info, we e-mailed back and forth casually. She wanted me to host a charity event for her organization in Atlanta, and I was hoping she would be a guest on my show.

Months later, I changed the course of our budding friendship. I was smack-dab at the wrong end of a breakup. I was crushed, devastated. Basically, I was a wreck. I was desperate to talk to someone who had been through the fire. Jane was that perfect person. I was not messing around here. At that moment, I needed real advice from a woman who we've all seen go through extreme ups (winning Oscars, creating a successful fitness empire) and downs (high-profile breakups, media backlash) and is able to keep it moving. So I sent her an e-mail asking if we could hang out one-on-one. Jane invited me to the house where she was staying, told me not to bring anything, and asked if I had any dietary restrictions. I was so looking forward to spending time with this American legend and getting to know her as a friend more than as a fan.

Jane greeted me at the door in casual clothes. She wasn't wearing makeup, but her hair was perfect. Here's someone that I've idolized my whole life, and here I am in sweatpants and tears on her doorstep. I opened with, "I'm out of my mind right now."

She responded, "I can tell. Come on in."

We went right to her office/work area. She told me that this was a writing day for her. Her office is a room off the kitchen where she sits on a recliner with her laptop. Jane said, "Pull up that other recliner and we can talk. I'm shacking up here at my boyfriend's house for a while." Her office was more like a traditional man cave, which I thought was hilarious. *This is working*, I thought. *I'm sitting here in Jane's office / boyfriend's den, and she seems perfectly happy.* I was hanging on her every word. I asked her to give me some advice about how to best deal with emotional turmoil while still working in the most public of fields.

She whipped off a grocery list of advice, and I took notes. I actually took notes! I'll give you my knee-jerk reactions in italics because I was in a frame of mind that was questionable:

"Don't make any major decisions right now."
So I shouldn't join Doctors without Borders?
"Don't sell your house."
But I'm pretty sure I could get a billion dollars.
"Don't buy a house."
I'd be perfectly happy in one of those tiny houses I've seen on the HGTV channels.
"Don't move across the country."
What? I could pull my tiny house on the back of a U-Haul and drive to Bangor, Maine, to start my new life.

"Don't jump into a new relationship."
What about a booty call with one of those Backstreet Boys?
"Don't do anything dramatic for one year."
I'm hungry.

We moved to the kitchen where she made me a quesadilla while continuing to rattle off advice. I sat at her cozy kitchen table and watched her as she got a tortilla from the fridge, pulled out some cheese, and casually asked, "Do you eat chicken?"

She confided in me about several of her relationships and why she had come to the conclusion of waiting a year before doing anything substantial. I never knew I would get to know Fonda in this way. She was so nurturing and kind and helpful.

It was a window into her world that few get to experience. There were plenty of jokes, too. I teased her about reading an article one time where someone asked her if she ever binged on junk food, and her response was, "Sometimes I have too much peanut butter." We laughed, but she was always focused on bringing it back to the simple task of a new friend being there for a friend.

Jane plopped down the quesadilla on a plate in front of me, and I couldn't resist saying, "I'm not gonna lie: it's a little bland. This quesadilla is terrible. This is a very WASPy quesadilla," hoping she would laugh. "No wonder you're so thin and fit."

She came back with, "Yeah, yeah. Whatever. Look, kid, stay the course. Steady as she goes. Make sure you stay super active and put yourself out there. Keep reaching out to friends. Girlfriends. Guy friends. Check in with me and let me know how you're doing."

I got in my car, drove home, and thought about everything she told me for one year. That's right. I took Jane's advice because she was absolutely right. I think about that day and how content she seemed sitting in her boyfriend's rec room, writing and juggling television and film roles while still being able to tap into her own experiences and offer me such thoughtful support. I owe Jane Fonda a hell of a quesadilla.

FORD, GERALD
Former President, That Should Be Enough

Only once have I ever been glad to be ignored by the media regarding a big event. In 2001, my friend Camryn Manheim took me as her plus one to a charity fund-raiser called "A Family Celebration" that was so celebrity-packed it blew my mind. We're talking super-duper A-list: Elizabeth Taylor (who I'd never seen in person before), Calista Flockhart and the whole *Ally McBeal* cast (which was THE show at that time), *NSYNC performing at the height of their *NSYNC-ness, Britney Spears in tow, Michelle Pfeiffer, David E. Kelley, Sylvester Stallone, and even a couple of former presidents,

Gerald Ford and Bill Clinton. At one point Camryn jokingly whispered to me, "Oh my God, Bill Clinton *is* sexy." I was nervous about shaking the hand of a world leader because I wasn't some big donor, just a comedian/sitcom star/plus one, but Camryn set me straight: "If Bill Clinton wants to shake hands, you shake hands." Then I shook President Ford's hand, too! He was older, of course, but very distinguished. A nice strong presidential, respectable handshake. I went home on a total high.

Cut to a few years later: I'm sitting in bed watching my newsmagazine shows, and there's a piece on who organized that event, some guy named Aaron Tonken. Well, that *some guy* turned out to be a gigantic con artist, stealing millions from these fund-raisers, and he went to prison for it. So when I say I was glad to be ignored, that meant I was watching this ABC News piece, which featured red carpet footage of that "Family Celebration" event, and thinking, *Please, please, please, don't show me.* Thank God I wasn't famous enough to make the cut on ABC News of all the A-listers who sincerely thought they were attending a legitimate charity event. Including two frickin' presidents. Oh, I fly, but sometimes I'm just under the radar.

FREEMAN, MORGAN
I Can't Wait for Him to Read This

I think Morgan Freeman is one of those guys that people truly want to know about. What is he like in real life? I can tell you.

Morgan Freeman is a stately dude. There is a presence about him. Everything about him just reeks of a man of a thousand experiences and stories. I think that is part of the Morgan Freeman mystique. Obviously, there are lots of jokes about him being God. He has even parodied that himself. I once saw him give a really funny interview about how he was jokingly bitter about not winning the Academy Award for Best Actor yet, even though he won the Academy Award for Best Supporting Actor for *Million Dollar Baby*.

I am happy to report I have seen Morgan in several different settings. He is everything you would hope he would be. He looks you directly in the eye, he plants himself on the ground when he speaks, and the minute he opens his mouth, you turn your head because his voice is so iconic. But what I love the most is that he has a great sense of humor. I was at a dinner thrown by Beverly Hills heavyweights Arnold and Anne Kopelson, and there was Morgan Freeman—Academy Award winner, voice of God, living screen legend, favorite actor to many, and so on. I was at a great table. I was seated with Sharon Stone and the great Don Rickles. Morgan approached a sitting Don Rickles from behind and threw his arms around him. Don turned around and gave him a friendly, "Hey, you bastard!"

Morgan said, "Don, I've been waiting all night for you to call me a hockey puck."

Let me stop for a minute. Obviously, if these two old pals are joking around with each other in a way that you can only do with someone you go back a long way with, then I want to watch with eyes wide open and ears pricked up. I just want to be honest and tell you I was quietly losing it inside to just be looking at Morgan Freeman. He's one of those legends. I can't be cavalier about my run-ins with Morgan because they are always very significant to me. He probably would laugh at this, but I'm just telling you, he's one of those big-time stars that would stop anyone in their tracks.

Of the many times I've had brief encounters with Morgan, there is one that he probably doesn't remember but stuck with me. I was hosting an awards show, and he was picking up an award for his film with De Niro, Michael Douglas, and Kevin Kline called *Last Vegas*. When he came onstage, in the off-microphone moment it took him to walk up to the podium and I went halfway to meet him with the award, he simply said to me, "Hey, Kathy! How have you been?"

I responded, "Great, Morgan. It's good to see you." It may seem like nothing to you, but I must have told the story of that small exchange to thirty of my friends. It has engendered every response from "Oh my God, he knows your name!" to "What is he really like?" to "That is just cool!" and I agree. I was giddy like a schoolgirl simply because Morgan Freeman said my name.

Back to the party. Morgan continued to Don, "What's going on? Are you off your game? I've been here two hours! I'm waiting."

Now, witnessing that exchange, it was like I got a hopeful glimpse of what I hope starts right now. When you've put as much time in as I have, watching these two gave me hope that I'm reaching that place where these folks that I put in my act actually come around and have a laugh at it. I'm looking at you, Jacob Tremblay (the kid from *Room*). Morgan was laughing at everything Don said. Don was on a roll. And that's how it should be. The guy we think of as God, wanting Don Rickles to bust his balls, was for me a sign that if I keep at it, I can still do what I do when I'm that age. Morgan and Don's rapport spoke of longtime friendship, mutual respect, and a bond over whatever makes you laugh regardless of the tenor. It reminded me of seeing the Don in his documentary *Mr. Warmth* and how Clint Eastwood just lit up talking about him. Ballbusting will never get old, and since it's what I do, I'm planning on sticking around until celebrities beg me for it. Let's just say, when I'm ninety, the goal is for me to have my Morgan Freemans chase after me at an event and say, "Kathy! I'm right here! The night's not over till you roll your eyes at me and flip me off!"

GARCÍA, ANDY
Cuban Royalty, Movie Star, Oh, Those Eyes . . .

The greatest joy of my career has been introducing my beloved mother, Maggie, to some of Hollywood's best and finest. But no good deed goes unpunished.

In 2014, I concocted a scheme I was very proud of. Gloria Estefan, a close friend of mine who I met when I hosted Bette Midler's Hulaween charity event in 2008, wanted to make my mother, Maggie, a very special invited guest at her Hollywood Bowl concert. Glo was promoting her album of standards, and since these were classic songs from Mom's era, Glo thought she'd have a particularly good time. But you can't entice Maggie with private box seats and backstage access to Gloria Estefan. Mostly she only wants to be anywhere that's close to a bathroom. So I had to trick her and essentially kidnap my own mother. So I invited Maggie to my house, then made up something like, "Let's go to church and then bingo for a glass of wine," or whatever. We threw her in the car, and as we approached the Hollywood Bowl, I heard Maggie say, "Oh, look, there's the Hollyw—"

I said, "Great! Let's go check it out!" and swerved into the entrance and up the back ramp for VIPs.

Before we knew it, Team Estefan had arrived with a wheelchair, and may I just say, it was incredibly touching how sweetly Emilio Estefan and everyone took care of Mom. Glo took time to say hi to us before the concert, and Maggie called her "the girl singer" in the band, after which I wanted to throttle her. They then escorted us to our awesome seats, Maggie requested a bland turkey sandwich, and Glo went on to give one of her greatest live performances. My talented friend had something special in store, too: she dedicated the song "Young at Heart" to Maggie from the stage. (She even referenced Mom's "girl singer" comment, which I loved.) Before the show was over, we wheeled Maggie backstage so she could watch Glo close out the concert from the wings. Glo literally waved good-bye to thousands of people, walked offstage, and said, "Maggie!" It was too adorable. We then went to Glo's dressing room for a tiny get-together with her, Emilio, their daughter, Emily, a couple of key Team Estefan members, and . . . Andy García.

The movie star had made a surprise appearance during the concert as a bongo player. "Maggie, I have a surprise. Look who's standing right behind you—Andy García."

Mom turned to him, and Andy—piling on the charm—took her hand and said, "What a pleasure to meet you, Mrs. Griffin. Don't you look wonderful."

I thought, *Oh, Andy, you have no idea what you're in for. Let's get this shitfest started.*

Maggie promptly said, "Oh, you're the one on the bongos! You were terrific. That's a good line of work, too, because every proper band needs a bongo player."

Andy's eyes narrowed slightly.

I said, "Mom, it's Andy García, the movie star, who came out as a special *guest* to play the bongos. He's not just some percussionist on the road. He's a big-time actor."

"Mmm, I don't think so," she said as only Maggie could.

I said, "Andy! Tell her some of your movies."

He said, *"The Godfather: Part III?"*

Maggie was drawing a blank.

He said, *"When a Man Loves a Woman."*

Maggie said, "No . . ."

Andy was now starting to look at what he thought was a sweet, fluffy old lady with something closer to the hardened stare of some of his darker roles.

I said, "You have to do better, Andy."

"Ocean's Eleven," he said.

Maggie's eyes lit up. "With Angie Dickinson!"

He clarified, a tad dejectedly, "I was in the one with George Clooney."

Maggie: "Oh."

I shook my head and said, "Way to go, Andy. You were in the shitty *later* one. Try harder. She's ninety-five. Mention a costar an old person would be impressed by."

Finally, he said, "Sean Connery?"

My mom brightened again. "Oh my goodness," she said. "Sean Connery? That must have been something. I hear he was quite the ladies' man! You were in one of his films, huh?"

Digging in, I said, "Yeah, Andy, what were you in with Sean Connery? Hmm . . . I can't seem to remember."

Andy García, who now looked like he wanted to kill both of us, muttered, *"The Untouchables."*

I said, "Speak up?"

He said, "I WAS IN *THE UNTOUCHABLES* WITH SEAN CONNERY. I WAS THE ROOKIE COP."

And Maggie, unaware of the dagger her words had become, said, "Oh, isn't that nice."

GIFFORD, KATHIE LEE
Christian Doppelganger, TV Hostess

When I first subbed for her on *Live! with Regis & Kathie Lee*, I took a real liking to Kathie Lee's hair and makeup person, Eve, to the extent that on a different day, when I needed to go to an event, I asked Eve if she'd do me up for it. She said yes, but only if I showed up early, when Kathie Lee wasn't around. We arranged a time, but it didn't matter, because as soon as I settled in, Kathie Lee barged in and very flamboyantly barked, "There's only room for one redhead in this chair!" I was laughing, but Eve had a look on her face that said, "Really, get out. Now. Seriously."

Look, I know Kathie Lee's disliked me a long time. She thinks I'm vulgar, blah blah blah, and even when I'm on TV with her and there's laughter, she always has to get in a chastising comment. I thought she might have a legit sense of humor because she was friends with Joan Rivers, but even when the opportunity arose at a Broadway premiere for us to get a picture together—something the hyper Mario Cantone was clamoring for ("This is a picture everybody's gonna want!")—she wouldn't do it under any circumstances. Fine. As for the name confusion, we've both had to deal with it.

I've been called by her name and she's been called by mine probably too many times to count.

But it reached a very surreal apex one August day in 2015 when I began receiving a string of cryptic tweets with a Christian tinge that were inordinately heartfelt and often came accompanied with the hashtags #blessings and #heaven. "Sending you #blessings." "He's in #heaven." "Dear @KathyGriffin, you are a #blessed lady who loves the lord." Jesus-y statements like, "#LoveIsPatientLoveIsKind." Don't tell my mom this, but I think I may have uttered these words out loud: "Jesus, who writes this shit?" I then wondered what strange prank one of my comic friends was up to when I noticed a few of the tweets mentioned condolences. It got me thinking, and then I went straight to the Google machine. Yes, on the day that Kathie Lee's husband Frank Gifford passed away, legions of her fans sent well-wishing tweets to me, a foul-mouthed, gay-friendly atheist. For a day, I was bathed in the holy love of grieving, religious, probably much, much older social media newbies who *didn't know Kathie Lee Gifford's actual name.* I'll admit, the tug-of-war in my dark soul between "Awwww" and "This is hilariously wrong" was immense, and if I say that tears were streaming down my face that day, I'll let you wonder whether they were from sadness or uncontrollable laughter. Although I am genuinely sorry for Kathie Lee's loss, I would like to believe—since time heals—that she'd find this Twitter-support hiccup amusing in some way, but I'm guessing not. For all I know, she's had to erase hundreds of mean tweets from crazed Lovatics, Beliebers, and Swifties looking for me. Maybe she and I should do a PSA together about the pitfalls of social media? Or maybe Kathie Lee Gifford's superfans should ask themselves why they couldn't take at least one moment to check the spelling of her handle. I get it . . . when you are typing into Twitter, auto-results will come up, and, obviously, her fans did not mean to reach out to @kathygriffin. (I have often wondered if Kathy Bates had the same surreal experience that day.)

GOMEZ, SELENA
Singer, Actress, Taylor Swift Girl Squad Member

She's a good sport, and I like her. It couldn't have been easy to get caught lip-synching at the Jingle Ball concert and then to have a hot mic capture her saying, "WHAT THE FUCK?" in

response to the screwed-up sound issue (I encourage you to look it up). I'm okay with cute-as-a-button Disney girls cursing onstage. More, please.

Anyway, I'm even more impressed that she survived dating Bieber. At the height of that craziness, I saw her on the red carpet at an awards show, and this was when the Beliebers were so out of control some were sending her death threats. She had an insane level of security, it was that bad. She walked up to me, we said hi and hugged, and then I said, "Jesus, there's more bodyguards for you than for President Obama. What's going on? Are you going to get assassinated tonight?"

She laughed, like, "HAHAHAHAHAHAHAHA," and then instantly turned deadly serious and said right to my face, "Don't say that."

I guess that one was a little too close to the bone.

GRANDE, ARIANA
Singer Extraordinaire, Ponytail Extraordinaire

Local radio station KIIS-FM throws a big, star-studded holiday concert every year in LA at the STAPLES Center, and when I attended in 2014, I was determined to get a photo with Ariana and Jessie J for a "Bang Bang" reunion in which, in my mind, OBVIOUSLY, I'd be Nicki Minaj. I could only secure pics with them individually, but when I met Ariana backstage, she could not have been nicer. I found out why. She confided to me that years ago, she'd sent me a fan letter that I read out loud on an episode of *My Life on the D-List*. "You probably don't remember it," she said, "but I love you, and I'm your biggest fan, and because we were in the same hotel once, I wrote you a letter and put it at the door of your hotel room. I was your psycho stalker! So you can't imagine what it was like for me to be watching *My Life on the D-List* and see you read it!"

Like I remember every fan letter. What am I, Bobby Sherman? So I lied. "Of course, Ariana! It's my favorite fan letter! Now let's get this selfie out of the way." What cracked me up

about the photo was that this twenty-year-old with flawless features was as obsessed with the angle and lighting as Barbara Walters. She was all "It's got to be from up here" and "It's got to look this way," and eventually I just said, "Trust me, Ariana, not only do you look gorgeous, but I'll be Photoshopping it so much that when it's done, *I'm* going to look twenty, and you'll look around nine years old."

GREEN, BRIAN AUSTIN

Actor, Rapper, 90210h-boy

In 1998, I hosted the Billboard Awards in Las Vegas at the MGM Grand, and afterward, there was a party with hundreds of people. I don't know what I was thinking by going, but at least this was the age before cell phones. Nowadays, if I were hosting something big like that, I'd probably only go to a more private and controlled wingding afterward rather than some free-for-all anybody could sneak into. But I was naïve. Also, there was a hot young guy named Brian Austin Green I had my eye on, and I intended to make out with David Silver from *90210*. This was no unattainable dream, either. I'd met him a couple of years earlier when I was a regular on the short-lived Roseanne sketch show that Fox scheduled to compete opposite *Saturday Night Live*. Anyway, when we met then, he was a guest star, and backstage we had a fun, impromptu, half-kidding make-out session. You know, for camp value. (I tell my boyfriend now, "Hey, it was the '90s.") This time, at the Billboards party, our eyes met, he said, "Hi," I touched the lapel of his outsized suit, we stepped behind a large fixture, and started kissing. It's going well, he's moving to my neck, he's kissing it, kissing it, and then . . . Yee— OWWW! He fucking *bit me*! That was an artery, thank you! Okay, there was no blood. I'm exaggerating, as I sometimes do. *Twilight* hadn't even been written yet! I guess second base for Brian Austin Green isn't touching my tits—an appropriate next stage of intimacy—but branding me by leaving a mark, behavior which should be left behind in frickin' high school.

"Ugh, you BIT ME, BRIAN!" I yelled. He was probably drunk.

Once I got away from him, I locked eyes on Lance Bass from *NSYNC and thought, *Hmmm, he's cute*. And while obviously nothing was going to happen there, which I didn't know at the time, I'd have certainly been better off playing board games with Lance Bass than fending off the skin-ripping jaws of a ravenous B.A.G. (That's his rap name and how he wants you to refer to him. Enough said.)

The day after the Billboards, I had to show up for a table read at *Suddenly Susan* with an effing turtleneck to cover my giant hickey from a *90210* cast member and then for show taping wear beard cover makeup like an extra in *Planet of the Apes*.

I heard he married a hot chick. Good for him. Time heals all wounds.

GRIFFIN, MAGGIE
My Mom, American Treasure, Boxed Wine Connoisseur

Wherever I go, people want to hear the latest Maggie story. They don't just want to hear that she's fine; they want to know what she said, what she did, and who's on her shite list. If I could just put her onstage in her muumuu and collect the check for her, I would. She's that beloved.

Very recently, she came over for a lunchtime visit and a nice bland turkey wrap—the only other alternative is a nice bland turkey sandwich. When I asked if she wanted a glass of her treasured boxed wine, she said, "No."

Huh?

"Kathleen, I'm sick and tired of you spreading the word through your unfair comedy that I drink too much wine. People think I'm a wino!"

I said, "Mom, first of all, no one uses the word *wino* anymore. Everyone thinks you're adorable."

"Fine. I'll have a glass of 'skey." Whoa, Maggie just kicked it up a notch. (She has always called whiskey *'skey*, just like we all call coffee *'ffee*, right?) As always with Maggie, the conversation moved from politics to pop culture, and I realized there was an opportunity to broach a certain topic with her.

"You know, Mom, everyone wants to know, since you're such a fan of the Kardashians, what your thoughts are on Caitlyn."

What surprised me at first about her response was that she

tried to evade the premise: "I don't watch the Kardashians anymore! That show has just gotten too ridiculous! And I don't want you telling people that I do watch it anymore, because that's another lie from your comedy routine that I don't appreciate."

Pause.

Fermented, distilled truth juice kicking in . . .

"But I might have watched one on Saturday."

Aha!

"And I do think it's probably better that Caitlyn decided to go back to being Bruce."

Um? This is the part in movies when you hear the needle scratching a record.

"Mom, I don't think Caitlyn went back to being Bruce," I said a bit worriedly.

She said, "No, no, I saw it Saturday. Bruce was back to being Bruce, with the ponytail and the whole thing, and they were all fighting like they always do on that show. And I just thought it was better that he went back to being Bruce, because it's probably less muss and fuss with all that hair and makeup to put on every day. All the dresses and the high heels. I can't walk in those anymore, and Caitlyn's no spring chicken! It's probably just easier for everybody." (Glug. Saltine crackers. Glug.)

That's when it dawned on me that she had been watching a marathon of reruns of *Keeping Up with the Kardashians*, a programming concept, by the way, that immediately brought to mind what I believe our military refers to as "enhanced interrogation techniques." I tried to tell her she'd been watching an old episode, that Caitlyn was absolutely still Caitlyn, and she said, "No, no, see, this is where you get in trouble, because I saw it with my own eyes on Saturday. You of all people should have known this." Yes, why hadn't I been made aware of this stunning reversal that took place in only a week? Scooped again by Maggie.

"Mom," I said, "do you think Caitlyn could have transitioned back in a week?"

"I don't know all the details of that newfangled modern medical hocus-pocus," she said.

End of discussion.

I couldn't help but imagine Caitlyn Jenner stomping into Cedars-Sinai Medical Center along with Candis Cayne, Kate Bornstein, Chandi Moore, Dr. Jenny Boylan (and maybe Candle and Francine Jenner) laying down the law to the hospital staff: "Hi, fellas, I need to be back to Bruce by episode twelve. And we're shooting eleven now, so hop to it. Let's get the reassignment team back together. Or the re-reassignment, I should say. Thank God I can return all those dresses to Tom Ford. Look, I think we can keep this hush-hush until it's revealed on the show, right, guys? High five!"

Oh, Maggie, please never change. That's why I love you.

GROBAN, JOSH
Singer, Player, Chosen One

I'm a big nerd fan of Grobes. I'm his fan base. It's not young girls. They're a part of it, sure. But the meat of it is middle-aged women, and they're *obsessed*. I'm the fan who sits and cries while watching YouTube videos of him singing "The Prayer" with Celine Dion. I watch all the videos from his tour where he says, "Would anyone like to do a duet with me?" And then some nervous girl goes up and then she sounds like Susan Boyle, and it's a shtick, but I love it.

I remember when I first heard him, and this is going way back. It was at the 2001 charity event where I shook hands with Presidents Gerald Ford and Bill Clinton. Music impresario David Foster came out and introduced this kid he'd discovered, whose debut album hadn't come out yet, and frankly, he looked like he'd lost his yarmulke. I always tease him now, "You know that first night I saw you, I wondered if you'd been told you were at a bar mitzvah. You didn't exactly look like a traditional up-and-coming pop star." Well, of course, he started to sing, and that voice came out!

The other thing about Grobes, though, is that as long as I've known him, he's gotten the hottest pussy of anyone in Hollywood. Besides Michael Bolton, of course. You don't hear a lot

about this because he's not like John Mayer. He's just always been with a gorgeous chick whenever I've seen him, and he's always had a great sense of humor about his popularity. He can take a joke. He's too rich and successful to be bothered by the likes of me.

One night he brought a date to come see me, back in my comedy club days, and came backstage to say hi. He said, "This is my girlfriend, January." As in Betty Draper—January Jones, hot blonde of note.

I couldn't resist. "How did YOU get HER? She's out of your league, Grobes."

When Jimmy Kimmel hosted the Emmys in 2012, Kimmel invited me to his post-party at the Soho House, and Grobes was there, so I started teasing him again. "You're out of control, you know," I said, and I brought up his stage bit bringing audience members onstage to sing with him. "Jesus, Grobes, how bad has it gotten? You're on tour, but the pickings are so slim you're trying to screw some chick in the crowd who can't even sing 'The Prayer'?"

He looked at me, and without skipping a beat, he joked, "Look, honey, this cock isn't going to suck itself."

Ladies and gentlemen, Josh Groban.

HAMM, JON
Actor, Nemesis

You'll never convince me to like Jon Hamm.

I'll admit he was great on *Mad Men* and deserved the Emmy they finally gave him in its last season. But that's it. I get that this makes me the loner. Pretty much in any group I've ever been in, when I start bitching about Hammy, people act as if I've just strangled Jesus. But I've known him since before *Mad Men*. You see, he's bros with some comedy guys I know, and I have to say the vibe I've always gotten from him is cold and somewhat disrespectful . . . toward me. I'm suggesting he's one of these hot guys who's mildly funny but actually thinks he's comedian-level funny. You know the type—there's probably one in your office or family. He just reeks of that. It's an entitled air. When Hammy wants to be funny, he's, well, *not*. And again, I'm not saying he hasn't been good in his comedy appearances on *30 Rock* and so on, but in my experience, the harder he tries to be funny, the more he's not funny . . . to me.

Case in point: a dinner at the legendary talent agent Sue Mengers's house, in which I was privileged to be invited. It was only eight people, and one of them was the great Jack Nicholson. So when Hammy showed up, too, inside I thought, *Oh, great.*

He even said to me, "What are *you* doing here?"

I said, "I earned my seat at the table. What are *you* doing here?"

He was in hair and makeup, because he'd just come from the set of *Mad Men*, where he'd been directing the episode as well as acting in it. (And yes, I'll even admit, he's a little talented.) But he proceeded to get very drunk during the coffee table portion, and then when it was time for dinner, Sue had sat him next to me. But at least Jack Nicholson was there, and I could focus on hopefully getting to know one of the great actors of our time. Then Jack, who usually directs whatever he says to seemingly the world at large, focused on me when he went off on a tangent about Rupert Murdoch almost getting a pie in the face during a parliamentary hearing in England. I was asking him about why he was so interested, and he started doing an imitation of the right-wing media mogul, and I was in heaven. And Hammy picks that moment, when Jack is talking *to me*, to start whispering boozy yammering into my ear. First it was, "You know your Emmy isn't a *real* Emmy." I let that one go, but then he whispered, "You're so o-o-o-o-ld."

I said out of the side of my mouth, "Not now."

But he kept going, saying things like, "Do you know how o-o-o-o-old you look?"

Finally, I turned and barked, "You can't keep up. You're outclassed. Now *zip it*; Jack's talking."

The impression I got from him was, *I'm not going to let her have that moment,* and I will never forgive him for stealing my moment with Jack from me. And look, I've been told I'm old and not funny by a lot of guys—a lot of hot guys, too— but not when I'm in an intimate conversation space with frickin' Jack Nicholson, an opportunity I figured I'd never get again; that's the real reason I can't stand Hammy. The double whammy of cruel but not playful comments and the horrible timing. Again, he's not a comedian, folks. Hopefully done with the drink, but probably still Don Draper-y. I'll also admit that I get a perverse joy in making him a nemesis, because it simply hasn't been done by anyone else. I've cornered the market on convincing the jury that there is at least reasonable doubt regarding Mr. Hamm's character.

HASSELBECK, ELISABETH
My Best Friend

It's easy to forget that years before we had our "Bring it" exchange on *The View* in 2010, Hasselbeck was a *Survivor* runner-up who expressed to me many times in her early *View* days she loved it when I came on the show and that I could get away with things that she couldn't say. How quickly they turn, especially when they don't have an identity, and they learn that spouting odious Republican talking points becomes the fastest way to earning the drooling love of old, white Fox News viewers.

I distinctly remember an early *View* appearance when I was trying to persuade Barbara Walters that she should have Gloria Steinem on, because I believed that nobody had taken up the mantle of feminism for the younger generation in the way that Gloria has, and Hasselbeck didn't know who Steinem was! Fair enough. Wait . . . did I just say "fair enough"? I was distracted by one of my dogs who started chewing on a cushion. Okay, what I meant was, how the hell do you get a seat on the panel of *The View* with the great Barbara freaking Walters and keep your job after having just admitted that you don't even know who Gloria Steinem is? So I described Steinem to Hasselbeck and said something like, "But for your generation, Elisabeth, I don't really know who that person would be now. In my opinion, it would be great if you and your sisters [using a real word from the real movement] could find someone to take the baton."

Then she said, "Oh, someone like Mandy Moore?"

I was so thrown by that, I had to clarify.

"You mean, the singer who sings 'Candy' and the gal from *A Walk to Remember*, or do you mean there is some other Mandy Moore somewhere in Berkeley right now teaching pro bono classes to disenfranchised single moms while she lives in a tree while researching her next appearance before the Senate, trying to get equal rights for women?"

She meant Mandy Moore the pop star.

Really, over the course of my time on *The View*, Hasselbeck's stupidity never ceased to amaze me. As she became the right-wing mouthpiece, I personally saw and heard her getting the Fox News / Republican party talking points for that day from one of the executive producers. Hasselbeck used to be friendly to me. Then she just became a mean girl. There are people who aren't bright but are at least aware at what they're good at and what they don't know. I think I'm bright about some things and am always kicking myself over the things I don't know. Elisabeth struck me as someone who, while she deserves credit for being ambitious, before my very eyes became someone who was a perfectly nice person that morphed into someone who was strident, yet unabashedly armed with Fox News–fed sound bites. I am sure she is a true believer in many ways as I am a true believer that she is a moron. I don't care whether you're on the left or on the right; you shouldn't be on a daily television show that purports to offer news if you don't know who Gloria Steinem is and think Mandy Moore is the modern equivalent. (Nothing against Mandy, incidentally, who's probably a lovely person. Icon of can-do, activist feminism, though? Exactly.)

Of course, our dustups have been popular with our respective fans—and the aforementioned "Bring it" moment makes for an audience-energizing part of my preshow clip reel—but I also know how much being on television adds to the spice of a "feud." When I was at a very small charity event recently, I was hanging with my friends Ali Wentworth and Jessica Seinfeld, and we saw Hasselbeck walk in. They started teasing me, saying, "Uh-oh, here comes trouble for you."

I said, "No, no, it's not like that. I may not get along with someone publicly, but ultimately we're pros. People like her know that off camera, we can all be civil."

I went up to Hasselbeck to say hello. I stood there patiently waiting for her to finish up a conversation to the point where it just got awkward and she didn't say a word to me—just walked away. I had to go back to Ali and Jessica and sheepishly say, "I was wrong." What would Mandy Moore have done?

HAWN, GOLDIE
Actress, Giggler, Activist

When my former beloved assistant Tiffany worked for me, she started an unofficial assistants' union and through that became friends with Goldie Hawn's assistant, Iris. When I heard about this connection, management (me) contacted labor (Tiffany) and demanded a sit-down with the legendary, Oscar-winning comic actress (Goldie Hawn). It was years in the making. In late 2014, the opportunity finally presented itself. Goldie wanted to know if I'd host her inaugural charity fund-raiser Love In For Kids, which, I know, sounds like a pedophile convention, but in reality was a benefit for her Hawn Foundation's MindUP Program Transforming Children's Lives For Greater Success. Yeah, that one's a mouthful. I just call it HFMUPTCLFGS for short. Well, I sent word through Goldie's assistant, Iris, that I wasn't doing it until I got my face time with the legend.

I knew Goldie was something of a recluse, but this was the deal—take it or leave it. Well, she took it, and we agreed to meet at a Melrose restaurant called FIG & OLIVE, which is not a place where you show up in workout pants, which is what Goldie wore. Her hair looked like she had just rolled out of bed with Kurt Russell. Hopefully she had. Based on her attire, I started teasing her.

"Um, do you have your yoga mat with you?" I asked. "Where's your ball gown?"

She cackled and said, "Oh, I don't do that stuff! You're a

riot! Siddown!" Ballsy, those legends. She started talking about the event, but I cut to the chase.

"Look, honey, I don't give a crap about the event. Do you know how many of these I've done for you people? What do I get?"

She looked confused. "I thought this was it!" she said.

I continued to tease her and kiss her ass at the same time. "I've always wanted to meet you because I think of you as a unicorn," I said. To me, a unicorn in the Hollywood sense is a mythical being that one does not often see and is someone whom after seeing such unicorn makes you want to run to your phone and tell all your loved ones about the sighting.

"I *am* a unicorn!" she immediately responded while simultaneously pointing to herself. It was her lack of hesitation and utter willingness to agree that she is a unicorn that made me fall in love with her.

I still had to set her straight about one thing. "Unless you have $300,000, we are not done. Give me the lowdown on the sequel to *The First Wives Club* and who I'm going to play. I'll call Bette; you call Diane." She just laughed and laughed, and

Iris initiated our Twitter pic, which I insisted be taken only after Goldie put on at least a measure of lip gloss.

ICE-T
Rapper, Cop, Refreshing Drink

In the days when I was getting my sea legs as a stand-up and working at the Groundlings, I became a staple on the radio show *Loveline* when Riki Rachtman and Adam Carolla were hosts along with Dr. Drew Pinsky. One night, the topic arose of rapper Ice-T's admitted past as a pimp, and I launched into a rant that amounted to "What's so great about that?" and went so far as to accuse him of lying. I was saying things like, "That's the type of thing you say when you want to have street cred. You think Ice-T was Huggy Bear from *Starsky and Hutch*? I don't buy it." He was already a wealthy music guy by this point, so I didn't think twice about it. But he responded, and in a newspaper article! He called me out by name with a "how dare she" and "she doesn't know me" tone, and doubling down on his claim that he was a badass pimp before he became a rapper. That was one of my early experiences in which I realized, *Uh-oh, the person actually heard what I said.*

Cut to some fifteen years later, if not a little more, and I got cast on *Law & Order: SVU* in a guest star role. Ice-T's a middle-aged man now, and in my mind, I'm foolishly thinking, *I'd better be ready, because he's been waiting for this day, to put me in my place since 1994. It's probably all he thinks about.*

We were filming on the streets of New York, and during a break in filming, we ended up sitting at the same table at a restaurant the production had rented. He just started talking to me, and he was essentially acting like a kind uncle, asking about stand-up, if I was having a good time on *SVU*, whether I wrote all my material, and complimenting me on doing my own thing. He was as nice as can be. So of course I had to bring up what was going unspoken. What else could I do? Remember when Ice-T had that rap feud with LL Cool J? In my head, his watch list was 1) LL Cool J, 2) Kathy Griffin. It's in my nature to break the perceived tension with "Remember when I pissed you off? Well, let me remind you if you don't." So I just said to Ice-T, "Come on, have you forgiven me yet? It's been long enough. We need to make up now. Are we cool after that whole thing?"

And he just looked at me and said, "What are you talking about?"

So I filled him in, because he has, after all, filmed 600,000 episodes of *SVU* and probably can't remember a time when he wasn't doing the show.

"Oh, that's funny," he replied. "You said that? Oh, man . . . and I responded? Oh, that's too much. Girl, you are crazy!" He chuckled.

I could tell this guy brought to the table the kind of demeanor that you can only get from decades in the music and television industry. Here we were, having a nice actor conversation, and I had to wind the clock back to a comment on a radio station when people were buying CDs and Clinton was president. Contrary to the Academy Award–winning song in the film *Hustle & Flow*, maybe sometimes it's NOT hard out there for a pimp.

ICE, VANILLA
Home Improvement Star, Rapper, Madonna One-Nighter

I pride myself on bringing my comedy to the real America, damn it, so naturally I booked a gig in Stuart, Florida. Don't pretend you know where it is, because I didn't. But they had a theater, and people there wanted to laugh, so I went. That's how my business works, people.

The theater was nice, although the backstage was small. The night I was performing, one of the theater employees said to me, "Vanilla Ice is here." When you're on the road as often as I am, you live for words like that.

"What do you mean *here*?" I asked.

"He's here at your show. He lives nearby. Everyone around here knows him."

Vanilla Ice bought a ticket for Kathy Griffin? I wasted no time. "GET HIM!" Then I clarified for this startled guy: "Tell him to bring his wife back here, we'll get a backstage photo, an exclusive!"

I'm not sure why I was speaking in a rapid-fire style as if I were in an outtake from *Newsies*, but it was minutes to show-time, and I was on a deadline.

Seconds later, Rob Van Winkle and his then wife appeared. He looks just like he did in the rap days. Besides his head, he looked like a casually dressed Florida-type dude. He said, "Hi," and I said, "Hi, I assume your wife wanted a picture."

He said, "Yeah. She loves you."

So we did the picture, and I made my small overture. "So,

you know, I would just love it if you could bring me out when I have to go on."

"Sure!" he said with an ease that can only come from surviving an alleged one-nighter with allegedly Madonna where they allegedly may have had sexual contact.

"You don't have to rap or anything. I'm just saying it would be fun for you to introduce me, because I'm really flattered that you came to see the show. All you have to say is 'Ladies and gentlemen, let's give a big Stuart welcome for the hilarious Kathy Griffin . . .'" I knew it would be wonderfully kitschy—even though he'd just started his new TV life as a home improvement show host—and yet make the audience happy. A truly great road moment.

But it was even better than I had hoped because he actually went out and into the mic said, "STOP, collaborate, and *listen . . .*" and then proceeded to sing half of "Ice Ice Baby"! He freestyled new lyrics that used my name and then said, "So give it up for . . . KATHY GRIFFIN!"

Everyone went crazy. I went crazy. I kind of forgot I had a show to do in a moment. I felt like I was at HIS show, and I had to remind myself to put one foot in front of the other and actually do MY show because this moment was delicious. The vibe in the room was awesome. I thought it was so cool that he knew what everyone would want and just gave it to them. It's Mr. T knowing not to lose the Mohawk and chains. God love him. To this day, it's one of the greatest intros I've ever had. Maggie would have to rap "Anaconda" at Carnegie Hall to top it.

———

IRONS, JEREMY
"Actor!," Borgia, French Lieutenant

In 2010 while dining with a friend at the Wolseley, a fancy restaurant in London, I spotted Jeremy Irons at a pretty big table. It's not exactly proper in the UK to walk up to celebrities and bug them, so I kept watch and waited. When he stepped outside for a cigarette break, I paid that frickin' check mighty fast. I grabbed my friend Derek and bolted for the door. Thankfully, the only people out there were a puffing Jeremy Irons—dressed in a vintage but elegant suit, like he'd just stepped out of a Merchant-Ivory period film, and leaning against the building, menswear-ad-style—and the restaurant's fancy greeter/guard, crammed into a red coat. A real British postcard, these two. As for approaching the Oscar-winning actor, I thought it would appear less threatening if Derek and I acted like a couple. (No, we didn't make out. Or have a screaming argument. We just looked familiar with each other.) We also hit upon the idea that instead of making the fawning, aren't-you-so-and-so approach, we should pretend we didn't know who he was.

Be patient, people. As always, I have a plan.

Since Derek is twenty years younger than I am, it seemed more likely he wouldn't recognize Jeremy Irons, so he walked up and very innocently said, "I don't mean to bother you, but would you mind taking a picture of us?"

Jeremy Irons said, "No problem." He took a few pictures, then even suggested we get one with the guard, and we all joked about how it had to be okay with him, ha ha ha, and it was all pretty collegial.

Then I said to Jeremy Irons, as if he were some random stranger, "Well, you might as well get in, too!"

He smiled and obliged. As he was posing with me for the photos, I was feeling very proud of myself because my scheme had played out in my favor. Jeremy Irons, who went to the Sherborne School in Dorset (yeah, I looked it up), was outsmarted by this sassy firecrotch as they all will be if I stick around long enough.

I said, "By the way, I obviously know who you are, and I just want to acknowledge that you've been so gracious. I'm a comedian in America—"

And then he interrupted me. "Of course I know who you are. I recognized you immediately."

OMG! The star of *Reversal of Fortune* AND the voice of Scar from *The Lion King* knows who I am, and he's just been playing along this whole time! Yeah, I felt pretty famous and realized I truly do have a global reach. This little ploy turned out all right! I asked if we could get a photo together, and we did a funny pose. Naturally, Jeremy—or Jer as I call him now—wanted a funny pose with one of his all-time favorite comedians. I get it. Suddenly we were chatting like two people in the biz, and it was really cool.

As we parted, I said, "I'm glad I finally came clean about knowing who you are, so thank you very much for indulging me."

And he said, "So long, Jackie!"

A-a-a-and . . . back to earth I tumbled.

Screw you, Scar.

JACKO, WACKO
Dancer, Singer, Regular Dude

In 1991, I was cast as a background dancer in Julie Brown's Madonna spoof for Showtime, *Medusa: Dare to Be Truthful*. I was the only nondancer amid real ones, some of whom had actually worked for Madonna. To rehearse, they booked us into a dance studio in Hollywood, and because I was simply the worst dancer—I was there to be funny, not wow everyone with my moves—I needed a special dance captain, much to the amusement of my temporary fellow dancers. Two male dancers even jokingly called me "heifer," after which I'd make fun of them right back, accusing them of being the ones who had gained half a pound over the weekend. We became fast friends.

One day, we didn't have parking spaces, because moving into the rehearsal room next door to us was Michael Jackson's "Black or White" video shoot! Suddenly the place was buzzing, because our choreographer was a talented woman named Smith Wordes, who'd worked with Michael in the past (in "Captain EO" and the "Smooth Criminal" video), and the feeling was there might be a chance to meet the King of Pop. Being an actress, I was just as excited to meet the video's director, the comedy filmmaker John Landis. And yet that first day, Michael didn't show up at all. This was a big-budget video, too. I remember walking past Michael Jackson's set, I looked in and noticed John Landis sitting on a folding chair by himself, reading a newspaper. I guess that's what you do when Michael is a no-show. That whole day, their choreographer, frequent Michael and Madonna collaborator Vince Paterson, kept coming over to our set and ended up helping us (and especially me) out. Then he said, "Do you want to see the choreography for the music video?" HELL YES. So we all got to go over and watch Vince (filling in for Michael Jackson) and the dancers do the "Black or White" choreography in full, as it was *supposed* to have been taught to Michael that day. It was one of the most dazzling performances I've ever seen, and because our dancers knew their dancers, the whole vibe was collegial and fun and a privilege to witness.

The next day, Michael showed. I heard they'd lost a million dollars because of his absence. A good portion of that must have been on the catering. I'd never seen anything like it. Our chips and waters had been transformed into a super vegetarian display, and I even became a fan of grilled, skewered tofu from that point on. (We got the okay from their production to eat their food.)

Then Smith dropped the bomb on us: "Do you want to meet Michael?" HELL YES HELL YES. So a small group of us—Julie Brown, me, and four dancers—went to the catering room. What follows is a series of things that surprised me.

Michael was in the room by himself. No bodyguards and no entourage. He and Smith hugged, and you could tell their relationship was warm and genuine. But my impressions of the legend himself went as follows: 1) He was not as surgerized-looking as hype and photos had led me to believe. I expected to see a nose halfway toward falling off. Instead, I would say he looked 60 percent himself, 40 percent "assembled." 2) He exhibited a thoroughly normal sense of humor and conversational ability. I remember that he joked around with Smith and never gave off that weird, timid affectation where he looks like if you said "pee" or "poop" he'd giggle and put his hand to his mouth. He was talking dancer shoptalk and didn't act shocked or shy. 3) The big one: his voice register was *nothing* like his high-pitched acceptance speeches and mousey interview moments. It was lower and not airy or wispy. Dare I say normal? If my back had been to him on the street, I wouldn't have known it was Michael Jackson talking; *that's* how different it sounded. Standing in that room, watching and listening to him chitchat and catch up with Smith, completely unfazed by total strangers being close to him, I was quietly flabbergasted. He was in his element: working, talking with colleagues, away from prying cameras. It was revelatory. And yet he'd been a no-show the day prior, costing the production a million dollars because—as newspaper photos revealed—he'd been at the mall with Macaulay Culkin. So . . . um . . . not *totally* normal.

JACKSON, MICHAEL
King of Pop, I Was There

I, Kathy Griffin, was an extra in the Michael Jackson Pepsi commercial in 1984 where his effing hair caught fire!

I have two points to make.

Point 1: You know what a Forrest Gump moment is, right? It's when you happen to witness or be present during an iconic moment in history, good or bad. I've had a few of those, and this was one.

Back then, I did as much work as an extra as I could, because it was the closest I could get to feeling like a part of show business. On a side note, not only was I never destined to be an overnight success, but I spent years as an extra for $35 a day just to have the opportunity to try to get my foot in the door. I did this while I was taking acting classes, improv classes, and keeping my day job at whatever nine-to-five office would have me considering I have absolutely no office skills. Needless to say, I was excited when I got the call in late January for a two-day shoot in downtown Los Angeles at the Shrine Auditorium. Two days at $35 a day was $70!

Not only was the money fantastic, but, when I learned it was a commercial with the Jackson 5, I was the first in line. I was one of a thousand in a standing-only crowd that day, watching Michael Jackson do take after take of him making his big stairway entrance onto a glitzy rock-and-roll-like set and jamming with his brothers to a reworked version of "Billie Jean," incorporating "You're the Pepsi Generation" into the song. It was fascinating to watch Michael Jackson at work. Of course, I grew up with his music, but it was quite an up-close and personal experience to just be in that audience watching how a really big commercial is made with one of the biggest stars in history.

At one point, I noticed my buddy Jon Lovitz in the crowd— we were both in the Groundlings then—and when I asked why he was there, he introduced me to *his* pal Miko Brando, son of Marlon and one of Michael Jackson's bodyguards.

Point 2: This was all before the Internet, social media, TMZ, cell phones with cameras, all of it. The public wouldn't know of a news event of this magnitude until much LATER. So when people ask me about what it was like to be there that day, I have to remind them of this. Here's what happened that day from an extra's point of view. Keep in mind you can see it online now, because *US Weekly* got hold of the footage of when a pyrotechnic effect went off too early and posted it in 2009. Anyway, the last thing a production would do following an accident like this would be to announce to hundreds, if not thousands, of extras something like, "There's been a horrible accident. Everybody go home!" I just remember we were all abruptly excused for the day. By the time I'd driven my parents' Toyota Corolla back to our Santa Monica apartment, it was all over the news, and I could hardly believe it. Over the years, it's been very strange to realize that I had been there for a momentous showbiz incident—one many believe led to Michael Jackson's debilitating addiction struggles and tragic death—and not known what had happened at the time. I still believe he molested all those kids, though.

JENNER, KENDALL
Model (By Today's Standards, Let's Be Honest)

First off, I call her Candle, which drives her insane.

Speaking of driving, the lanky, somewhat soft-spoken, very homeschooled, up-and-coming model / reality star / whatever and I were leaving an event at the same time, so the valet guys brought our cars one right after the other. Candle's SUV was in front of my car, and when she backed up slightly to maneuver out, she came perilously close to my front bumper. This is what I call an opportunity, so I yelled out, in front of all the waiting celebrities, "Candle! Candle! Don't kill me! This isn't the night!" I grabbed Rosanna Arquette, who was nearby. "Rosanna! You've got to be a witness! Candle Jenner is trying to kill me!" I'm pretty sure Candle waved as she drove off, a gesture from a stone-cold assassin that said, "Next time!"

I know you're wondering: my Maserati was unharmed. Shaken, but okay.

JENNER, KRIS
My Biological Mother

When it comes to Miss Kathy Griffin's style of highbrow comedy, the Kardashians get it. Not in the way you're thinking. I mean, Kris Jenner *really* gets it.

I'm the least of the Kardashians' worries. They're juggling all sorts of tabloid newsworthy topics ranging from sex tapes to relationship drama and paternity suits to the academic rigors of Ph.D. dissertations. There might have legitimately been a time when the subject of Kathy Griffin warranted an "Oh no, not her." But now they say hi, and I honestly don't think I've had a Kardashian mad at me in years. This is not something I am proud of. Let's see if this book can break that streak. At least the main Kardashians haven't been mad at me in years. I can't keep up with the younger ones who seem to be multiplying. (I'm looking at you, Saint.)

Case in point: A few Christmases ago, I found myself at a star-studded party where I was embarrassingly under-dressed. As in, I'm in jeans, and it's supposed to be formal wear. My big idea was to sneak off to a room, call my assistant, and get him to drive over and throw a Carolina Herrera gown through the window. I find a door, open it, and inside is Kris Jenner, the three main Kardashian girls, Candle floating around somewhere, and Francine, who may have been in the room, but at this point, she is, how shall I say, unrecognizable. They really do clump together like the Mafia, or some bygone Irish band of toughs from *Gangs of New York*. I started right in joking with them, and they let me go on, even though by a certain point I realized they'd kind of encircled me, and the brief thought of a blood sacrifice ritual entered my mind. But really, they were all friendly and just wanted me to entertain them. Nobody was mean. Khloé even came up and squeaked out a "Hi, my favorite!"

I said, "What's up, Loch Ness?" It was as if I were the attraction at some weird Hollywood petting zoo.

Anyway, Kris piped up at one point and said, "You know, I was just in another conversation, and we were trying to figure out how you would classify our family. I noticed you were here, Kathy, so I thought, *She's going to be able to come up with something right away!*"

I pretended to think about it, then said, "I'm going to have to stick with 'dirty whores.'" They all cheered and laughed.

As I thought, *They get it.*

JONAS, NICK
Singer, Former Has-Been, Current Hit Maker

When I first met the Jonas Brothers, it was at the Grammys, where they played with Stevie Wonder, and I thought they were embarrassingly horrible. Stevie Wonder may have wanted to be deaf as well as blind that day. I really couldn't get over how they'd been shoved down our throats: the stadium tours selling out, dressing alike, talking alike, being anointed somehow "better" than your average boy band. It was manufactured, time-tested showbiz formula, which worked very well for them for quite a while. Also, dating famous young women in a rotating tabloid-friendly fashion also accomplished two goals: staying famous and staying in my act. But then, for various reasons, the Jonas Brothers, as we knew them, faded away.

During this period, Nick wound up being seated at my table at a charity event, and he was sweet and humble, even calling me "Ms. Griffin" (which I love) and sporting a white-boy 'fro, and for all intents and purposes acting like a nice young man who didn't care anymore about the spotlight. "Damn right, it's Ms. Griffin, Jonas!" I reminded him. As you know, the Jonas Brothers decided to part ways and move on to their next musical projects. Nick just couldn't help himself. He hit the gym, got a haircut, sent one Instagram pic of his abs into the universe—you know you've seen it, LGBTs, okay, mostly Gs—and now he's hot again (and all that a certain person whose name rhymes with "Banderson Booper" can talk about).

I ran into Nick again after that, and I had to let him know. I yelled, "*I know your game!*" He flexed a bicep, smirked, and went along his merry way.

Just a word of advice, Nicholas, Aunt Kathy wants you to know that if you gain ten pounds or turn even the least bit doughy with your now-famous upper-body physique, the Gs are going to dump your ass and remove you from their cell phone screen savers.

I say this out of love.

———

KEATON, MICHAEL
Birdman, Batman

Something happened with Michael Keaton that's never happened to me before with a celebrity run-in. I saw him in 2016 at a black-tie soirée, and since I've always loved him—how funny he is, how great an actor he is, how he's weathered the ups and downs and always come back stronger—I wanted that interaction to happen. Especially since I loved *Spotlight*, which would go on to win the Oscar for Best Picture weeks later.

I went up to him and, in my ready-made fast-talking mode, said, "Hi, my name is Kathy Griffin, I really want to meet you, I just think you're so amazing, I'm going to bug you for a picture, and just, your work, your movies, they're so great . . ."

And as I was rapid-rambling, he interrupted me with that patented shy mutter of his by saying, with his head slightly down, "Uh, I've actually met you, but you probably don't remember."

Pause. Oh, wow. Oh my God. For a brief moment, I was *Speechless*. (Had to get the name of a Keaton movie in there.)

Here's the funny thing: *of course I remembered meeting him*, but it was barely a "meeting"—and it was ages ago! It was during the *Suddenly Susan* era, twenty years ago at a party, and Keaton was talking to Brooke Shields and I was standing nearby, smiling, nodding, probably thinking, *Holy shit, that's Michael Keaton*. And now, here I was, acting like I'd never met him, because *I assumed he wouldn't have remembered meeting ME!* He isn't allowed to be the misremembered one!

"Yes! Of course I remember! I assumed *you* wouldn't remember!"

He said, "Oh, well, I just thought . . ."

So yes, we had a brief, "no, *I'm* less memorable" exchange, which was absurd. Believe me, that has never happened before. It made me wish there was a camera there to capture it. In a way, there was, but I was so taken aback my cell phone wasn't ready. By the time it was, Keaton and I had moved on to a serious conversation about *Spotlight* and pedophile priests and Catholicism. So serious, in fact, that his brow was in full furrow, and then I said something like, "Time for a selfie!" and he had to go, "Whoa! Whoa! Transition!"

Then I decided he needed photos with different people, so I started pushing him toward the likes of Jane Fonda, Alice Cooper, and even Sammy Hagar. He played along—"Oh my, Sammy Hagar!"—and all the while I just couldn't get over how an Academy Award nominee thought I wouldn't recall meeting him. Believe me, in those situations, it's always me going, "Um, we've met several times, I made you laugh, sat next to you on an eighteen-hour flight, hosted your charity event, made out with you several times, and saved your dog from drowning. Fine, you don't remember me?" But Michael Keaton did.

KENDRICK, ANNA
Twilight-er, Pitch Perfect-er, Could Be Nice-er

I'm sure this was an isolated incident. Or at least I'd like to think it was. I was at the Toronto Film Festival in 2011, hosting an amfAR event, and I attended one of the parties as the date of a movie publicist friend. I saw Katie Couric, who let me hijack her phone so I could scroll through pictures, and that was fun. Jessica Chastain was a not-yet-famous up-and-comer then, and she ran up to me and said, "Aaah! I want to meet you. You're so amazing!" That was cool. Then my friend wanted to say hello to Anna Kendrick, who was at a booth nearby.

I walked up and said, "Hi. It's nice to meet you." Then I think I complimented her on *Up in the Air* and her Oscar nomination for it. Really simple chitchatting, maybe thirty seconds. Then there was a pause, and since I'm not afraid of pauses in conversation, I just kept talking.

Then she looked at me and very unabashedly said, "Um, I have to ask you to go. My cousin's here visiting, and we need to catch up."

And ladies and gentlemen, at that moment, I just wanted to DIE. I had nothing. I probably said something like, "Oh! Uh . . . that's cool! Yeah! . . . Uh, ha ha . . . ," and bolted. But seriously, if there had been a security guard in the vicinity, I wouldn't have been surprised if Kendrick had snapped her fingers to him and had me forcibly escorted away. It was that weird, and, to my mind, rude, and, as Maggie would say, "a little high and mighty." I mean, it was a party. I was nice to her. She's a winner in life: a star on the rise, breaking out of those *Twilight* movies, and I was acknowledging her for that. It wasn't even my initiative! A friend had walked me over to her booth! I wasn't some drunk fan barfing on her tits. I get that she had a relative there, but I pride myself on reading a room, and I clearly had that one wrong and I don't know why. I also pride myself on being the sassy aunt to the fun younger gals like Meghan Trainor and Aubrey Plaza, so this diminutive ice princess's tone caught me off guard. I would have fully expected that reaction from Katie Couric, and probably ten feet before I'd ever got close enough to say anything. Plenty of famous people have given me leeway, watched me step over the line, then had to say, "All right, enough." Never in a million years would I have expected Anna Kendrick to give me the "do I have to have you removed" look after less than a minute of friendly praise. I wish I could tell you I had a snappy comeback, but I just skulked away like a high school nerd rejected at the cool kids' table. I still think she's talented. I love the *Pitch Perfect* movies. But the next time I see her, I might just have to barf on her tits, just so when she tells me again that I have to go, it makes more sense.

KNIGHT, SUGE
Former CEO of Death Row Records, Can Give a Death Stare

One night I was talking to my pal comedian Katt Williams on the phone, and he said, "What are you doing right now?"

"I'm in my pajamas, and my boyfriend's watching sports."

"I'd like to send a car for your people, if you want to come over."

"Well, 'my people' is me and my boyfriend," I said. "But I can drive my own car."

As we were getting ready to leave, I joked to my boyfriend, Randy, whose upbringing is very much Orange County Caucasian, "Look, we're going to Katt's in Malibu. He's had some legal issues, and there's a chance, just a chance . . . it probably won't happen . . . but this evening could resemble the *Boogie Nights* scene with armed Alfred Molina and the gaysian throwing firecrackers."

"What?" Randy asked, utterly confused.

I tried to reassure him. "But probably not."

We got in the car and drove to Katt's, and as we pulled into his driveway, I noticed a few Lamborghinis and two cages on the front lawn that housed giant mastiffs. I thought, *I've never had a boring moment with Katt Williams, and this won't be the first.*

Katt met us in the driveway and escorted us inside, where he had a smorgasbord of Italian takeout laid out. "Do you want some fettucine?" he asked.

He was being a very sweet host.

There were two imposing men in the corner, and Randy whispered, "That guy looks like Suge Knight."

"That's because it is," I whispered back.

The color drained from Randy's face, which was my cue to go, "Soodge?"

Katt started laughing, so I said, "Soodge! What are you doing here? My God, I miss you!"

Suge Knight looked exactly as you might expect: ill-fitting golf shirt, chains, and jeans with mysterious bulges that didn't look anatomical. A man of few, measured words, he didn't say anything, then walked over to a table and picked up a box of Popeye's fried chicken. So I did the slow clap, approached him, and said, "Really, Soodge? You're a black man who's going to eat Popeye's fried chicken in front of a white comedian? Welcome to my act."

Katt was laughing even more, saying, "Oh, Suge, now you did it! Now you're in trouble. White lady's gonna say anything, you know how that white lady is." (*White lady* is Katt's term of affection for me.)

Randy, of course, had his "please stop talking" expression working overtime, because my teasing Suge was admittedly on the edge.

Suge really hovered over Katt the whole time we were there, bodyguard-style, to the extent that I said, "Soodge, is it time for my pat down?"

Katt was the perfect host, and we had a great time hanging out, and when it was time to leave, he walked us out to the car. Right before getting in, though, I said, "Soodge, have you met my boyfriend, Whitey?"

I could tell Randy was thinking, *We're so close. The finish line is right . . . over . . . there . . .*

Then I asked, "Soodge, do you know what just occurred to me? When was the last time you spooned with a lady?"

Katt chuckled and said, "I don't think that's what he's into."

"You know what?" I said. "I think it is. I think someone here is afraid to ask for a spoon."

I walked up to Suge, took his arms, wrapped them around me with my back to him, and said, "Just breathe, Soodge. Enjoy something called tender loving care."

Then Suge—again, a man patient with his communication skills—said, "Normally I like PUSSY."

I nodded and said, "I know, I know. But tonight, you're going to have to be satisfied with gentle spooning from your friend Kathy."

I looked at Suge as I got in the car and said, "Good night, Soodge. And remember who to call when you need a little spoon."

I know many people might be surprised that I wanted to engage with a convicted felon as somebody adorable, but I believe I changed him. And yes, since that night he's been shot, and arrested for theft, and been involved in a fatal car accident that led to another murder charge, but I know what gets him through his trials: the affectionate redhead who opened his eyes to spooning.

KUTCHER, ASHTON
High-Tech Nostradamus, Douche Bag

When Kutcher was pushing Twitter hard in its early days, saying it would change lives globally, I tweeted out, "Does Ashton Kutcher have stock in this company?" Obviously, the guy has his finger on the pulse of all things Silicon Valley and has venture capitalist chops to prove it. But in my experience with him, this social media champion is a tool.

We cohosted a charity event in 2005 for uBid.com. The event was star studded with everyone from Jessica Biel to Mila Kunis, and it had an extra spark because this was when Mila was still dating Macaulay Culkin (take that in for a minute) and Kutcher had just married Demi Moore. Jesus, I have been present or involved in some pretty crazy-ass moments. But I digress.

The point of this story is Kutcher, my cohost, did not speak to me once. If you're wondering how exactly that works, join the club, because I don't, either. At least three separate times, we were standing in the wings, waiting to go out and present, and I'd say something like, "Hey, what if, when we go out, we do this . . . ," and suggest something, and he'd just ignore me. We might as well have been strangers standing next to each other in a subway car, which makes the one who starts talking sound like the insane person, especially when the other one refuses to react. At least two times we were out at the podium together, and the silence had been enough for me to almost say, "Ladies and gentlemen, wait a minute, I have to talk to the happy groom . . . ," just to force him into talking to me, but I didn't. Because oddly enough, I understood his skittishness about being a high-profile newlywed. And yet if he said five words to me the whole day, I'd be surprised. It was bizarre and rude and made me feel as if he thought I was beneath him, someone not worth talking to in the slightest.

Three years later, I'm grabbing something to eat from the little Mexican takeout place in my neighborhood, and who should walk in but Kutcher and Demi Moore. I smiled and waved. Nothin'. If you won't say hi to me in the Mexican takeout joint, you're a d-bag.

Another time, I was talking to P. Diddy, and Kutcher stepped directly in front of me and started talking to Diddy as if I wasn't even there.

So that's three incidents. Do I loathe him? No. He's just someone who's made it perfectly clear to me that I have absolutely nothing to offer him during his precious time on earth.

By the way, I encourage you to look up the photo of us hosting this event because it is one of those photos that just says it all.

LANSING, SHERRY
Studio Chief-ess, Model, Jane of All Trades

Trust me, I am as equally in tune with the groundbreaking

women who are behind the camera as well as the women in front of the camera. Sherry Lansing was the first woman to head a major Hollywood studio. She started as an actress, became a producer, then president of Twentieth Century Fox, then later was CEO of Paramount for twelve years. I've gotten to know her through the Beverly Hills "mafia" sometimes referred to as the Loop Group.

Sherry knows how to work a power luncheon, which she hosts often. On one of those luncheons in attendance besides Sherry were Bette Midler, Anjelica Huston, Sidney Poitier's wife, Joanna, and *Vanity Fair* editor Graydon Carter—and little ole me. I've always gotten the impression Graydon finds me classless and vulgar. Of course, the reason this bothers me is because I have been a longtime and loyal subscriber to *VF*.

Often these lunches are all about the seating arrangement. I was happy to be seated next to my pal Sherry, who, by the way, is a great laugher. When Graydon arrived and took his seat next to Sherry, she said, "Graydon, Kathy Griffin's here. What a treat and a surprise." Nice tee up, Sherry. Let's see where this goes. Sherry obviously has the gift of seamlessly putting people together and that day proved herself to be a true friend. I had told her I was nervous about meeting the formidable Graydon Carter.

Next thing you know, as will happen at a lunch party, people started mingling and shifting chairs. I found myself seated between Bette Midler and Graydon with Sherry to his right. I tried to bring my A game in the conversation department. Politics, pop culture, and, most importantly, quoting not one, not two, but three of my favorite *VF* pieces.

Sherry chimed in, "Isn't she great? I just love her. Her mind is so fast." (Thank you, Sherry.)

Graydon finally asked how I knew Sherry.

I said, "I know Sherry because she respects me tremendously." And he laughed at that. Then I said, "But I don't know if Sherry knows that she's married a crazy person."

And Sherry said, "What?!? (laughing) You think I don't know THAT?"

Sherry is married to Academy Award–winning director William Friedkin, who made *The French Connection* and *The Exorcist* and who—while being an incredibly great filmmaker—has a notorious reputation for being a somewhat volatile perfectionist. Look, Linda Blair's head didn't spin itself. I've teased him about it, even.

Sherry continued, "Let me tell you my story. I married Billy four weeks after I met him, and twenty of my best friends called me and told me I was making the worst mistake of my life. Then another friend called me and said, 'You'll never be bored!'"

I loved that story. And yet I said to Sherry, "When I see Billy, he's always kind of warm and fuzzy, but I just want you to know, there's darkness there."

Sherry laughed and said, "That's why I married him. Isn't she great, Graydon? Isn't she great?"

Graydon? Graydon? I'm ready for my cover . . .

LATIFAH, QUEEN
Actor, Rapper, My Friend Dana

In the *Suddenly Susan* days, I remember a moment waiting for an elevator at a hotel, and Queen Latifah came up to me and said, "I'm watching you"—*Uh-oh*, I thought—"and you're really funny!" *Whew.* "I really like your shit. You're really funny!" I never expected anyone to know who I was in those days, and I remember thinking, *Queen Latifah knows who I am!* It was really sweet of her.

That led, years later, to appearing on her daytime talk show. Many hosts don't bother checking in to say hi or meet their guests, but Latifah did. When she came to my dressing room, I shouted, "Come on in, Dana!" knowing I was buck naked. I do love to shock a talk show host—I always have. I have a REAL body. Real boobs, real everything. Gravity does exist. And that is what Latifah saw. I was rushing to finish the full hair and makeup process, which required full nudity. I had a strange, half-done rainbow colors of pale effect in that my arms and legs were covered in very dark bronzer, which would have off-set the pale, near-translucent canvas display of my naughty parts in a probably very disconcerting manner. Basically, I'm assuming I looked like a strangely iced gingerbread cookie, or a stripper who fell asleep that day at the beach. I've been in this business long enough not to give a rat's ass who sees me naked anymore. If you think I'm going to wait for you to clear a fitting room before I shed my clothes, you're sorely mistaken. I'm there for a fitting, not to play demure.

Back to Latifah's reaction, which was swift and genuine. A lot of "Oh no! Sorry, I should come back later! Are you naked? Kathy, you are too much!" Mission accomplished. I had shocked the host and stayed on schedule with my full-body-bronzing process. I was more than a little flattered when she blurted out, "Dang, girl, you still got it! No wonder you got a young boyfriend!" With that lovely compliment—a nice bookend to her "You're really funny" intro all those years ago—I half considered forgoing the dress or any of my clothing for my segment. But I decided to wear clothing because 1) it was daytime, and 2) she's royalty.

LENO, JAY
Comic, The Tonight Show Host, Confidant

Jay was one of my guys. He had me on *The Tonight Show* multiple times, and with my history of talk show banishment, it was a relationship I'd come to cherish. It had its rocky period, too, as fans of *My Life on the D-List* well know. During an appearance on *The Tonight Show* in 2005, I was doing a bit with a picture of me and Carmen Electra, and how she wouldn't stop calling me for beauty tips, and Jay threw in his own crack, calling the photo a "before-and-after" picture. To this day, I can't fully explain why I cried about it in the NBC Studios parking lot. It surprised even me. And yet there I was welling up and needing to calm down. I called him out on it afterward as a below-the-belt joke, to which he argued that I should be able to take that kind of humor if it can be said to a man, too. (Our conversation was accidentally recorded by the *D-List* crew, and I tried to get it played on the show, but I heard the network put the kibosh on it. Can't confirm that, just heard that was the case.) It was just an all-around horrible scene, and I was off that show for a while.

But then I got invited back, and I have to say, ever since then, it's been a lovefest with Jay. Since that fight, he's been one of the kindest, most generous people and a terrific champion of mine. I know he has his detractors, but my personal experience with him is that of an attentive, thoughtful colleague, one who took the time to visit me in the dressing room before every one of my appearances on his show and initiate private chats in which we could talk about anything. It became a ritual. During hair and makeup, he'd stroll in, make a joke, and I'd say, "You know what it's time for!" Then I rudely kicked everyone out, and Jay and I would settle in on the dressing room couch next to each other and get very candid about whatever was going on in our lives. He opened up to me about what he was going through during the feud with Conan O'Brien, and I could ask him about anything. He even called me up personally after my guest star stint on *Law & Order: SVU* to tell me I was great.

After my talk show was canceled and I was in a dark place, he told me, "Look, kid, this is what I think. It was a good show, but it was so under the radar, it's not a fail. Don't think of it as a show that was canceled. Think of it as two seasons of a talk show that gave you that experience." Maybe the most valuable thing he said to me was after I'd been complaining about some career slight, not getting a sought-after TV gig that had once again gone to "the other girl," and he said, "I don't get it! You're first chair on *The Tonight Show*, you've got the awards—you won! Be careful what you wish for, because most people I know who end up truly realizing every dream, they went down the toilet very quickly." And boy, do I think about that a lot. His advice was, "You want to keep the struggle."

Here was a guy I'd had a rough start with, and now, all these years later, I cherish our conversations. I like talk show hosts who want to talk, you know? To this day, if Jay and I happen to be headlining at the same casino a night apart, I will go in a day early, or stay a day late, just so I can get our precious one-on-one shoptalk.

LETO, JARED
Actor, Singer, National Oddity

I have an unspoken arrangement with Jared Leto. It's not enough for him to be gorgeous and a great actor; he's still got to have the frickin' band. I remember when Sixty Seconds Over Tokyo, or Thirty Seconds Above Pluto, or whatever his ridiculousness is called, was playing teeny-weeny clubs in town, and Leto was bragging about turning down film and television roles, and I just thought it was absurd. I would look at his guyliner and dyed hair and think, *Get a Casio, put it in the basement, and do it on weekends when nobody has to be embarrassed for you.* But God love him, he made it successful. Like Jennifer Hudson, he told Hollywood, "You're going to love me," and it worked.

Now, it doesn't mean he loves *me.* Our friendship is very much one-sided: I'm friends with Jared Leto, even though he isn't friends with me. I'll explain it this way: after seeing each other repeatedly over the course of many celebrity-packed events, we have a thing. It's not sexual, it's not even necessarily collegial, it's . . . like I said, an arrangement.

The thing is, when he was making the awards-season rounds with *Dallas Buyers Club*, I saw Leto at everything, because he has feet in the acting and music worlds. He'd be at the Screen Actors Guild Awards, and then the Grammys. I'd run into him at a British Academy of Film and Television Arts (BAFTA) luncheon, and then he'd be at iHeartRadio. So enough time had passed and events transpired at which we'd exchanged pleasantries, that I realized it was time to ramp it up a bit. I can't remember the first time I homed in and gave him shit, but I do recall at the Eagles concert at the Forum he was sporting two-tone long hair and wearing a poncho, as if he were going to be called onstage to sing "Desperado" that night. He looked like he was in costume, for Chris-

sakes. I yelled from my seat, "LETO!" He looked back and up and gave me a tentative "hi" wave, and I said, "Hey, Khloé Kardashian called. She wants her hair back!"

Leto said, "Thank you, Ms. Griffin," and kept walking.

I thought to myself, *Damn straight. The hot guy A-lister takes the joke on the chin because Mrs. Kathy has earned it, and it wouldn't be right to beat up on her. Game on.*

Two weeks later, I was doing my regular walk in a park. A park! I wasn't going for a walk down a red carpet or through a movie studio. I was pretty much in the middle of nowhere. No cameras around. Just going for a hike—nothing Hollywood about it. I see, of all people, Academy Award winner Jared Leto walking toward me in costume. Yes, I said in costume. I don't know what you work out in, but my new boyfriend Jared Leto was rocking a man bun, wearing what looked to be those Kate Hudson–brand colorful jeggings with a paisley print, skimpy tank top, and a red fanny pack. I said, "LETO!"

He just stopped.

"I'm sorry," I said, "is there a Cirque du Soleil rehearsal I'm missing? You're in a canyon. *Act like it!*"

He just put his head down and said, "Thank you, Ms. Griffin," and walked on.

Thank YOU, Mr. Leto, for hiking into my act.

LETTERMAN, DAVID
Talk Show Legend

Those of you familiar with my bestselling memoir *Official Book Club Selection*—and that's all of you, right? I thought so—know of my heartbreak when I was banned from David Letterman's show after I swore on air and my thrill at being asked on again all those years later. Well, that welcome back was permanent, as I became a true friend of the show through the rest of Dave's tenure, and I loved it. I remember talking to Tom Hanks once about appearing on *Late Show with David Letterman*, and he said what a lot of us felt about sitting in that lead chair: "I actually rehearse for David Letterman. I want to go there prepared." It's that legend factor.

Well, of all my appearances, my favorite story has to do with him showing everyone a picture of Cher and I swimming together. He asked me about it, so I told him about going on vacation with her, and Dave just couldn't get over it. It's all he wanted to talk about. A lot of stars would tell you about how you weren't supposed to talk to Dave during the commercial breaks, so I never initiated anything. But that night, during the break, he grabbed my hand, pulled me toward him, and continued his flabbergasted tone:

Dave: I just can't believe it. You go to Cher's *house*? [Keep in mind, the audience can't hear any of this.]

Me: Yes! Dave, what's wrong with you? You've interviewed every American president, and you had an on-air fight with Madonna!

Dave: I'd be *terrified* to go to Cher's! Come on, is that true?

Me: Dave, everything I say is true; you know this.

Dave: But this? This is true? Come on? This really happened?

Me: Yes!

Dave: You go to her bedroom and you guys just . . . *talk*?

Me: Yes! We talk politics and movies and laugh. What don't you get about this? This is what you do for a living!

Dave: I could never go to Cher's house! I'd be scared she'd eat me alive! I can't believe you just . . . *talk* to her.

Me: And I can't believe you're so freaked out about Cher! I'm going to text her everything you said.

Dave: Hold on, hold on, *please* be careful how you say it.

Me: Oh, okay, Dave. I'll be extra careful 'cause she's so

scary. FYI, you're a thousand times scarier than Cher.
She's a breeze. You're a tough cookie.

It's true. He was much more intimidating. Who knows what was going through Dave's mind regarding Cher? The fact that she called him an asshole on his show all those years ago probably had something to do with it. Dave and ballsy, outspoken women always made for great TV. (Again, Madonna.) Maybe to him, as often as he has been called a legend, he thought of her as the bigger legend, the one with a genuine mystique. It was like the modest Indianan in him was coming out, but only for 120 seconds. (Remember, it was a commercial break.) It was cute, in a way, how bewildered he was.

Later, my text to Cher was along the lines of:

Well, thanks a lot. My whole interview was about you. I could barely push my new TV special.

LOVATO, DEBBIE
Pop Star, Slugger, #TooConfident

One night, I got asked on Twitter who I thought was the "biggest douche celebrity." This is not a question I take either extra seriously or that jokingly, so I usually just go with recent history. A certain Disney Channel star had been unfriendly to me for no good reason at a few different events (i.e., we wound up on the same guest bill at *The Tonight Show* once, and I made a point of walking over to her after she performed to say, "Congratulations on your new song," to which she sneered back, "What?" I repeated myself, and she repeated the snarling, "WHAT?"). *Okay*, I thought, *so you're just an asshole*. Thinking back on this and other brief encounters, I said into my iPhone, "Demi Lovato," and Siri translated it as "*Debbie* Lovato," which I thought was funny. So I call her that now, because Apple products are always right.

Lovato had been in my act because of an incident on a plane in 2010 in which she'd punched a backup dancer named Alex Welch in the face, then suddenly went into rehab to allegedly deal with a lot of things—cutting, eating issues, substance problems, bipolar disorder (serious stuff, I GET IT!). These issues obviously trigger very genuine emotions in fans (or . . . in my humble opinion as a professional stand-up comedian who is covered under the umbrella of the First Amendment of the United States Constitution under satire—and trust me, Debbie, I know that First Amendment better than Larry freaking Flynt); I am merely suggesting that I have long held the opinion that Debbie may have gone to rehab to help everyone forget that she punched a girl in the face when she got mad at her. Quick question for you, reader, if you were in this same situation: do you think you would be sent off to rehab or, I don't know . . . jail?

So I admit, I'd had some comedic fun in my shows with the theory that jail time didn't sound too appealing to Debbie, but settling quickly and going into rehab right away worked out nicely, and how many civilians who assault someone can get away with that? (Judge: "Do you have an album dropping soon?" Civilian: "No." Judge: "Lock her up.")

Anyway, the day after I called her the douchiest celebrity on Twitter, my phone blew up with supportive "Are you okay?" texts and e-mails from friends, enough to make me think someone had died. Then I checked my Twitter feed, and it had more tweets than I'd ever received, and they were not what you would call friendly. Here are some examples:

@kathygriffin: I will burn your house down cunt.
@kathygriffin: I will come to your house and rape you bitch. #lovaticswantkathygriffinraped
@kathygriffin: Don't you ever talk shit about my Demi again or us Lovatics will kill you in your sleep

. . . and I'm not making fun of this topic at all, but I will be honest, I involuntarily may have chuckled in shock when I read this one:

@kathygriffin: I really hope you commit sue of side.

Meet Debbie's "fan army" (by the way, kids, you're not in an actual army, so stop acting like it). The Lovatics are a thirty-million-strong bunch that are passionate and clearly not fazed by being labeled with a suffix that conjures up a medical condition and the need for treatment. Whatever happened when Debbie went into rehab after settling with Alex Welch, she freaking somehow came out with an image makeover that's turned her into a Sheryl Sandberg for teens. ("Lean in" when you punch people, I'm assuming is the message.) But it's an image, as calculated and successful as it's been, that's contradicted by the level of hate and vitriol her fan army can whip up, and I refuse to believe Debbie herself doesn't realize this. So when the LAPD became involved and detectives were sitting in my living room, they expressed that they had considered some of the posts from certain Lovatics to be "credible threats"—posting pictures of my home online, showing enough knowledge of my daily routine to suggest people go to certain places and throw bricks at my head until I'm dead, and so on. I wonder when Debbie feels like it's time to call off the dogs. I believe she can. Since then, a security team has kept and continues to keep profiles of certain Lovatics. In my mind, she escalated things not long afterward when she tweeted a selfie from backstage at iHeartRadio (long before this dustup began) in which you can see me in the background watching Rihanna perform, and Debbie in the foreground making an "ick" face and pointing to me. Thanks, Debbie. She quickly deleted it—millennials always think they can hit a button and go, "We're all good now"— but I allege she very much inflamed things even more. Look, I've poked fun of them all—Beliebers, Directioners, Swifties, Barbz, Smilers—and never experienced anything like this. By writing this, I probably made the worst of them think, *Yassss!! We slayed her for stanning our kween!*

LYNCH, MARSHAWN
Beast Mode, Super Bowl Champ, Big KG Fan

I took on Beast Mode!

It was March of 2014, and the Seattle Seahawks had just won the Super Bowl. Apparently, heterosexual men get very excited about this football contest. All I remember is that the Bruno Mars halftime show was fantastic.

Anyway, I was cohosting an event in San Francisco that happened to have a lot of star athletes and pro sports team owners as donors in the audience. It is not uncommon when hosting a high-profile charity event that I am asked to mingle with high donors prior to the event or if there is any down-time between acts. I've had many times in my career when someone with a headset just yells, "Go out into the audience and vamp!" That means I have to choose someone at random, bring a wireless microphone, and improvise with them for a moment until the next musical act is done setting up.

Halfway through the show, I was asked to do just that. Since I am not so up on the sports figures as the seventeen straight guys reading this book are, I asked for a photo cheat sheet. I picked out one guy who just looked like he would be fun to play with. I had my cheat sheet and was running up the aisle with a microphone in a long red Valentino gown, yelling to the entire audience, "Where is this guy Marshawn Lynch? Is that how you say it? Marshawwn? Or Mar-shan?"

Two things happened simultaneously. I found him quite easily. He is a rather imposing, gigantic African American man with dreads, who stood out in a room of primarily white, diminutive men in their hedge fund suits. The second thing was that almost every dude in that audience immediately started gasping, freaking out, and pulling out their cell phones and taking pictures. I knew this was going to be good!

I ran up to Marshawn and proceeded to do what I do best. I kept putting the microphone in his face and asked him rapid-fire questions while flirting with him, throwing my arms around him, telling him he was absolutely adorable, asking him what he did for a living, asking him if he could picture seeing Marshawn and Kathy Lynch monogrammed on his bathrobe. The crowd kept their cell phones on. I was highly inappropriate, and all he had to do was stand there like a champ.

And guess what? My new BF Marshawn Lynch was a good

sport and a teddy bear that night. He played along like the pro he is, and the audience ate it up. I mean for God's sake, this is a professional football player who has a Super Bowl ring. He deals with the public constantly. He deals with the press constantly.

Uh-oh. Record scratch. After my triumphant vamping with the clearly tamed-by-me Beast Mode, I triumphantly returned backstage to hear a choir of heterosexual crew dudes start shouting at me. "How could you pick him? Don't you know how shy he is?" As if I care about a celebrity being shy at a public event. I mean, come on, what does that really mean? Everyone in the audience seemed very excited to see my abilities at making Marshawn Lynch really come out of his shell. I don't know too many athletes who are introverts. Well, the crew told me right away. Apparently, my Beast Mode is well known for not wanting to be questioned, bothered unless it is his choice, had recently been fined tens of thousands of dollars for refusing to talk to the media throughout the season, and has no history that he enjoys a crazy redhead randomly running up to him with a microphone asking him a minimum of fifteen rapid-fire questions.

I am proud of this moment. First of all, I didn't know I was supposed to have Skittles in my bra. Second of all, at not one point during our harmless, yet clearly romantic, encounter did he say, "I'm only here so I won't get fined." I'm *his* Beast Mode. Take that, sports nerds. I tackled the Beast and turned him into a KITTEN. Deal with it. He probably wrote a bigger check that night just to get me away from him. Where's my Super Bowl ring?

MACKLEMORE
Bundled-Up Rapper

I don't just love making my second-favorite Vanderbilt laugh every *New Year's Eve Live* on CNN; I'm always looking for any and every comedic opportunity.

December 31, 2013, I spotted Macklemore performing on the ABC big stage nearby (damn you again, Seacrest!). Wait, screw you, Seacrest, because Macklemore and Ryan Lewis walked right over to where our modest operation was. I live for these impromptu moments.

I actually looked up the transcript of my conversation that evening on air with Macklemore:

> Griffin: Hey, I was at Jingle Ball when you guys were there. Remember when Selena Gomez said what the F-word really loud and then, boom, threw the mic down à la Chris Rock style?
> Macklemore: I did.
> Griffin: Confirm it, yes.
> Macklemore: I watched it on the Internet.
> Griffin: Wasn't it great?
> Macklemore: It was impressive.

Then my overactive brain started worrying about another odd element: fur. I was wearing a real fur, a rented sable, and I knew that Macklemore liked wearing fur, but what I didn't know was if he was into the dead-animal kind or the faux

kind. Because if he's Mr. PETA, and I'm sporting a carcass, then I needed to keep my trap shut about the topic. Sure enough, during the commercial break, Macklemore won't shut up about my fricking outerwear.

"Oooh, girl, that's a fly coat. Where'd you get that coat, girl? Is that fur? What kind of fur is that?"

I just kept nervously laughing and saying, "It sure is cold up here! It's no 'Thrift Shop'! HAHAHAHAHA!" I was panicking. The last thing I need is PETA and a bunch of activist rapper fans pelting me—excuse the pun—with balls of paint. But all was good. He was a great guest, it was a big get for us, and later I Googled him and learned that he does wear real and faux fur. The video where he shows off ten fur jockstraps with tails stuck with me. He may be missing one next New Year's Eve.

MANGANO, JOY
Inventor, Entrepreneur, Literally the Joy in Joy

I loved *Joy*. Stories about successful women really get to me. When I hosted a high-profile, high-celebrity-octane awards presentation in 2016, I knew I might get a chance to meet the real Joy, because she was there to present David O. Russell with a screenwriting award. Well, I didn't recognize her at first, because even elegantly attired for a Hollywood event, there's nothing Hollywood about her, which is refreshing. She had teased hair and a black shift dress, but I remember looking at her gigantic scoop necklace and long earrings, wondering if the diamonds were real, because if they weren't cubic zirconium, Mangano had to have been sporting the most expensive bling in a very expensive room that included Catherine Zeta-Jones, who I doubt would know costume jewelry if you threw it at her adorably bipolar head.

When Mangano sat next to me at first, it took me a second. "You're Joy from *Joy*!"

She said, "Yes. Don't you remember, we met at HSN?"

She was referring to the Home Shopping Network audition episode of *My Life on the D-List*, and frankly, that day was a blur. But I told her, "I'll tell you, I wasn't looking too good that day trying to put that vacuum cleaner together. I wish I'd had your mop!"

She laughed, and then she turned on the nurturing tone that Jennifer Lawrence clearly adopted to play her so well and said, "We have to do something together! There's got to be something you and I can do together that you can sell!"

She was so charming and genuine. Really, it was as if I were in the movie and sitting across from her in her home office as was portrayed near the end of the film. This was my wet dream, because I immediately started to feel like I could be one of the women she lifts up to help realize her business goals.

I had to be honest with her, though. "Trust me, Joy, I would love nothing more than for my money to make money and be a brand and have a product"—you know, to be Diddy with Cîroc vodka, or Jessica Simpson with her shoe line—"but unfortunately, I only have a bucket of dick jokes. I've only been able to make money the boots-on-the-ground way, doing stand-up or being on television." But she wouldn't let go of the idea of us working together, and I loved it. I'm sure my quick-fire idea in the moment didn't go over well—"How about instead of a bucket, a *can* of dick jokes?"—but I'm brainstorming now, believe me. Kathy's Bottle of Freckles? Kathy's Troubles-Be-Gone Juice (ingredients to be determined later)? Kathy's Lesbian Flats? (Bad name, but you know what I'm talking about.) But it will not be a line of funny dog clothing. If one more person suggests that, I'll hit them with a Joy mop.

MANILOW, BARRY
Bathhouse Pianist Made Good

I know there are fools who may think of Barry as a guy who once had a top-of-the-charts heyday and is now a has-been. But let me tell you, he is not. He's insanely rich. That publishing money—that's what you want! He even wrote the song "I

Write the Songs." Let me put it this way: When Barry shows up for Clive Davis's Grammy party, which is in Beverly Hills, he takes his jet. FROM PALM SPRINGS. (It's twenty minutes, tops.) Look, maybe he thinks it'll save him time so he can write more songs. He lives music 24-7. It's one of the things I love about him. He has to be reminded to do things like, oh, eat. (He is a tall, rather lanky man.) The other thing is that Brooklyn accent, which is hard to forget. Sure, there's the whole look: the feathered hair, the tanner, the padded shoulders, and all that. But when you hear him talk, he turns into Tony effing Soprano. That said, he doesn't do a lot of talking. When you sit next to me, though, at a party, you're going to answer my questions. He and I have played this game multiple times.

One year, I said to him, "So, Bar, every Grammy nominee's performing here tonight. So many greats. So many legends. So many new faces. Who are you looking forward to seeing?"

"Jennifuh."

Jennifuh? Oh. "Jennifer Hudson?"

"I luh-v Jennifuh."

"Yeah, she's incredible! Never lip-synchs. She'll be great."

"So-o-o-o lookin' forward to Jennifuh . . . an' I wanna see Johnny."

"Johnny?"

"Johnny *Mathis.* Johnny's gonna sing 'Chances Are.' I wanna see what Johnny's up to."

I admit. This one was my bad. I kinda thought Johnny Mathis was dead. (Oops.) Instead, he was performing? This was incredible. Seriously, I'm a kid from Forest Park, Illinois. I never thought I'd see this in my lifetime. I was practically crying. And yet that still didn't stop me from thinking I was talking to a mob boss, with the whole "I wanna see what Johnny's up to" Brooklynese. Is there going to be an offer that can't be refused? I meant "re-fyoost."

"Barry, that's amazing. By the way, you must be excited about Jennifuh . . . er, *Jenni-FER* because she'll be singing her new duet 'Trouble' with Iggy Azalea."

Pause. "What's an Iggy?"

Before I could start laughing, I said, "Well, Bar, an 'Iggy' is an Australian white girl who's also a rapper. She and Jennifer have a duet, and I think you're going to like it."

An "ugh" escapes, then he jokingly added, "Is dat the tawk-singing?"

I said, "Yeah, that's the talk-singing."

"That's when they lose me."

Ooh boy. Well, when Jennifer Hudson came out and sang, Barry did this thing I've seen only a handful of these top music guys do. He leaned forward, elbows on the table with hands clasped, and rested his chin on his hands and closed his eyes. Clive Davis does this, too, and so does Quincy Jones. They're purists about the music, about listening. They don't care about the outfit or if somebody is being drunk or obnoxious nearby. They know how to tune it out. It's pretty great to watch. Well, Barry did it for Jennifuh.

Then Iggy started.

Barry opened his eyes, turned, and said, "Get the jet."

Manilow OUT.

MARS, BRUNO
Filipino Jersey Boy

It's getting harder to do, but when I'm at a star-studded awards show like the Grammys and stuck sitting in the back with fans, interns, and assistants, I'll jump up, run down to the front rows where the big names are clumped together, and grab a departing celebrity's seat faster than you can say, "Shut up, Kanye." The last time I successfully did it was 2012, when I stole the seat of a country singer who lost and left. (Why, oh why, would anyone leave???) I was on the aisle, a choice spot for being in trolling cameramen's shots, and for craning one's neck to see who's around me, and for bolting if security realizes what I've done. In this case, after my self-actualized upgrade, I noticed that Bruno Mars was across from me to the right, maybe five feet away, and a few feet away to the left of me was my buddy Dave Grohl. Now, Bruno had already approached me earlier before the show and said complimentary things, which I thought was sweet. He was in a good mood. After all, he was up for at least five major awards, including song, record, album, pop performance, like, everything. But this was also the year someone else was up for all those same awards, a certain singer named Adele. Remember now, the televised Grammys don't give out a whole lot of awards, but of the ones they do, most are in those big categories. I may not have had a legitimate front-row seat, but I did for the spectacle that was Bruno Mars getting visibly pissier every time he lost an award.

The first time he lost, he made a mildly stifled show of discontent, but then he looked at me, and I shook my head and mouthed, "You were robbed." Which is maybe the worst thing you can do to somebody in that situation, fan the fires of their indignation when they're supposed to act like they don't care. So I did it again. Second loss, third loss, Bruno's barely suppressing his outbursts and looking back at me with a "Can you fucking believe . . ." look and I'm all "Right back atcha" with an eye roll that says, *This is BULLSHIT.* Now, I knew that Dave Grohl was watching me do all this, because his eyes bored right into mine, and he made the slice across the throat with his finger, as if to say, "Too much. Not cute. Not funny." I got it. But I have to say, part of me both loves the show I got to see and admires how this massively gifted star just wasn't going to be anything but openly honest about being a sore loser, something I have absolutely no experience with whatsoever.

For the final award of the night, for which Bruno Mars was also nominated, he lost to Adele again. Bruno was still backstage after his performance when the live cameras caught his extremely candid reaction to losing once again. If I could have, I would have run backstage to "console him." It took the full force of the Foo Fighters to shut my ass down.

MERCHANT, STEPHEN
British Bean Pole, Almost Fiancé

Ricky Gervais once suggested I go out on a date with his writing partner, the freakishly tall, nebbishy-looking, brilliant Stephen Merchant. They collaborated on the original British version of *The Office* and the HBO show *Extras*, and Merchant did his own HBO series called *Hello Ladies*. Dating him seemed a remote possibility, literally, since Merchant lived in England. But Gervais liked the idea, especially because, he said devilishly, "I talked to Stephen about you one time, and he's scared of you."

I rolled my eyes and said, "Well, can you also tell him that there's my act, but there's the human me?"

I spotted Merchant for the first time when I was having lunch at the outdoor patio of the Chateau Marmont in Los Angeles. I walked up to him and said, "Merchant?!"

He turned to me, and it was as if all six feet seven inches of him began to shrink. "Oh no," he said in that perfectly clipped British accent of his. "No, no. Scared of you. No, no. Scared. Please. No, no."

It was so funny I couldn't stop laughing. I was charmed by him instantly, but nothing came of it.

Then a little while later, I booked a one-day role on the Farrelly brothers film *Hall Pass*, which Merchant costarred in, and on the set, I ran up to him to get a selfie. As I was pulling him to the side, he continued the bit from before: "Oh dear. No, no. Petrified. Don't want trouble. Please help. No, please. Someone. Anyone."

I even got the Farrellys involved, telling them within his earshot, "Will you talk your skinny star out of being scared to fuck me? I mean, what's the big deal? I could crush him, true, but other than that . . ."

And Merchant would keep chirping away, "See! See? This is what I mean. Hello? Haven't said anything negative about you! Don't want to be in your stage show! You look lovely!

See! Being nice. Hello? Help. Don't want trouble . . ."

Gervais really had put the fear of God into him.

MILLAN, CESAR
Dog Whisperer, Trainer of Humans

Look, I'm not a paid spokesperson for Cesar Millan, but I can tell you, he has come to my house twice and actually whispered at my dogs to the point where they behaved so well that I wished they could speak so they could tell me exactly what he said to them to convince them to act like completely different, perfect, magical dogs. My mistake was never getting him to train my ninety-six-year old mother. God knows she doesn't listen to me.

Where was I?

After I got to know Cesar, he came to my house to interview me for one of his books, and basically, he wanted to know why an obnoxious comedian has a bond with dogs. I told him that I'm as normal as anyone else, that when I'm on the road, what gets me in my gut is missing Maggie and my dogs. It'll be 3:00 in the morning, I'll have just finished a show, had a meal, and what brings me to that calm, relaxing place is looking at videos of my dogs. Cesar welled up listening to me talk like that, and that's why I love him. He's the real deal about canines. "That's what I want people to get," he told me. "Dogs save lives."

I admire that Cesar has written about vulnerable issues and even attempting suicide, which is another reason people worldwide love him: he's a successful guy who's honest about his feelings.

That being said, he's also a great sport about my sense of humor. On the early seasons of *Dog Whisperer*, he was operating out of a South Central neighborhood that looked scarier than any of the dogs he was dealing with.

I told him, "Cesar, it looks like a fucked-up doghood." I know, that is a very un-PC expression. I was just trying to make him laugh. I do think he should make an animated all-dog version of *Boyz N the Hood*, though.

He said, "Well, I'm not afraid."

I said, "Of course not. You've got eighty pit bulls!"

But he really does have the touch. My dog Pom Pom is a secret assassin (possibly funded by Oprah Winfrey Inc.) who will not allow another dog into the home. And yet when

Cesar visited—when I still had Chance and Pom Pom was new—he brought five dogs, and the effect was almost comical: Pom Pom sat like a princess on an imaginary tuffet, and Chance drooled. It was like Cesar brought the instant hex. He really will get your dogs to do things they've never done before, and I was that person saying, "Oh, wow. Pom Pom has never done that before!" I know, I sounded like every person who's ever been on any episode of any of Cesar's television shows. Look, I obviously don't have the touch, and I admit I don't follow up on the training Cesar tells me I'm supposed to. The minute he leaves, it's back to the bad doggy behavior. Fine, maybe it's my fault. But, I can't resist joking to Cesar, "Look, why don't you make the tagline at the end of every one of your episodes a little more honest? 'I am Cesar Millan. I am the Dog Whisperer . . . until I leave your house and you're screwed.'"

Cesar, if you're reading this, you still have a standing offer to just move into my palatial mansion whenever you want. Just don't leave. I need my sofas intact.

MORGAN, TRACY
Comedian, Next President

I once had a five-day commercial gig as part of a group that included me, Jim Gaffigan, Michael Ian Black, Debra Wilson, and Tracy Morgan. It was a great ad campaign, fun to do, and it's where I met the indomitable, unforgettable Tracy.

My time with him was magical, because even though he was up and down—laughing one day at something inappropriate, crying the next over something that touched him—he said the kind of hilariously crazy things that kept you on your toes. He was exactly the way you'd think he'd be and could even joke about it. "Now, *Kathy Griffin*, I don't know . . . if my *queen* doesn't dole out my *pills* right, I'm not sure what's gonna happen!"

Weirdly enough, I feel as if I share something in common with Tracy, in that we're both 24-7 comics, almost out of necessity. If he and I happened to run into each other on the worst days of our lives, we are able to riff. With him, there's no downtime. Comics are not always wild about other comics who are always "on." But I will riff anywhere, with anyone, and Tracy's such a genius—unfiltered in the best way—it's fun to bite whenever he says something nutty.

"I'm about to get you PREGNANT, Kathy Griffin! That's how FINE you lookin'!" You don't respond to that by thinking, *How dare he objectify me!* If you're Kathy Griffin, you say, "Tonight could be the night, Tracy. Let me find that last remaining egg somewhere deep, deep in my ovaries." He clearly had no shame about his issues, whatever meds he was taking, and so on, so I wasn't surprised that he allowed the producers of *30 Rock* to make his over-the-top character Tracy Jordan a heightened version of himself.

If he offends people, and he has, I'm telling you, he doesn't know it. Backstage at the Kennedy Center when Eddie Murphy was getting his Mark Twain Prize, Tracy's appearance there was all anyone could talk about. He'd just made his triumphant return to *Saturday Night Live* the night before, after the debilitating truck accident that nearly killed him, and even Eddie Murphy was asking, "How is he?" But Tracy came out guns blazing and kicked ass, ignoring the producers' ban on using the N-word by telling a joke that had that whole stuffy Kennedy Center audience in stitches.

I got a quiet moment with Tracy backstage that I'll always cherish. We started reminiscing about our week together doing the commercial shoot, remembering details, talking about how much fun we had, and it gave me hope about the traumatic brain injury diagnosis he got from the crash. He needed to sit down for a second, and he admitted he was hurting, that doing *Saturday Night Live* and the Eddie Murphy tribute two nights in a row was hard. But he also said, "You know how it is, Kathy. As long as I can be making people laugh, that's all I care about." And I'm pregnant.

MULLALLY, MEGAN
Actress, Pal

I've known Megan for a long time, as in doing-student-films-together-in-the-'80s-and-'90s long time. She's a dear friend, the kind who will only trot out the Karen voice from *Will & Grace* for my mom.

Well, during one of those long-ago student film shoots when we were struggling actors, she told me about auditioning for Warren Beatty's *Dick Tracy* movie, and for years afterward, I loved telling people what happened to her.

Megan's an incredible singer, so I'd get all excited regaling friends, acquaintances, and talk show hosts with how she won the role of Breathless Mahoney after auditioning at Beatty's house. And how she'd get those famous Warren Beatty phone calls at 2:00 A.M., asking if she'd want to come over. (*You know, for SEX!*) And how Megan was a struggling actress but not inclined to accept his advances, so on the third such phone call, after his "It's Warren, do you want to come up?" she politely replied, "Warren, have I ever wanted to?" And how Madonna then swooped in and stole the role of Breathless from Megan because, well, she *did* respond to those phone calls in the affirmative. Can you imagine? Thinking your career was going to change overnight and that you'd be starring in a big-budget musical film only to find out Madonna used her fem-

inine wiles to ruin the life of the adorable Megan Mullally in one day. Oh, how Hollywood can be BRUTAL! I just loved that story!

I had a feeling Megan hadn't told me everything, though. We were together somewhere years after this story of hers had been a part of my repertoire, surrounded by people, and I said, "Megan, why don't you tell the real story? You were banging Warren, then Madonna caught wind of it, and she stole the role from you! Are you so afraid of Madonna that you can't be honest?!"

Megan's eyes got wide. She laughed out loud and said, "Kathy, I love that you think my life is so exciting. But let me remind you what actually happened." She told me she had auditioned for Breathless Mahoney. Warren Beatty did tell her that he'd be happy to take her to lunch or dinner anytime in a platonic way. And obviously, the role went to Madonna. Apparently, Madonna did not "steal" the role of Breathless Mahoney from Megan. According to Megan, she was never actually given the role. My version of this story is so much better that I have no shame about having told it to anyone that would listen for years. Come on, my version is torrid, juicy, and I haven't met a gay man yet who didn't believe it. After she heard the version I'd been generous enough to spread over the years, Megan said, "Okay, 10 percent of that story is true." Ten percent is all I need, honey.

MURPHY, EDDIE
Comedy Giant, Recluse

I had a few lines in the movie *Shrek Forever After*, and as part of the promotion DreamWorks honcho Jeffrey Katzenberg gathered the big four—Mike Myers, Cameron Diaz, Antonio Banderas, and Eddie—and those of us who voiced new characters, for a group photo at the Soho House in Los Angeles. The photographer only had ten minutes to get all of us, and I happened to be lucky enough to get seated behind Eddie.

I had heard all the rumors about him being unapproachable, that he doesn't do appearances and whatnot, so this felt like maybe the only chance I'd get to meet one of my comedy idols. He was mellow enough and seemed to recognize me—"Oh yeah, you're great. So glad you're here"—and I realized I could walk away saying I met the great Eddie Murphy and that he was nice and not weird. But then we had some downtime, and I recognized a chance to initiate more talk. But all I could come up with was a lame "Hey, how's everything going?" Not proud of that, but I was in proximity to brilliance—I can't tell you how many times I've watched his stand-up classics *Delirious* and *Raw*—and Kathy Griffin the fan can get nervous.

Well, of all chitchatty questions to actually take seriously, Eddie chose that one. He turned and quietly said, and I'm paraphrasing here, "Well, most days I wake up in my mansion around 3:00 P.M., fight depression, and try to work up the strength to even get out of bed." Whoa. Then he turned back around for the rest of the photos.

Needless to say, that honesty floored me, and it hit home to me what a guy like that has gone through. He's a talent who's had the highest of highs and the lowest of lows, and I absolutely loved how brutally frank he was in, of all places, a photo shoot, and to someone he didn't even know. Was it that maybe something like that could only be said comic to comic? I have no idea. Five years later, when I was asked to pay tribute to Eddie at the Kennedy Center when he was given the Mark Twain Prize, I knew I had a great personal story about him.

(But first, quick sidebar, I also want to let you know the night before the Mark Twain taping, Eddie and his family were incredibly sweet and welcoming to me. We were both staying in the same upscale hotel in Georgetown. Of course, Eddie had the penthouse. How do I know this? Dave Chappelle made the mistake of pointing out Eddie's room number to me. In the moments before I put on my fancy cocktail dress for a dinner honoring Eddie, I was hanging out in my room in my pajamas. It was only 5:00 P.M. Why would I be dressed yet? I can't help it. I love walking the halls of fancy hotels in my not-at-all-fancy penis-repellant pajamas. It always gets a laugh from strangers and, damn it, it was going to get a laugh from Eddie Murphy. I marched up to Eddie's room and bum-rushed him. He then put his arms around me and said to the amusement of everyone in the room, "Oh, okay, you're one of those eccentric people." I spent quite a few hours in their suite with Eddie's crew, Dave Chappelle and Arsenio Hall, hanging out and laughing our butts off.)

Now, back to D.C. and the Mark Twain night. I had to find some way to not bring the place down or sandbag the amazing Eddie Murphy with his darkest feelings he had shared all those years before. So I admit, I fudged something for the greater good of a loving tribute to an extraordinary comedian. I kept the part about him telling me he had bad days, but changed the ending into a complete fabrication, which is that he leaned in and whispered, "But otherwise, I'm still Eddie fucking Murphy." I labored for weeks over what to say that would get righteous applause for a hero of mine, stay somewhat true to the nature of our small exchange, and still sound like it came from Eddie. I'm coming clean about it here because I want you all to know that Eddie's actual candor in an unexpected moment was meaningful to me and reflective of what comedians have been known to go through. He may not have said some of those words I told the Kennedy Center audience, but in that brief moment at the photo shoot, he really was Eddie fucking Murphy to me.

NICHOLSON, JACK
Legend, Joker, Cuckoo

Holy shitballs! I'll bet you never thought your Kathy Griffin spent an evening seated next to the great Jack Nicholson at an exclusive, small, eight- to ten-person dinner party . . . twice!

I am as aware as you are that this man has always been shrouded in mystery, riddles, enigma, and public and private scandals, but most importantly is recognized as a cinematic icon and larger-than-life person. I'm going to give you the reason you bought the book. I'm going to describe what it's like to be in a private living room when he walks in. Because when people speak in clichés about movie stars or the "it" factor, I can tell you I felt it in the air, and it was tangible. Even the hostess herself announced his presence with a not-so-subtle, "The king is here!"

I couldn't take my eyes off him. Okay, I get it, you're thinking, *No kidding, Kathy, neither would I.* Jack Nicholson has that quality that is truly magnetic. It was fascinating to watch him enter the room in a suit and tie with all the quirks, mystery, and Nicholsonisms you could ever hope for. So what do I do? Try to make him laugh, of course. Did I succeed that first time? No.

Here was my attempt:

I had just won my first Emmy, so I brought it with me and tried a bit in which I said to Jack upon first meeting him, "Excuse me, Jack, but I don't know if you've seen a REAL LIVE Emmy in person. My name is Kathy Griffin, I'm thrilled to meet you, but just know that if you want to touch it or take a photo with it, that's fine. I don't mean to rub it in, but an Emmy is physically larger than an Academy Award." He looked at me like I was from Mars, and since he's from Mars, I was fine with that. Even my friends call me an acquired taste.

He carried himself as if he didn't realize how imposing he was and yet still came across like a younger, dapper man. He was clearly there to hang with his old pals. The hostess told a story I found unbelievably charming about how she and Jack had gone to a local down-and-dirty, well-known LA burger joint called Tommy's. Maybe they had the munchies. I don't know or care. What I wish I had was security footage of the dude working the counter at Tommy's Burger taking an order from Jack Nicholson.

At the dinner table, I was seated between Lorne Michaels,

whom I barely know, and Jack, who didn't know me at all. Though I could easily talk to Lorne because we have comedy in common, I really wanted to just listen to Jack. He talked movies, a little bit of politics, and occasionally he'd just laugh at nothing in particular.

Thinking I'd missed something, I'd turn to Jack and say, "What? What'd I miss?"

He'd just say something like, "You look good, honey."

At one point, I turned to Lorne and said, "So . . . is Jack like this all the time? He's laughed three times in a row now, at nothing."

Lorne was cutting a piece of meat and, without looking up, just said, "All the time."

The second dinner with Jack, though, I got to hear him talk about his own movies, everything from *The Departed* to the famous hot tub scene with Kathy Bates in *About Schmidt*. It was the stuff that dreams are made of. He even talked about *The Shining*. It was amazing listening to him talk about working with director Stanley Kubrick. He peppered these stories as usual by Nicholsonisms like looking away, seemingly lost in thought, then laughing. Being in that rarefied, cozy atmosphere, where a silver screen superstar is spinning yarns about his movies, was indescribably cool.

There was enough of a chumminess building up that I got a little bolder, turning to him once and asking, "Are you ever going to settle down?"

He said with a devilish twinkle in his eye, "I think when ole Paris Hilton turns thirty, I'll be seventy-five, and she and I will be exactly in tune, at exactly the right time for both of us." (Later, I told Paris Hilton this story. She gave me her signature blank stare.)

By the end of that second dinner, I got the sense that he

maybe knew who I was *a little bit*. I timed my departure to coincide with his, which meant he and I were in the driveway together as his driver was getting his car, and I was . . . being near Jack Nicholson.

I got up the nerve to say, "You know, Jack, I always love talking to you."

He said, "Kathy, you've never looked better."

I immediately got all flush. In all seriousness, he could have said any generic form of good night. But what touched me, and I know this sounds silly, was that he KNEW MY NAME!!! Look, for a Forest Park, Illinois, girl who went to all his movies, it doesn't get much better than that.

NICKS, STEVIE
Velvet Gypsy, Singer, Possible Wiccan?

I'm going to borrow a great expression my assistant, John, has for the icons he loves: "relevant in every decade." As much as I love the kids who pop up and blow everyone away, it's the legends who really get to me.

My second concert ever was Fleetwood Mac, back on the *Rumours* tour. Stevie Nicks has been my silver spring ever since. It was such a thrill to have her on *My Life on the D-List* in that great moment where Bette Midler calls her to rally Grammy support for me. I believe Cher's quote was, in full Cher voice, "Stevie's one of the good ones. She's always been a great girl."

At our first in-person meeting, we hit it off and already

felt like we knew each other. She was performing at a fancy post-Emmy party, and I wrapped my arms around her and we started chatting. We actually forgot that we were on a red carpet, and while the cameras were going off, we were having a fun and genuine conversation. She's one of those legends I just want to make laugh! She is a great laugher!

One night at the Fillmore in San Francisco, a legendary rock venue where I filmed my first HBO special, Stevie was doing a solo show, and my boyfriend surprised me with tickets. Stevie and I had talked about chatting backstage after her show, but I didn't know she was about to blow my freaking mind. There I was in the balcony fangirling out, and Stevie, draped in her full Stevie flowy, witchy, sexy getup, stops the show and says, and I am NOT making this up, people, "My friend, the hilarious Kathy Griffin, who has made me laugh so many times, is here in the audience tonight. So I'm dedicating this next song to her." And that song was a little tune you may have heard of called "LANDSLIDE"! I could not have been more excited and touched at the same time.

The last time I saw her, backstage at the Forum in LA, we got right down to business. We just love talking about all the rock-and-roll dudes who lost it all to failed marriages and baby mamas, and how the girls of rock and the girls of comedy are not all that different when it comes to holding on to the hard-earned dough. Is she on board and supportive of me traveling the road with my boyfriend who is also my tour manager? You're damn right!

Stevie will last a lot longer than a lot of others from that era because her audience never vanishes. LGBTs and women of all ages worship her, and she told me that whenever another date gets added—whether to her solo tour or the Fleetwood Mac tour—she loves it. "I'm grateful," she told me. "Do you know how many of my friends, who, like Fleetwood Mac, played stadiums back in the day, now come up to me and tell me they're playing two-hundred–seat theaters? It's not lost on me that we're still touring as a group and playing the Forum."

The fact that she and I talk about the road like we're peers just kills me. She said she's building a silver bullet trailer on the beach to be a perfect writing space, and when it's finished, she wants me to come over and write. Can you just picture the two of us sitting side by side in a silver bullet trailer with notepads? I can. Stevie will be writing haunting, beautiful lyrics, and I will be writing my dick jokes and running them by her to see if she laughs.

NIGHT STALKER, THE
Serial Killer, NOT My Boyfriend

1989 is more than just the title of the wildly successful Taylor Swift album. It is also the year I decided to turn to my then boyfriend, Andrew, and say, "You know, as an actress in training, I should get as much life experience as I can, and I just realized I've never attended a real live trial." The local TV news in Los Angeles was obsessed with covering the trial of Richard Ramirez, dubbed the Night Stalker, who had terrorized LA and San Francisco throughout the early 1980s with multiple home-invasion rapes, assaults, and murders. He was captured in 1985, and his trial started in 1988.

We made it downtown to the criminal courts building and managed to snag seats in the third row. Soon after, I heard the distinctive sound of metal rattling. I looked up, and there was Richard Ramirez wearing handcuffs and shackles around his ankles. I don't know what came over me, but I decided to indulge a crazy notion I had that I could stare him down. That's right, I gave him the "you're going down" glare that has terrified . . . well, probably nobody, ever. There's nothing to gain from staring down a captured killer who's undoubtedly so bored by now he'd find a curly-haired girl scowling at him amusing. But I was intent on staring him down, and I did. Ramirez stared right back. He did not smile. He looked straggly. His frame was tall and thin. He did not present himself as someone who was trying to show his innocence. Of course, I had seen him on the news, but up close, he truly stared me down in a way that anyone would label as menacing.

Andrew, under his breath, said, "Is he looking at you?"

"Sssh. It's starting."

Having seen plenty of TV shows and movies, I was expecting to see tears, pointing, loud objections, and gavel banging. Instead, it was over an hour of detailed testimony about Ramirez's sneakers! Granted, it was illuminating to see how a defense lawyer wears down a witness with potentially damning testimony: bog down the person with details and inconsistencies. "Well, what was it, navy or regular blue?" That kind of thing. Then they started down the same road of specificity about a blanket. A blanket?

Recess was called, and I was surprised to see that the attorneys for both sides, as well as the jurors and spectators, were all sharing the same space in the hallway. The lawyers seemed chummy with each other, and the jurors were talking to each other. Nobody was sequestered. This isn't what I was expecting at all. However, I took it all in as an exercise for my acting training. Remember, that was the real reason I was there.

I went to the bathroom right off the hallway, and after I emerged from the stall, I recognized a woman from the courtroom washing her hands next to me. I casually said, "Now, that last witness, do you think the sneaker they were talking about . . ." And she just turned and walked out. Rude! I thought we were all chummy at the Night Stalker trial! When I came out of the bathroom, I instantly felt hands on me. Sheriff's deputies yanked away my purse and searched its contents, while another pair of officers dragged me away as I heard Andrew—himself being held back by a deputy—yell out, *Where are you taking her!?*

I screamed, "I don't know!" Was I being kicked out? Worse! They ushered me into the judge's chambers. I was shaking so hard, I could barely concentrate on anything. I thought I was going to jail. I had been in row three among everyday people, and now I was facing superior court judge Michael Tynan for some reason. The attorneys for both sides were also in the room. Was this some horrible mistake? The court stenographer was there, as well, and when she started typing, that's what made me think, *Oh shit. This is official.*

One of the attorneys said, "Tell the judge about the incident in the restroom."

I was so scared, I swear I had no idea what he was talking about. Incident? Restroom? "I . . . went . . . to the restroom . . ." I was too afraid to talk. Was I going to prison based on what I'd say? Then the woman I had talked to was brought in, and a brief sense of relief washed over me. "Hey, you're the lady from the bathroom!" I yelled.

Again, the attorney: "What did you say to her?"

"Oh! I was asking about the sneaker, because I . . . ," and then I just described the bathroom scene, which to my mind was going to end this, because the lady would help clear it all up!

No one said a word for a while, and then Judge Tynan said, "We're going to return you to your seat, but you're not allowed to leave."

Back in the courtroom, I noticed that all the spectators were gone, and the jury had been excused. It was me, Andrew, the woman from the bathroom, both teams of attorneys, and Richard Ramirez, the Night Stalker. I could tell Ramirez's attorney was loving this.

When the judge called back the jury and audience members (the term they actually use for spectators), I thought my nightmare was over. Then Judge Tynan said, "Ms. Griffin, approach the bench." Oh shit. I got up, walked through the creaky little swinging gate, and heard the judge say, "Stop." I was now standing right NEXT to Richard Ramirez, who was staring up at me during the following exchange.

"What's your name?" Judge Tynan asked.

"Kathy Griffin," I said, barely audibly. Again, softly, I muttered, "2637 Centinela, Santa Monica, CA . . ." and as soon as the words came out of my mouth, I realized Ramirez *was looking right at me, and I was saying my home address out loud to the fucking Night Stalker.* This was so much worse than being afraid of going to jail.

"What is your relationship with Mr. Ramirez?"

"None," I said. *Oh my God.*

"Have you ever corresponded with Mr. Ramirez?"

"No," I answered. *Holy shitballs. They think I'm one of those psycho chicks that pursues serial killers.*

"Do you have feelings for Mr. Ramirez?"

"None, Your Honor." *I see where this is going, and it is not good for me.*

"What do you do for a living?"

And then I said, "I'm a loan officer in a bank." Let me explain.

That last answer was a lie. Yes, I had just stated out loud my home address in the presence of a psychopathic killer—which, incidentally, my late brother Gary, who was a trial attorney, told me later I didn't have to do—but I was certainly not going to admit in a court of law that I was an out-of-work, wannabe actress, because that would sound really stupid. Telling an unrepentant, still-not-convicted criminal where I live? That I would do. But saying, "Well, I'm taking commercials classes in Van Nuys—fingers crossed for that,

Your Honor, or a juicy nonpaying role in a student film—and I'm starting soon at the Lee Strasberg Academy . . ." *That* I deemed too embarrassing. "Ladies and gentlemen," he said, "we've had a case of possible jury tampering."

This is it. I'm going to jail—tell my mom and dad I love them.

Yes, readers, it was a member of the jury I'd started talking to at the restroom sink. And before you ask yourself, "Did she *know* she was on the jury?"—yes, I did. But, and this is one of the reasons I regret not going to college, I truly didn't think it was inappropriate to ask a juror any question as long as the question wasn't "Do you think that the defendant is innocent or guilty?" Learn from me, law students. Even worse, the trial had already had its issues with jury tampering, as the judge reminded everyone that day, adding, as he put it, "We cannot afford to lose another juror." In other words, naïve Kathy Griffin and her little sneaker small talk could have inadvertently led to a mistrial for one of the worst serial killers in recent memory. (During the trial, a juror was actually murdered, which eventually wasn't attributed to Ramirez, but it understandably had put that entire jury on edge for the whole trial.)

That judge really humiliated me. I just stood there and took it. It was crushing, and I was dutifully chastened.

"Why are you here?" the judge eventually asked me.

"I . . . uh . . . wanted to see . . . a real live . . . trial . . . in a real courthouse and everything . . ."

"WELL, YOU CERTAINLY PICKED A GOOD ONE! Take your seat."

That was my first and last time attending a trial. But somewhere buried deep in the court transcripts for the *People v. Richard Raymond Ramirez* is "Kathy Griffin" who lives at "2637 Centinela . . ."

O'DONNELL, ROSIE
Comedian, Talk Show Host, Pal, Connector

When I call my good friend Rosie a "connector," it's not just about someone who introduces me to famous people. What Rosie has is a skill for joining people together who are likely to develop meaningful bonds. If it weren't for Rosie, I wouldn't have met Cher, the Estefans, Bette Midler, or Rachael Ray, and these are now some of my closest pals in show business. She's like a chef, and her friends are ingredients she likes to toss together to make something special. That's how insightful and smart she is. But she makes good on those promised connections, too. A lot of people like to say, "Oh, you should meet my friend so-and-so," and then never do anything. She makes good on it, and that's rare.

We met in the mid-'90s when she was in Los Angeles taping episodes of her breakout hit of a daytime talk show, and *Suddenly Susan* snagged her for a guest role as herself. I'll never forget her telling me I was funny. After that I appeared on *The Rosie O'Donnell Show* several times, and if there was ever an instance when the show was already fully booked with guests, she'd say, "Come on as a surprise." One time, she even flew my mother and father out to New York, and they'd never been to the Big Apple in their lives. She put them up at Le Parker Meridien and had them make an appearance on her talk show, and to this day, Mom talks about that trip and Rosie's generosity. Rosie believed in me from the jump, and it was a serious boost to my confidence as a stand-up.

Of course, I love that she's outspoken and a showbiz pioneer as an out lesbian, but there was a moment from that *Suddenly Susan* taping that really hit home to me how unique her place was in the entertainment world.

We were filming scenes on Rosie's talk show set, with her audience still there—she'd asked them to stick around for us, and they happily agreed—and as we were getting ready to shoot, Rosie expressed dissatisfaction with a line in the script with a reference to the gay community.

"I won't say it," she said to someone on staff.

This staffer said, "Well, I wrote it, and I'm gay." Rosie wasn't out yet. And I'll never forget this, she was still miked up, so every crew member could hear her (but not the audience), and she said, "Look, I know. I'm gay. It's not that I don't know what being gay is. But I have small children, and I go and do stand-up comedy on the weekends in places where I would literally fear for my life and the lives of my kids if I became the openly gay talk show host and stand-up comic. It's different for me as a mom." Remember, this is just before Ellen DeGeneres announced herself as a lesbian but didn't have kids or a daytime talk show with which she was trying to win over heartland America.

Rosie's words struck me, because it meant she was out to everyone she worked with, and obviously to friends, but not to the world. It was as if she'd created this experimental staging area for herself from which she could plot the right moment to come out, and she did near the end of her show's run. I remember showbiz friends calling Rosie a hypocrite, pretending to have a crush on Tom Cruise and such. But secretly, I knew there'd be a bigger power to her coming out when it was on her own terms as a super successful TV figure. And it was indeed powerful, and I was incredibly proud of her.

She opened my eyes to the timing of a gay joke, and I feel as if I did the same for her when I helped her reconcile with Joan Rivers. Joan would make jokes about Rosie in a way that, let's just say, Rosie did not care for. She used to say to me, "How can you be friends with Joan Rivers? She's so mean." I would keep telling her she could feel however she wanted about Joan but that Joan had done so many things for me that I would always love her. Eventually Rosie saw Joan somewhere, walked up to her, and said, "I don't know what to do. Kathy Griffin has nothing but nice stories about you." And they made up on the spot. When Joan passed away, Rosie and I attended her funeral together with Rachael Ray and Kristin Chenoweth. Rosie even was kind enough to arrange a car and all the logistics for that day. Always connecting. That's who she is.

ORMAN, SUZE
Financial Guru, Girlfriennnd, Approved!

You haven't lived until you've had a Lesbian Super Bowl Party. There, I said it!

What I mean by that is my good pal Suze Orman and her wife, KT, were in Los Angeles coincidentally the day of the Madonna Super Bowl. I don't know who the teams were, and I don't care. I was just happy to have two of my favorite ladies visiting for the day.

Suze has been a genuine-not-Hollywood-but-actual-friend since I threw myself at her mercy and cold-called her. Ten

years ago, I was dealing with a complicated and very personal financial issue. Without skipping a beat, she said, "Come to my office and bring all the financials you want me to see." This woman knows her stuff. She lives it. She is a true believer and is on a mission to help people from all walks of life make the emotional connection between their financial issues and their everyday life choices.

Anyway, back to Madonna. Suze and I were goofing around holding hairbrushes singing "Like a Prayer" alongside Madonna. My boyfriend was looking at us like we were insane. We may have been making fun of him for being a heterosexual male just a little bit. When we sat down, Suze held up her phone and showed him an e-mail she had received from her friend Pat Riley. What?!? It was THE Pat Riley, legendary NBA player, coach, and at the time, president of the soon-to-be-championship-winning Miami Heat. I was confused. "What's Pat Riley e-mailing you for?" Suze told me Pat Riley had contacted her to make videos to speak directly to the players' moms. Not only do I find it hilarious that the implication here is that these big, muscular tough guys ultimately listen to their moms, but might possibly also be a little afraid of them. When I brought this up to Suze, I asked her if these players weren't dealing with big-time agents, accountants, stockbrokers, and so on.

"Girlfriennnd, Pat Riley knows how to train these young men into champions, and he knows that I know how to speak to PLAYERS' MAMAS!" she said in her signature singsongy voice. I've never heard of these supposedly famous basketball players, but she explained that she made videos for the moms of Chris Bosh, Dwyane Wade, and some guy named LeBron James. Is it possible that my bright-collared-jacket-wearing, firm-but-loving giver of the "Suze Smackdown" friend was helping Pat Riley assemble "The Big Three" into an NBA championship team in Miami? I imagine Suze making these videos, looking right into the camera, and getting right to the point, speaking directly to these women. Maybe something like, "This is the sum of money the coach has in mind, and this is how it's going to work: your son will be playing in a little state called Florida, which—guess what, my dear?—has no state income tax, which means he can keep a lot of it, invest most of it, and here's my number, and you call me . . ." Let me see if I'm getting this straight (pun intended). My gal Suze somehow was instrumental in putting together a championship dynasty? Is there nothing this woman can't do? Suze Orman, NBA commissioner? Suze Orman, president 2020?? Just think about it. Oh, and shocker, she and her wife also remodel and flip houses. (It's also my understanding that this LeBron James character was even able to segue into feature films.)

Suze, I issue a challenge to you: It's time for you to assemble the next "Big Three." Kathy Griffin, Ryan Gosling, Tyson Beckford. We'll call it the "Big Three-Way."

———

OSBOURNE, OZZY
He's Really Like That

In May of 2013, I hosted an auction/concert charity event benefiting women, thrown by rocker extraordinaire Linda Perry, who was able to get everyone from Natasha Bedingfield to Sia to the great Ozzy Osbourne. Now, as long as I've known Sharon, believe it or not, I'd never met Ozzy. I've seen Ozzy in concert with and without Black Sabbath, and let me tell you something, I do not think Sharon Osbourne gets enough credit. She is by far the most powerful and successful female rock-and-roll manager and has broken the glass ceiling for women in that part of the rock-and-roll industry in a way that is nothing short of dazzling.

I knew Sharon would be the perfect person to approach regarding how I should give her client, Ozzy, the best intro. We all know that Sharon is deliciously unfiltered, so it will not surprise you to hear her response: "Just get up there and say, 'This fucker better give the performance of his life because it's for an amazing cause.'" Easy.

I made my way to the Beverly Hilton green room, which is pretty small for a venue that regularly hosts so many high star-wattage events, and Ozzy was in there running around, chatting with his band, and sounding incomprehensible because I can never understand what he's saying.

I said, "Hi, Ozzy. I'm Kathy Griffin, and I'm hosting the event. Since I'm going to be introducing you, is there anything in particular you'd like me to say?"

He was speaking fluent Ozzy, which I did not take in high school, so I admit I could not understand a lot of what he said except for when he would keep repeating, with his very thick accent, the word "Ah-MY-zing!"

I said to him, "So perhaps . . . 'Ladies and gentlemen, the amazing Ozzy Osbourne'???"

He just kept saying, "Ah-MY-zing!"

Then I said, "Sorry to be *that* person, but can I get a selfie with you?"

Once the camera was out, he grabbed me, gave the full-on Ozzy smile-sneer, and again said, "AH-MY-ZING!"

As if that wasn't Ozzy enough, something else caught my eye. You often hear about rock and rollers having these crazy riders in their contracts with various specific and bizarre demands. In a room filled with typical, boring dressing room fare, such as a couple of bagels, a coffeepot, and a few bottles of water, I happened to notice something that had an actual Post-it on it. It was a pyramid of six little 5-hour Energy bottles and a note that said, "Don't touch. For Mr. Osbourne only." I had my intro! "With thirty hours of energy and an AH-MY-ZING amount of talent, ladies and gentlemen, the AH-MY-ZING Ozzy Osbourne!" And with that, he flicked the switch! He's one of those. He didn't just get through his set. He blew the roof off the place from "Paranoid" to "Crazy Train." I even barked at the moon.

PALTROW, GWYNETH
Beautiful Pill, Entrepreneurial Stork

There have been a few celebrities who've been a cloud of exasperation for me for so long, they should win some kind of longevity award. Oprah is one. Paltrow is another. There's an arc to our relationship, even though I'll bet she doesn't even know we're in one. Call it a subconscious intercoupling, if you will.

When I first encountered her at the VH1 Fashion Awards back in the early 2000s, unable to join in the fun with her mate Stella McCartney—who had no problem answering my silly red carpet questions—she was the kind of snooty celebrity whose antics helped me build a comedy career. I hated her, I loved her, I got comedy out of her. But at a certain point, you want a response. So years later, when I did a guest spot on *Glee*, she was there the same day I was, filming a different episode. I found her trailer, burst in, and said, "Paltrow?!? I'm here!"

She was looking at a magazine and getting her hair and makeup done, so I got the bare minimum, a "Hi." Look, I get it. She was in the zone, and me acting like her Make-A-Wish kid was finally here was probably a bit much. So later, I got a copy of a cheesy full-page picture of me in some tabloid magazine, went back to Paltrow's trailer when she wasn't there, and found her assistant and said, "I'm going to leave a present for your boss." This very statement may have sounded ominous to this visibly uncomfortable assistant. I added, "I need a Sharpie." He reluctantly handed over the pen, and I ripped out the full-page picture of myself. I proceeded to give her the gift of a lifetime. I wrote in big block letters over the entire page, "DEAR GYNNETTH, I WANT TO GIVE YOU AN AUTOGRAPH FROM YOUR PERSONAL IDOL. LOVE, KATHY GRIFFIN." I hoped she'd find the misspelling of her name amusing, since I'd read somewhere that she couldn't stand it when people misspelled her name. Push their buttons first, I say! Well, I got zero response. Did I misread our semiconscious thruppling? Did she go straight to the cops with what she perceived to be evidence of stalking?

The following year, I saw her at an industry party, and I couldn't resist. I went up to her and said, "What's up, Goopy? Everything goopin'? Everything gooptastic?" And finally, a decade after the frickin' VH1 Fashion Awards, she just gave in and laughed. She figured out how deep I really am. I approached her the way I approach every gig: if the audience laughs, I end the show. If they don't laugh, I'll stay up there for five goddamn hours until I hear it. Audiences have known it for decades. Now Goopy knows.

PAUL, AARON
Jesse Pinkman . . . Thanks to ME

You'd be surprised to learn who had a small role as Zipper in an episode of *Suddenly Susan*. It was a certain teenager named Aaron Paul. *Breaking Bad*? Ever heard of it? Yeah, I discovered him. Although I knew the character of Zipper could not continue on *Suddenly Susan*, I know raw talent when I see it.

I remember it like it was yesterday: he came on to our set with the intensity of a big cat, but he didn't know what to do with it all. You could just tell it was going to be trouble. We were a sitcom, not some brooding basic cable drama, and the studio brass weren't happy. They were going to can him, but I got on the horn with the bigwigs and said, "I can straighten him out! He's a kid! Let me at him. Kathy Griffin's been around. I've done the math. I can take him under my wing." I stormed onto the set, grabbed Aaron, and pulled him aside like a teacher with some delinquent. "Oh, well, heil Hitler, bitch. We're all on the same page. The one that says, if I can't kill you, you'll sure as shit wish you were dead. Look, whatever you're trying to cook up here, Captain, can it. We're not some lab where you can just try things out. You haven't earned your own trailer just yet, bucko. A show like this requires chemistry, so you'd better dial back the intensity. You look like someone poisoned your girlfriend's kid, for Chrissakes. So shape up and learn to love working in Burbank, or the next thing you know you'll be a crazy handful o' nothin' in some shithole in Albuquerque, where there's a lot of uncertainty, bitch. The sky is just as blue here, and the chicken places are better. Do we have a deal, you pathetic junkie? Answer me!" Then I threw him on the floor of the *Suddenly Susan* set, choked him out until he finally pointed to his pocketful of meth, which I promptly threw into the Warner Brothers decorative fountain next to the *Friends* set.

Okay, honestly, I have ZERO recollection of ever meeting Aaron Paul when he was only nineteen. I'm too famous. But he still owes me a lifetime of gratitude for putting him on the map.

PELOSI, NANCY

Speaker of the House, Secret KG Ally

Hillary Clinton and Nancy Pelosi have taken enough sustained smearing from mean, backward Republican men to last a few lifetimes. And I think *I* have it bad with pissed-off celebrities!

The first time I met Congresswoman Pelosi, she was unfailingly nice, complimenting me and talking about the importance of humor. In my opinion, a much better understanding of a solid chick comic than Paul Ryan ever will have! So when I was scheduled to go on a talk show on which I knew I'd have to defend her (don't come at me, Fox News, for respecting this woman's accomplishments, for God's sake!), I made sure I had my talking points ready on what a badass she is in the House of Representatives. She runs her caucus like a mob boss. My D.C. pals tell me that she's loyal as long as you don't cross her. Check and check. I respect her because at seventy-plus years old, she is still working her ass off. Oh, and she has a killer body. Does any of this ring a bell? I'm just saying . . . we have a lot in common. Kathy Griffin, Speaker of the House. Just think about it.

The great story, though, is when I was at an awards season party and a distinguished, handsome, gray-haired gentleman walked up and said, "Hi, I'm Paul Pelosi. My wife and I would love to say hi to you," I said, "Oh my gosh, I'd love to say hi to the Speaker!" So I went over to their table, and it was a power group, for sure: the Pelosis, Apple CEO Tim Cook, a few other true titans of industry, and some chick with hair like Ginger's from *Gilligan's Island*. Pelosi and I exchanged pleasantries, and then she said, "Have you met Lana?"

Suddenly it clicked who the redhead was. "Oh," I said. "You're the singer Lana Del Rey."

Lana made a forced cough sound and said, "Um, I heard what you said about me."

My mind started racing—is she even in the act?—and then she continued, "Uh . . . for your information, putting me on the worst-dressed list was preposterous because that dress was . . ."

Oh, okay. I get it. *Fashion Police*. At that time, I had done *one* episode, and not only that, someone else had put her on the worst-dressed list. It wasn't even my doing. I tried to explain this to her, but Lana's anger appeared to be escalating. Then Nancy Pelosi stepped in to do what she's had to do countless times in the Capitol: mediate. She said, "Lana, dear, it was a joke. Kathy tells jokes! She goes around the country and makes people laugh. I'm sure it wasn't a comment on you personally."

I said, "Lana, I think you're a very good singer. I do. A little dark, but . . ."

Nancy Pelosi kept defending me at the same time she was trying to comfort Lana: "The thing about fashion and humor is that they're both essential in their way, as is music. And Lana, dear, people are going to make jokes. If I could tell you all the things I've heard in the Senate!"

I loved how the Speaker was stepping in to soothe a hotheaded celebrity! It kind of emboldened me. It made me want to continue the dialogue with Little Miss Sourpuss, although I might have taken a little advantage of who was in my corner.

"Lana," I said, "do you know who this woman is? I doubt it. So why don't you practice your scales and enjoy your meal?"

Pelosi said, "Now Kathy, dear, that's not going to help."

Lana sat there, silently stewing. I felt like dragging in more big guns, so I looked at the Apple honcho and said, "And what kind of gay MAN are YOU, Tim Cook? Can't even help me out? Lana Del Rey wants to kill me! She even refers to herself as a 'Suicide Girl' in the song 'She's Not Me'! What's next, 'Homicide Girl'?"

Cook was laughing as Nancy Pelosi walked me away from the table, like a trainer at a boxing match. Everything was fine. Then sure enough, at the valet, there's Lana again, and she walks right by me Taylor Swift–style without so much as an acknowledgment that one of the most powerful women in the world played diplomat for our benefit. I guess Lana felt like she got her two cents in at the table and that's all that mattered. How in the world does Speaker Pelosi deal with those petulant wack jobs in the House? And for those of you who still can't be talked out of trashing Nancy Pelosi, I encourage you to Google Dennis Hastert. Yeah, that's what I thought.

PENN, KAL
Kumar, Actor, Canine Hero

One morning, Larry, my big lug of a dog, went missing, and I was in a state of panic. As in I couldn't stop crying. It really is not in Larry's nature to vanish. It's more his nature to lie around and wait for food, not try to find it somewhere. But he is a people dog, and I was sincerely hoping he hadn't found someone else. Men. You open up your home to them, let them eat your food, clean up their poop, and they take off. I imagined Larry being taken in by a frat house, because he'd be a perfect companion to a bunch of mentally stunted dudes who eat Cheetos off the floor and growl if you drink all their beer.

I put out the word on Twitter that Larry was missing, hoping someone would come forward, and someone did: Kal Penn! Kumar of *Harold & Kumar*! Obama appointee! (After famously campaigning for him, he took the position of associate director of the White House Office of Public Engagement, then later served on the President's Committee on the Arts and the Humanities.) I've never met Kal Penn, but apparently he was a neighbor. A neighbor my dog Larry must have wanted to meet very badly, as Larry wandered over to Kal's house for a hug and some White Castle sliders. Kal brought Larry back safe and sound. I was out of town, but my assistant took a picture of Kal with Larry, and after I tweeted it with my public thanks, my awesome followers showered Kal with their social media appreciation, which I thought was great.

Kal later tweeted, "Man, you get a shout out from @kathy griffin & your feed becomes a love fest. Thanks guys! Larry the dog was totally adorable in real life."

If Kal in any way during his brief caretaking endured a crotch nuzzle from Larry that left a slobber stain, he didn't say anything. I have nothing but gratitude, but I feel for comedic purposes, I must point something out. My hero, Kal Penn, was in possession of Larry the Dog for several hours, even though Larry had a tag with a phone number on it. I've often wondered if Kal did an adorable photo shoot where he acted as if Larry was in fact his dog in order to attract chicks.

Maybe he took a photo with Larry, sent it to the Obamas with a note that said, "Dear Barack and Michelle, I don't miss the White House one bit since I've adopted this big fella." Or maybe he used a photo with Larry for his Tinder profile pic? Come on, wouldn't you?

PENN, SEAN
Oscar-Winning Actor, "Experiential" Journalist

The sun was cresting over an earthquake-ravaged Haiti as I handed Sean Penn a shovel and said, "That drainage ditch isn't going to dig itself. Get to work!"

No, wait, that was a dream I had.

In reality, I was at the Women in Entertainment power breakfast hosted by the *Hollywood Reporter*, and Penn, who was giving a special award to Melinda Gates, showed up *looking a little disheveled*. I was at my power table near the front and said to anyone around me who'd listen, "Look at him. His hair is ridiculous." It was 9:00 A.M., and believe me, I'm no fan of getting up before midday, but he really looked like the guy who opens his eyes, throws on the suit from the night before, and doesn't even bother to check the mirror before going out to give an award to Melinda Gates. Kris Jenner, who was at my table—and by the way, I still maintain she gets my genius attempts at hilarity—dared me to bring Sean Penn to our table. Done and done, lady. This is what I do on a daily basis.

He was nearby, so I marched up to him in the middle of his conversation with Melinda Gates, which sounded very cerebral and save-the-world-y, and said, first to her, "Excuse me, Mrs. Wozniak." (Crickets from her.) Then I turned to Penn and said, "I don't mean to interrupt, but what's with your hair?"

He looked confused and said, "Why?"

"Well, you're at a big power women's event, you're giving an award, your hair looks like crap."

"What do you mean? What should I do?" he asked.

"Well, do you have any hair gel?"

"No," he said.

"Sean, you look like you lost your two Oscars on skid row. Look at the room. Barbra Streisand is right over there. Captains of industry are here. Get it together, Sean! Your hair needs shape!"

He started putting his fingers through it, as if that was going to help. So I wrapped my arm around him, as you would an old person going down a stairwell, and said, "Let's go to my table. They'll want to meet you. Come on, Penn. Excuse us, Melinda."

The arm around him was important, because he tried to get away, the alarm rising in his voice: "No, no, no!"

But it took only three steps, and then I announced, "Ladies, I give you Sean Penn!"

And my whole table—Rita Wilson, Meghan Trainor, Lena Dunham, Sarah Silverman, and Kris—went, "YAY!"

Why didn't I make that wager with Kris for a million? She has it. Probably on her.

Anyway, I loved that later Sean Penn then got up and called me out from the podium, telling everyone, "I walk in, and the first face I see is Kathy Griffin telling me my hair looks like shit," and everybody clapped. It worked! His comment got a laugh, and then he caught El Chapo.

PINK
Singer, Opinionated Acrobat

At the 2000 Billboard Awards, when I was hosting with
*NSYNC, Justin Timberlake and I were rehearsing a sketch
that needed Britney Spears, and we had her for a very short
amount of rehearsal time. We got maybe five minutes with
her. The three of us were running over the lines as many
times as could fit in, and suddenly up-and-comer Pink walked
up. (This was when she only had the one album and the hits
"There You Go" and "Most Girls.") She was in Britney's genre
at the time, and because we were slammed for time, I said,
"Hang on a second." The next day, the producer of the show
called and said Pink wanted an apology. I ran over the previous day in my brain and said, "But I didn't make a Pink joke!"
He explained how Pink was really good friends with Britney
and Justin, and she was just trying to say hello when I blew
her off, and she felt disrespected. I was livid. "I am not apol-
ogizing! Are you kidding me? I was rehearsing! I'm not apol-
ogizing to a twenty-year-old who's got her panties in a wad!"
He said, "Okay, what's the compromise? Will you at least talk
to the manager?" So I talked to the manager, said I barely remembered what happened because I was rehearsing, which
he took as "Good, I can go back to Pink and say you're sorry."
Fine.

Years later, I'm in the scenic Burbank Airport, about to
board a flight to Vegas, by myself, when I see a chick in a
baseball cap sitting against the wall. It was Pink, trying to

look under the radar. I went up to her and said, "Do you want to sit together? You're probably better off sitting next to me than some drunk dude on his way to his bachelor's party," and she said, "Cool."

We had a great time on that flight. She had just gotten married to motocross superstar Carey Hart, who was working in Vegas, and she said, "This is what it's like when you're in a long-distance marriage. Am I a good wife or what?" I agreed, and then we talked shop, specifically selling merchandise at shows. I had just started doing it myself, and she let on, "Oh, I make more selling merch at my shows than with ticket sales. I make more money selling glow sticks than I do from my ticket sales. After the show, I make the venue settle the merch and make them put the receipt under my hotel room door so I can go over it that night."

I was like, "Well, hello, Pink!"

She was so mellow and super smart and a good businessperson that those fifty minutes in the air were really fun and eye-opening. (You know I love it when the ladies know their biz affairs.) Ever since then, I look forward to running into her at events, and we have a great picture of us hugging after I won my Grammy. I guess when you're a mellow, super smart businesswoman, you forget about whatever made you angry at the Billboard Awards at the turn of the millennium. Well, *I* don't, per se, but I need the material. You understand. Now I know why Pink wants to get the party started.

PITBULL
Chrome Dome Homey

Team Griffin and Team Estefan cannot stop coming up with brilliant ideas.

The night of September 10, 2011, I was in a bad mood because I'd just lost (or rather, been ROBBED of) the Emmy for *The D-List* that year, and yet Emilio Estefan had arranged a limo to whisk me from downtown Los Angeles to a hangar at the Santa Monica airport, where the American Latino Media Arts Awards were holding their show the same night. That's because Emilio wanted me to be part of a surprise inside a surprise. Gloria had arranged to premiere her new song "Wepa" with a performance the audience didn't know about, and Emilio wanted me to surprise Gloria by sneaking onstage as a backup dancer. The plan was going well, but I started running into people—hosts Eva Longoria and George Lopez, actor Danny Trejo—who all pretty much said the same thing: "Hey, hi . . . wait, WAIT? What are *you* doing here?" My answer was pretty much the same, too: "I'm Hispanic now, since I've heard it'll help my career. I need you people. And you could use some redheads."

At this point, several high-profile Latinos were in on the Estefan/Griffin prank. At the crucial moment, Team Estefan (minus Gloria) had people huddle around me to shield

my presence. Emilio described what would come next. He said, "Once the dancers go on, we're just going to push you out there and see if Gloria notices." We found a small space in the wings where my protective little human shield wouldn't be noticed by Gloria's entourage, who were also waiting. But then out of nowhere comes Pitbull and *his* entourage, and we're now truly a traffic jam of posses. A Team Estefan guy named David, who's known Pitbull forever, starts yelling at him in Spanish to get out of the way, and then Pitbull starts yelling back in Spanish, and I am officially terrified. I don't know who are the Jets and who are the Sharks, but I know I'm not Officer Krupke. I'm worried that I've started a Cuban turf war, at which point Pitbull turns to me and starts screaming at *me* in Spanish, as if I were Lucy after some cockamamie scheme gone bad and he was Ricky Ricardo tearing me a new one. I turned to David with a nervous "What's he saying?" look, and David started translating: "You are the funniest *bitch*, mama! I *love* you, mama! You're so fuckin' *funny*, mama, I'd fuck you *and* listen to your jokes, mama!" Then Pitbull grabbed my shoulders and kissed me and walked away. Once my brain grasped David's translation of Pitbull's words, all I could do was snap out of it and yell,

"Um . . . *gracias!*"

That had to be the most aggressively scary compliment I've ever received, and to this day, whenever I see the Estefans, they love to bring up the time Kathy Griffin was frightened by superfan Pitbull, after which they do their impression of the terrified white girl. Ha ha ha ha ha.

A couple of years later, Pitbull performed at the Hollywood Bowl, and we arranged to go backstage and hang out with him in his private suite. I know he's supposed to be this big, scary Pitbull, or he's ferociously sexy to the ladies or whatever, but I can tell you he's also a guy that took time out minutes before his headlining performance at the Hollywood Bowl to host my little group of four. We took pictures and joked around. Real international love stuff. As he exited the room to start his performance, I yelled, "DALE!" And no, I don't know what it means.

POITIER, SIDNEY
Actor, Sir with Love, Lily of My Field

As you may know, I typically find myself in relationships with much younger men. However, let me be clear: I'd fuck Sidney tomorrow.

I bet you never thought I know Mr. Tibbs, did ya? Well, I do.

When you first lay eyes on Sidney, you just kind of have to take it in that he's actually in front of you. And then if you're me, you've got to start to work.

I introduced myself to him years ago at a fancy dinner party, and he said, "I love comedy." I tried to make him laugh, and

he laughed. What more do I need to hear? Ever since then, the Academy Award–winning leading man and civil rights icon has been a favorite of mine whenever I see him, and his lovely wife, Joanna, is always my partner in crime. He's cool, charismatic, regal, and has a giant laugh that fills up a room. Because he's such a pioneer for black people in the arts, he's a darling of Oprah's, and being the classy gentleman who can speak to the struggle comes easy for him, but in everyday life, he loves a joke. If I've really gotten to him, he'll double over, then get up in my face and say, "*You*, young lady, go too far! Don't *ever stop!*"

I'm always cornering him and asking when we're going to get it on, and Joanna Poitier typically chimes in with, "For God's sake, Kathy, take him off my hands for one night. That's one night I won't have to make him a bland chicken breast for dinner."

I get to say, "Sidney, let's cut the shit. Your wife is practically throwing you at me, and the Beverly Hills Hotel is ten minutes away. We can go knock this out."

He'll turn to my boyfriend, Randy, and say, "How do you

DEAL with her! NOTHING STOPS HER!"

Then Joanna says, "Well, I'm not going to stop her, because I'll get to go home early and read a book for once. Maybe Randy can join me."

Joanna and I then began planning the swap, and I've watched Sidney put his arm around Randy and say, "What will it take to get you and me to just go get a drink somewhere *alone*?" It's been years of these exchanges.

Even at Jackie Collins's memorial, which she had let friends know she wanted to be lively and not dour, he was bantering with me. I hadn't been there for very long before Sidney came up and said, "I have been looking at you for *five minutes* and you've been *ignoring* me!"

I said, "Fine, Sidney! It's all about you! First of all, who dressed you? Corduroy? Seriously?"

He roared with laughter and said, "Here's what I need from you—stop being so beautiful!"

I said, "Can't do it!"

I noticed Jodie Foster nearby. I don't know Jodie Foster. Has that ever stopped me? "FOSTER!" I yelled. Jodie walked over, and I decided to introduce them. "Foster, Sidney Poitier's here, did you ever meet him?"

She very humbly said, "No, actually, I haven't."

"Watch how a pro does it. Sidney! This is Jodie Foster! She's an actress!"

Sidney said, "How do you do? What a pleasure."

I turned to Jodie. "Come on, Foster, work it a little bit. He kind of knows who you are, but maybe not quite. *Sidney!* She's got *two* Academy Awards. Foster, don't screw this up. What did you win for? *Tell him!*"

Jodie Foster appeared somewhat shy. She may or may not

have wanted to be put on the spot at this very moment. Too bad, Foster, I can't help being a Goodwill Ambassador when I feel the calling.

"Uh, *The Silence of the Lambs*?" she quietly responded.

"Not to me!" I yelled. "I know that! Tell Sidney!"

She repeated it. I said, "Louder!" She said it louder, and I said, "What else?"

She said, "*The Accused*, sir. I won for *The Accused*."

"How about that, Sidney! But guess what she doesn't have? The Medal of Freedom."

He shook his head and said, "Oh no, you're not going to bring that up again . . ."

And I said to Jodie, "Foster, here's the thing about Sidney. He's great, but he's got to bring up that frickin' Medal of Freedom every two seconds."

Jodie looked shell-shocked at the exchange, but Sidney smiled and said, "*That's* the young lady I wanted to see tonight!"

The fact that a genuine history-making, massively gifted superstar like Sidney Poitier gets me is such a source of joy and contentment, it's hard to describe. If Oprah knew, she'd curl up in a ball in Gayle's lap and cry.

POVICH, MAURY
Secret Baller, the One That Got Away

This is a tale of two cities. One part your humble authoress (me) kissing my own ass for a piece of comedic genius that I feel I provided the world that did not get the credit it so de-

served. The other part is the story of a man you thought you knew for delivering the line "You are NOT the father" in a gray cashmere V-neck sweater.

Maury Povich is the shit. (Judge Judy . . . you are also the shit, just give me a minute here.) Maury's talk show—really a live relationship melodrama—has been a hit forever, he owns a production empire, and probably runs half of Montana, where he lives with his wife, the legendary television journalist Connie Chung. Here's the moment I want you to look up online and hopefully get a good chuckle.

Sometimes I just can't stop myself. I got the idea in my head that the greatest way to spend an evening would be to show up to a taping of *Maury* and sit in the front row in a disguise. No one was filming me, this was not part of any of my television shows—I just do this stuff for the love of the game.

I had someone from my team reach out to Team Maury and let them know they were in for quite a treat. They thought the idea was funny. I told them I would not disrupt the taping of the show in any way but that I had one request. I wanted a sit-down with Maury himself.

The plan was in place. I showed up at Maury's favorite restaurant a couple of hours before showtime. He has his own table at a quiet restaurant. The maître d' greeted me with, "Maury's table is right this way." He was sitting there by himself, and that alone was a relief. I really cherished getting to meet my idols one-on-one without a team surrounding them and prohibiting a real live conversation.

I had a lot to say to this man. The first thing was "Please tell me you are having as much fun as it looks like you are having!"

He laughed and told me, "I have so much fun doing this show! How could I not?" Check. Right answer.

I expressed to him how many longtime successful celebrities I had met who could not simply be happy with their jobs and how refreshing it was hearing from someone who had been so successful in the business for so long describe how fun it is. That's how I feel. It's that ease that comes with years and years of going up and down, up and down in the television business that I have found only comes with a certain maturity.

It took me five minutes to realize that this is a man who has a great sense of humor, a real sense of balance in his personal life, and happens to be a kick-ass businessman. Oh, why are all the good ones married . . . to Connie Chung?

He stopped the conversation and said, "What can I do for you?"

What?

Folks, this never happens. People who ask this question are not telling you they have some fucked-up agenda or that you are secretly making some deal with the devil that you won't find out about until later. Guess what? The good news is Maury Povich is one of my idols because he doesn't need anything from anyone, least of all me.

We talked about my dreams and aspirations, how I wanted my new talk show to aspire to a level of conversation that Dick Cavett used to bring to television, and he was interested to hear that. He told me he owned a company called Stun Creative, and that knocked me off my seat, because I'd done promos with Stun, and everyone thinks they do great work. He said, "Early on in *The Maury Povich Show*, the promos other people did were okay, but what I realized was that the promos and the commercials had to be better than the show. So I started my own company, and now we do all the promos for NBC Universal."

I raved about Stun, and he offered to help me put together a Stun-quality sizzle reel of existing *Kathy* content at no charge. It was such a generous offer, I couldn't believe it. He also told me something fascinating about his deal with NBC Universal on *The Maury Povich Show*: he used to own it, but it was such a hassle auditing NBC Universal every year to ensure they were being honest that he did the math and told them, "I know what it makes, so pay me this much every year, and you can own it." Jesus, I practically thought he was going to say, "Wax on, wax off."

I said a brief farewell to my sensei, as I had to don my disguise to live another dream of mine and get into character for being the greatest Maury Povich audience member you've ever seen. I played this role for two episodes in a row that night. I had the time of my life! I wore a short brown wig. I made my face up in a way that was befitting (how shall I say this delicately?) a true *Maury* show fan from the Deep South. She had a whole backstory. She proudly wore her "Who's

Your Daddy?" T-shirt, took several bus rides from the trailer park, and was fist pumping with anger every time she felt one of the participants onstage had done his lady wrong. Maury never skipped a beat. He wasn't distracted by my insane front-row behavior even though I did my damnedest. It was honestly one of the most fun nights I have ever had.

At the end of the taping, Maury really laid it on thick. "Ladies and gentlemen, I have one more secret to reveal about this sordid tale we've all been going through tonight." Pause.

Audience moans loudly, "Ooooooo."

"That's right," Maury continued. "There is someone else in our midst tonight who is NOT who you think they are."

Audience even louder, "Nooooooo!"

Maury continues, "Yes! This woman"—points finger at me—"in the front row is . . . the . . . great . . . comedian Kathy Griffin!"

Greatest intro ever. Audience went crazy. I ripped my wig off and hugged Maury onstage. Maury then boarded his private jet and went to the Masters.

QUEST, RICHARD
CNN Correspondent, Extreme Extrovert, Amateur Park Ranger

This entry is designed to make Anderson Cooper quake in his Prada shoes.

I insisted Anderson introduce me to CNN's lovably loony limey. That's a lot of alliteration, Richard, but I think you can handle it. I just knew Questy and I would fall in love. Anderson described him in terms that made him sound like a caged animal, and he's obviously very protective of Richard, so one of the conditions of that particular New Year's Eve live broadcast was that I not mention any, um, incidents in Richard's past. By that, I am referring to the following article from *The New York Post* in 2008: "CNN personality Richard Quest was busted in Central Park early yesterday with some drugs in his pocket, a rope around his neck that was tied to his genitals, and a sex toy in his boot, law-enforcement sources said." I agreed, because I am willing to give Richard the absolute benefit of the doubt when it comes to being arrested in a park with crystal meth and a rope tied to certain parts of the body. If that isn't the definition of a victimless crime, I don't know what is. It doesn't matter anyway because he's been back on CNN ever since, lighting up the channel with his over-the-top delivery, and I just find it amusing he's presented as one of their tent-pole global stars.

When we did meet one New Year's Eve, live and on the platform, Richard did the most charming thing: he brought a mistletoe that he wouldn't stop holding over my head. I am more than happy to open-mouth kiss this colorfully vested, roaringly accented Richard Quest, because well, Christiane Amanpour probably doesn't have the balls to do it. Richard was like your crazy uncle at Christmas, festively dressed and full of spirit, and when compared side by side on television with my Anderson, I couldn't have been happier to be the girl in the middle.

So Anderson need not have worried about me referencing the *New York Post* article.

———

QUINTO, ZACHARY
New Spock, Loves Pussy

Zachary looked impeccable in his suit and tie when I came across him at the CNN Heroes event. I needed to point it out. He said it was a Louis Vuitton, tailor-made for him. I was in a form-fitting Zac Posen full-length gown, and Zachary complimented me on how chic it was. Realizing we had younger boyfriends in common, we talked about that. (His is thirteen years younger, mine is eighteen.) We talked about how gorgeous they were and how good they looked in suits. Then we talked about our houses. I mentioned my eight-thousand-square-foot home in the Hollywood Hills, and he described his new Greenwich Village townhome that he and his lover were redoing. We discussed house flipping, the pros and cons. Then it was time for him to go because he had to get onstage and present an award. He looked at me, chuckled, and said, "Wow, this has really been a gay exchange."

QUIVERS, ROBIN
Radio Host, Stern Wrangler, New Age Health Experimenter

I've been enjoying my visits as a guest on *The Howard Stern Show* since 1996, and I can say that I felt an instant nurturing connection with Robin. (Already we're talking about an un-

usual atmosphere, because "nurturing" and "morning radio" are words that don't typically go together.) Obviously, part of her role is to be the clear-eyed, reflective, cheery counterpoint—and sometimes, laughing audience—to the glorious unbridled rants and activities Howard throws himself in, and it's earned her plenty of accolades as a multifaceted broadcaster. But it's also a great cover, too, for when she decides to be naughty. She'll be on your side for a good part of the interview, and then—zing!—she'll challenge you. Hers is a very particular skill. Off the air, she's an angel, even though we've really only had personal moments in the hallway at the studio.

Remembering that Robin was a captain in the air force, I sought her advice when I performed for the troops in Afghanistan and Iraq. So let me remind you, this is not just another story about me telling you about another woman who works in a male-dominated field. She has literally been in the trenches. Oh, and she works with Howard.

Sometimes I'll do my best to pry and ask, "C'mon, Robin, who are you dating now?"

She'll say, "Yes, I'm dating someone, but that's as far as this is going."

I said, "Seriously, Robin, I'm not going to ask you if you take it up the butt. That's Howard's job."

She'll say, with her signature laugh, "Yes, but I also know who I'm talking to here."

Fair enough. We've talked dieting a lot, and she's famously become a vegan who's promoted a cleanse that involves lemon, maple syrup, and cayenne pepper. And I have incredible admiration for how she's survived child abuse and cancer. I'm especially fascinated, though, by how she's navigated a boys' club for over thirty years.

When I talk about female influencers of a certain age, I think of Robin, too, as someone whose example has taught me that it's still a grind. Robin's job is probably no easier than it ever was—she has to deliver as much as Howard, she has to give as much shit as she gets—and for that, I'll always gravitate toward Robin whenever I show up for an interview. I remember the backlash, too, she used to get from women of all colors saying she shouldn't let Howard say the things he says. But I've always understood the amount of finesse it takes to roll with this crew hour after hour, day after day, year after year. We're not talking about elected offices here. I love that she's this rock, this mainstay, a monument to hard work (when the cancer was at its worst, she did the show from home) and recognizing what her strengths are. We all know Howard wouldn't be anywhere near as successful without Robin, so in my mind, after all these years, it's pretty clear who the real winner is.

Robin, as you can see, I laid it on REAL thick here. Why? Because I know it's going to *kill* Howard. Because I know Howard is going to read this passage verbatim the next time I'm on his show and take umbrage to something or challenge me on labeling you an "angel" without irony. Hey now!

RAY, RACHAEL
Personal Chef to Kathy Griffin

I have Rachael Ray's house keys. Don't call the police yet. I can explain.

Whenever I see them in New York, whether I'm at home with them or out and about, Rachael and her husband, John, are that special kind of couple who never make me feel like I'm a third wheel. They are true friends and incredibly gracious hosts.

The first time they had me over for dinner, Rachael pulled out all the stops with a gourmet meal that took way more than thirty minutes to make and cost a lot more than ten dollars, and I joked, "Rach, half of this stuff I can't even eat. It's too exotic. I really was hoping for a good old-fashioned tuna melt." The next time I went to their apartment, she made me the most delicious tuna melt I have ever had! Also, the fanciest tuna melt I'd ever eaten, with eighteen ingredients from around the world, so I had to keep up the joke: "Okay, Rach, let's keep it simple next time. Enough with Thai shallots and gribiche aioli. I just want tuna and cheese, and the cheese has to melt."

Rachael, who's as down to earth as they come, has her fun, naughty side when it comes to humor and always teases me about my tastes, which I love. But she knows me and knows what I like. When I was performing my sold-out limited run Broadway show, *Kathy Griffin Wants a Tony*, at the famed Belasco Theater, I reached out to Rachael and said, "I can't

eat before the shows, I can't eat after the shows, I'm changing my material every day, and it's thrown my nutritional habits all out of whack. I have a hotel room with a microwave. I'm starving, and I don't know what to do. I can't keep food down because of my nervous stomach." So she sent me a tray of the most incredible homemade, all-natural, mouthwatering mac and cheese that I lived on for the week. It was nourishing, thoughtful, and tasty.

Rachael would have preferred I just stay with her and John. They have a spare room off their apartment that's really its own spare apartment, and one time she started giving me shit about not taking them up on their offer. I said, "As flattered as I am, I'm never going to stay with you. I know you have a gorgeous apartment, and I can spend weeks hanging out with you, but do you know how loud you guys are? You talk louder than anyone I know! That's why you had voice surgery—because you yell everything! The husband's no better! Besides, I sleep late, as in 1:00 P.M., and you two are up at 6:00 A.M. every day to go to the damn gym! Plus, you're a cabinet slammer. Yeah, I said it. I don't care if you cook every meal for me. I'm not staying here!"

Then she pulled me into the guest apartment, saying, "JUST LOOK AT IT! LOOK AT THIS BEAUTIFUL APART-MENT!"

"You can have it, lady!" I yelled back.

So we'd gone back and forth with that routine many times, until one night over dinner at her place, she simply gave me her house keys. "I'm tired of this argument," she said. "I'm just giving these to you. Next time you're in town, whether *we're here or not*, you've got the keys to both apartments. Just give me one day's notice by text, and we'll clear out the one next door."

I just shook my head and said, "You're like a crazy person! What are you, nuts?"

"TAKE 'EM!" she said.

It was like your aunt trying to give you the five-dollar bill: she's literally shoving them in my pocket. I said, "Okay, I'm going to take them. But I'm going to mail them to you tomorrow."

She said, "Now *you're* crazy!"

I was walking back to my hotel that night, Rachael Ray's house keys jangling in my pocket—even her keys are loud!—and I texted her: "I have your house keys."

She texted back, "I want you to have my keys. Why aren't you getting this?"

A few days later, back in LA, I called her and said, "Hi, this is Kathy Griffin, and I have your house keys. They're with me now, but when you get a FedEx package from me and it sounds jingly, it'll be your keys."

"Don't you *dare*," she said. Which, I'll admit, sealed our friendship forever.

So now I don't know what to do. When I see her now and I even start to say, "By the way, Rach, do you still want me to . . . ," she says, "YES!" No celebrity has ever given me the keys to the house before. And that includes my mother.

Do I worry that Rachael will be burglarized and that my fingerprints being on her keys, which are in a safe-deposit box, will make me the prime suspect? Yes. But do I also imagine an apocalyptic future, perhaps because Lovatics have taken over the world, and I need to hide out at Rachael's à la Jodie Foster in *Panic Room*? Yes. I could live on tuna melts, absolutely.

REDFORD, ROBERT
Actor, *Hubble (Not the Telescope)*

In 2012, I was asked to present a career achievement award to *Hollywood Reporter* editor Janice Min at the Los Angeles Press Club's awards dinner, which was being held at the Biltmore in downtown LA. What was also exciting, though, was that my friend Jane Fonda was getting a Visionary Award that night, and her presenter was going to be the great Robert Redford. I was going to meet him, come hell or high water, even though I knew his publicist would valiantly try to keep that from happening.

Well, Redford was late, and nothing could start without him being there, which I knew would be driving the publicist up a wall. Then I overheard someone say, "He's just pulling up." Time to have an urgent need to hit the ladies' room. It was my only chance to get face time. I ran up to the hotel's glass doors as Redford was coming through with his publicist, and I thought, *She's not going to stop me from saying hello.* From my perch near the restroom, I darted right up to him and said, "Hello, Mr. Redford. My name is Kathy Griffin, and it's a pleasure to meet you! I know you're giving an award to Jane. Well, I'm giving one to Janice Min, so we're both giving awards tonight!"

Redford said, "What's your name again?"

"Kathy Griffin. I'm a stand-up comedian, and I think tonight is going to be great, and Jane is so excited to see you. By the way, the restrooms are right over here if you want to use one first." I wasn't obnoxious. I didn't ask for a photo or an autograph. And he was completely mellow about it and very nice.

Well, the presentations started, and Redford did his speech for Jane, which was terrific. Then I did mine about Janice. About two lines in, I decided that I should abandon and just free-style instead, which worked great, and I got big laughs. Whew! I sat down, and Robert Redford, who just looked fantastic in his tux, came up to me and whispered in my ear, "You're not just funny, you're sexy as hell."

Whaaaa?!? Oh, Bob! I shot back, "Bob! My boyfriend's right here, and guess what? He's going to kick your fucking ass!"

He just laughed and said, "That's why I love her! Sexy and funny! You're a lucky man, Randy! Do you know what a great combination that is?"

And it doesn't stop there. Years later at a Women in Entertainment power breakfast, Redford was giving an award to Barbra Streisand, and as he was going over her career, he got hung up trying to remember the club where he met her.

Redford, wondering aloud from the podium: "What was that place you played, Barbra?"

Streisand, from her table: "The Bitter End."

Redford, not hearing her: "What was the name of it?"

Streisand, again: "The Bitter End!"

Redford, still not hearing her or even grasping that she's speaking: "Little place in the Village. Everybody played there. Lenny Bruce . . ."

Me, standing up and shouting: "BOB, IT WAS THE BIT-TER END!"

Redford, now hearing: "Who was that, anyway?"

Someone in the crowd: "KATHY GRIFFIN."

Redford, my new boyfriend: "Oh yeah . . . she's terrific."

My heart: pit-a-pat, pit-a-pat, pit-a-pat . . .

RICKLES, DON
Mr. Warmth, Fearless, Genius

The night I met the one-of-a-kind Don Rickles, it was like a Rat Pack experience. His beloved late son, Larry, worked on *Suddenly Susan*, and one day, he said, "By the way, my dad is Don Rickles, and he invited all of you to Vegas." What? Seriously? Yes, please . . . I'll have some more!

The whole cast went—Brooke, Nester, David, and myself. We sat in a classic Vegas showroom booth at the Flamingo. Brooke Shields was engaged to Andre Agassi at the time. Having watched Don Rickles famously pick certain people out of audiences on countless television specials and lovingly rib them was something I could have only dreamed of actually witnessing in person. About halfway through the show, sure enough, Don did the old-school "Ladies and gentlemen, we have some special guests in our audience tonight. The beautiful Brooke Shields [applause] and her fiancé, tennis champion Andre Agassi [more applause]!" *Here we go*, I thought. *This is going to be freaking classic.* And it was.

Don was on fire. He made every joke you could possibly think of from Brooke's Calvin Klein ads to Andre Agassi's mullet. When you make fun of people that are in the audience, it is truly a high-wire act for the comedian, the subjects of the jokes, and the audience. It is a skill. Don is not an insult comic. He has the ability to work the room that extends from his own work on the stage to his "subjects" he's poking fun at in the audience and the actual crowd that is witnessing this complex and dangerous exercise, which he executes with the excitement of a teenager.

Well, that's not how Agassi saw it. Gulp. Brooke loved it, and Agassi was livid. I couldn't have been happier: I'm laughing at a legend who's still got it and relishing how pissed off that flashy tennis-playing bore was over being teased about his mullet and dating Streisand. (Now that we know a little bit more since Agassi's book came out, he was probably coming down from something. Allegedly.)

Afterward, we were invited to his dressing room, and Don couldn't have been a nicer host. I was gushing. We all were. Well, except for a certain US Open, Wimbledon, blah-blah-blah winner—oh, what do I care? I have no time for some annoying athlete who can't take a joke from the great Don Rickles. Brooke was at her most charming, and Agassi was still a stone-faced pill, even backstage when we had the privilege of hanging in Don's dressing room after the show. Brooke had to *explain* it to Andre: "It's an honor when he makes fun of you." Oh, good God!

Anyway, as I've gotten to know Don over the years, he's been wonderfully supportive, telling me to be who I am and say what I feel. Don has tried to fix me up with guys, mostly because he thinks I shouldn't be with younger men. Every time Don sees Randy, he says, "When's this gonna be over? It's run its course. Come on." He busts Randy's balls endlessly. "Why don't you let the kid go take his SATs?" Then there's Randy's tall Germanic presence. Don will say, "Can I trust him? Is he in the Party?" Then, to Randy, "Hey, kid, how's the Third Reich? This look familiar?" At which point he'll put one finger under his nose and give the "heil" salute with the other. I love it all, and Randy does, too.

I want everyone to appreciate the no-holds-barred, fast-on-his-feet comedy that Don made his own and that I've always found inspirational. When I got the call to present an award at the Emmys alongside Don Rickles, it was as great an honor as I could have hoped for outside of winning one. Backstage that night, it was so dark that Don was worried about falling, so we walked out with me holding his hand. It brought an air of fragility that I felt needed counterbalancing, so I yelled out to the jaded celebrities in the auditorium, "GET UP!" And BOOM, the whole place stood. I'll never forget that moment, and later, Don was super sweet and appreciative that I not only helped him avoid tumbling, but that I made the crowd show their respect. "You know, kid," he said, "I'll always remember that." Hey, Don, I was just, as you say, being who I was: your biggest fan.

RIVERS, JOAN
My Friend

Look, it was hard to pick one Joan Rivers story for this book. I'll always miss her. I have countless meaningful and hi-

larious memories of our time together. But here's a story that will blow your mind. It may have a couple of surprises, but I think it encompasses so much about Joan that I loved.

In 2011, she called me and said, "Chuck and Camilla are having a two-night event, one night at Windsor Castle, one night at Buckingham. It'll be very fancy. Do you want to come as my plus one?"

WHAT?!?   (Kathy moves around schedule furiously in under thirty seconds.) To this day, it's one of the greatest, most generous invitations I've ever received.

I was determined to make Joan proud and do it up right. I packed a knockout Oscar de la Renta gown for night one and a Carolina Herrera gown for night two. I'd already booked my room at a swanky modern hotel when Joan called and said, "I want you to move into the Ritz so we can get adjoining rooms. You can even use my hair and makeup people." I should have known that Joan would think of every detail for both of us! She really wanted to make a girlfriends' weekend of it, which I was touched by. Now, I knew Joan was friendly with Prince Charles and Camilla, but what I didn't know was that she *hung* with them, as in, she rolled deep with them. As in, she went out to Balmoral Castle on a painting vacation with them. Seriously. Hence, calling him "Chuck."

At the hotel, with our adjoining rooms, we were like a couple of teenagers getting ready to go to the prom. We had so much fun shouting across the room at each other and making jokes about who was going to sneak into one of the spare rooms and cuddle with Chuck. We took bad cell phone pictures in our hotel room after we'd gotten ready for the first night, and we headed out to Windsor freaking Castle. Have I mentioned I'm from Forest Park, Illinois? And now I'm sitting next to Joan Rivers in a car driving through the gates of Windsor Castle.

When we got inside, I was a nervous wreck. My eyes were like saucers. Joan immediately started cracking me up by making fun of Sarah Ferguson, the Duchess of York, who divorced Chuck's brother Andrew. "Can you believe her? How stupid. How *stupid*! She could have had this . . . forevuh!"

I played along and fanned the flames. "Maybe she was unhappy," I said.

Joan was all, "Ugh! Please! Ugh! How could she . . . *stupid, stupid, stupid*!"

I loved it. I can tell you it's quite nerve-racking to be standing inside Windsor Castle, but Joan was prancing me around, acting like it was her vacation home. She gave me the lay of the land, pointing out the global movers and shakers in attendance, the secret old-money types who aren't famous but have this kind of access. Now, I realize that gay men everywhere are all about Harry, but for me, it was always Prince Charles. Sorry, boys, Chuck and Camilla are *my* royals. When

Joan introduced me to Charles, she said, "This is my friend Kathy, and she's a very outspoken, outrageous comedian in the United States."

Then Charles pulled me in and said, right in my ear, "Well, if it weren't for comedians and journalists, who would keep us honest?"

Way to go, Charles! We don't hear that from power brokers, much less royalty.

We also don't hear a comment that I admit was in the back of my mind when I was speaking to him. I'm only human. I'll tell you right now, I've always found the surreptitiously recorded remark he made about wanting to be Camilla's tampon to be nothing short of charming. Seeing how obviously thrilled he was to see Joan that night was very moving. It was obvious they had chemistry. He put his arms around Joan, and she was politer than I've ever seen her. Someone made a joke: "Well, it's a good thing Camilla's not here tonight, because in fact, Joan is the love of Charles's life!"

Later, alone, I said to Joan, "And you thought Sarah Ferguson was stupid? You're the one who blew it! Charles could have been your tampon!"

The evening was nothing short of thrilling, and we got to do it all over again the very next night at Buckingham freaking Palace. I was just as nervous in the car with Joan passing through those gates. Can you imagine? I couldn't either. But my pal Joan Rivers made this happen for me. Camilla Parker Bowles, you know, the Duchess of Cornwall, was there the second night for the Buckingham Palace event, and it was even more fun because Camilla made a beeline for her good friend Joan. Charles came up to me and said, "I saw you on *Graham Norton* last night." You're the Prince of Wales, and you watch comedic talk shows? Oh, Chuck, are there cracks in your marriage I should know about? Just let me know. Now, he could have had his doyenne whisper that fact in his ear, but who cares? He addressed me by name. *He really does love comedians*, I thought.

When it was time to eat, Joan and I were seated in separate rooms, but Joan told me why. "I'm going to sit with Charles, but you'll sit with Camilla, because she's a great laugher. Say anything you want." Joan was giving me a window into her relationship with them, which I could see was special to her. She never made me feel like I was lucky to be there. She even told me to make sure I took home a menu, since they were hand painted.

At the end of the night, someone wanted us to accompany them to a nightclub, and we joked, "Sure thing. We'll be right over. You go first." We laughed—obviously we weren't going to an EDM nightclub—but what I didn't realize was Joan had something else in mind: she wanted to stop by a hospital to visit someone she was close with, who was dying. We were quite a sight in our ball gowns in a quiet hospital after visiting hours, taking funny pictures with this ill friend of Joan's who was so happy to see her. She made him laugh, and then we left.

Joan had been in her element over those two nights: funny, friendly, supportive, enlightening, and oh so energetic. She mostly kept this part of her life private and sacred, and I understood: she'd been open about a lot, but if you can't keep some things to yourself, how do you know what's an act in life and what's genuine? Joan knew.

Chuck's comment about comedians keeping us honest is something Joan Rivers did for all of us for so long. She never gave up when life and show business weren't always so kind, and her example will never cease to inspire me. When Joan passed away, I was devastated. It took me some time, but I finally worked up the courage to ask her longtime assistant, "I'm curious, have you heard from the royals?" She told me the Queen, Prince Charles, and Camilla had all called. Of course they did.

ROCK, CHRIS
Comic, Director, Lil Penny

I'm going to take you inside baseball. A lot of people ask me during interviews what comedians are really like to each other, which comedians support which other comedians, what comedians hang out, and so on. When you're a fifty-six-year-old chick comic, there is no one answer, but let me tell you one time that was super meaningful to me.

One night, years ago, the late, great Prince was doing a secret performance at a small club in Vegas. I snagged a VIP booth. I see Chris Rock come in with his friends and sit down at a nearby booth. This is always an odd moment for someone like me. Yeah, he and I are both comics. Yeah, he and I even play the same venues sometimes. But let's cut the shit. I'm me (no complaints, no whining). But he's Chris Rock. I get insecure in those situations because I'm a little bit of a peer, a little bit of a fan, but I have enough understanding of celebrity to not want to bother Chris Rock sitting at a booth at a secret Prince show! Chris made a point of getting up, walking over to me, and literally took my left hand in a gentle grasp with both of his hands and simply said, "I just wanted to come over and say hi. You're doing great." That meant the world to me.

Chris and I have since become pals. I admit, I am such a stand-up comedy geek that when I was standing in a circle backstage at a high-level comedy event in Washington, D.C., surrounded by George Lopez, Tracy Morgan, Kevin Nealon, Dave Chappelle, and Chris, I was giggling like a schoolgirl. I was also the only girl. Again. But enough about that. Chris had this insight about my eighty-city Like a Boss tour:

"DAMN, Kathy, what the fuck you doin' eighty shows a year for? Do you owe child support?"

It was one of those moments when I was in the mood to tease him and all the other boys about anything that came into my head. Chris was in my crosshairs. "CHRIS!" I yelled. (By the way, he was standing right next to me.) "Why do you always ignore my boyfriend, Randy? He's standing right here next to me, we've been going out for five years, and you've met him several times. Why do you have to be such a racist?"

Chris casually said in his most Chris Rock–y performance voice, "Kathy, here's the thing. Randy seems nice for a white guy. Why? Cuz you seem happy. And if you're happy, I'm happy. Cuz you're not bitchin' to me about how you can't get a man. Now, the minute you break up with Randy, I'm gonna run all over town yelling, 'Fuck that white guy!'"

And then Chris and Randy took a selfie.

RUSHDIE, SALMAN
Author, Fatwa Survivor, Swims Against the Stream

I just did a phone interview for my tour for the Lincoln, Nebraska, *Journal Star* a few minutes ago (they can't all be *Van-*

ity Fair covers), and I was asked a question I often get asked. "Tell us something we don't know about you." Today, I answered, "I know Salman Rushdie."

I know we've all had bad days, but this dude had (and still has) a fatwa on his head. According to *Merriam-Webster's* dictionary, a fatwa is defined as "a legal opinion or decree handed down by an Islamic religious leader." *That can't be that bad,* I thought. I've dealt with tough crowds. Comedy is dangerous.

Rushdie, a British Indian novelist who angered a lot of Muslims with his 1988 novel, *The Satanic Verses*, received a fatwa from the Ayatollah Khomeini in 1989, which ordered all Muslims to KILL the author! That is way tougher than an angry bachelorette party that I've had to deal with at a Vegas show. I admit it. I remember that whole controversy vividly and at the time thought if I ever had the chance to meet Rushdie someday, I'd want to talk to him about how he dealt with it: the hiding, the fear, his gradual reemergence into the world. In fact, he even has a famous cameo in the 2001 film *Bridget Jones's Diary,* so I figured he was comfortable being out and about in public on some level. Comedians are routinely in positions where what they say stirs up shit, and I've certainly joked about my propensity to do that. One New Year's Eve, I said to Anderson Cooper that my goal that night was to get a fatwa on my head, and he quipped, "That wouldn't take much effort on your part."

When I was promoting my memoir, *Official Book Club Selection,* my dream came true and we snagged a sit-down with Rushdie for *My Life on the D-List.* We filmed it at the big Manhattan Barnes & Noble, and I'll admit, when he walked in, I was fearful for him. Would someone shout "Infidel!"? And point *at both of us*? I didn't know if he was going to be openly and visibly jittery and paranoid.

He walked in very casually. We spoke on and off camera. On camera, he was a great sport answering my silly questions. He really played along with the setup, that I thought I could sell more books if I had a fatwa. I thought he might walk off the set at that question, but he did not. It was a great scene for my little show, and I want to tell you about our conversation when we stopped taping.

I asked him to come hang out away from the crew, as I wanted to have some private time with him. He talked openly about why he chose to come out of hiding, and he said, "I finally got to the point where I thought, if they're going to get me, they're going to get me." He said living under that kind of terror made him snap, but in the opposite way. "Instead of getting angry," he said, "one day I said, 'This isn't getting me anything, so I'm going to live my life the way I want.'" (A couple of years after our talk, he published a memoir about his life under the fatwa, called *Joseph Anton*.) At one point, Rushdie confessed to being nervous about our talk, and I thought, *Uh-oh, he is scared about being out in public!* But instead, he said, "I thought you were going to ask me about my ex-wife." What? Oh, that's right. He was married to *Top Chef* host Padma Lakshmi from 2004 to 2007. I had to assure Rushdie that that was the last thing I would bother him with when I'm talking to a man with a fatwa on his head. He laughed, thank God AND Allah.

But the truly cool moment was when we were having our private chat, and suddenly my phone buzzed with an incoming text. I said, "Well, well, well . . . here I am talking to the great Salman Rushdie, but I have to ask you to wait, because I have a text from *CHER!*"

I showed him my phone, and he said, "Oh my. That's very exciting!"

I said, "Yeah, I roll with the big time. Authors, living legends."

He then grabbed his cell phone and showed me a text he received from Lou Reed (remember, this was 2009) and said, "Every time I get a text from Lou Reed, I want to show somebody, just like you did! I hold my phone up to whoever I'm with and say, 'Lou Reed just texted me!' I worship him and think he's a genius."

By the way, that fatwa still hasn't been revoked, and in fact, more money was added to it in 2016. You know what Salman Rushdie taught me? We all have our "Cher" in life. We all have our "Lou Reed." We all have our Ayatollah Ruhollah Khomeini of Iran issuing a fatwa ordering Muslims to kill us. Right?

RUSSELL, DAVID O.
Filmmaker, Fighter, JLaw's Svengali

I know a photo op when I see one! Damn it, if the press isn't smart enough to create it, then I will.

Please tell me you have seen the infamous viral video of my friend Lily Tomlin and my other friend the great director David O. Russell GOING AT IT in an epic way on the set of *I Heart Huckabees*. Now both Lily and David (who went on to direct *Silver Linings Playbook, Joy, The Fighter* . . . you get it) are going to be pissed that I even brought this up again, but stay with me. I have discussed this incident with both of my friends separately, and they both have confirmed several times that while that was a difficult shoot, the video going viral was something neither of them ever predicted, and the two of them have since made up and can have a laugh about it. I don't think this is something most people are aware of. That's where I come in.

Even when I am busy hosting an award show, I still have an eye out for things like Lily Tomlin and David O. Russell sitting three tables apart in the audience. I'm a real multitasker. In a very star-studded room, everyone from Michael Douglas and Catherine Zeta-Jones to Bette Midler and Jane Fonda, I still wanted to test the waters and see if David and Lily would be up for the official "We've made up due to our good friend Kathy Griffin" photo. At one point during my hosting duties, I actually ran into the audience with a microphone and straight-out asked Lily Tomlin how she felt about having David O. Russell a few tables away. "I love David," Lily said. "That was a long time ago." And trust me . . . that room filled with movie stars and directors knew exactly what I was referring to. Step one accomplished!

Later on, after David had accepted his award for *Joy*, he stopped backstage to give me a kiss on the cheek before he was about to leave. I had met David O. Russell in 2011 at an awards season luncheon. He was with his wife, and he approached me and said, "Hi, I'm David O. Russell, and I directed *The Fighter*." He said it in that very direct way that I now notice in his characters. He cracks me up every time I run into him. He's very intense, even if we are just having small talk. He seems to have no sense of personal space, which I find charming because he always has something interesting to say.

Anyway, back to the story. Before he left the backstage area, I unloaded on him. "DAVID! This was your big chance to publicly look Lily Tomlin right in the eye and, even though she has nothing to do with *Joy*, randomly let the world know that you guys are pals and have made up. Jesus, David, do I have to do everything, including sell the popcorn?"

He's a pussycat. He laughed and said, "Oh shit. I really meant to thank Lily."

I told him to go back to his seat and wait for five minutes when I would return to the stage and save his career once and for all. I went back out there and proudly announced that I was about to publicly bring back David O. Russell and Lily Tomlin in a sign of solidarity for actresses and directors everywhere. "David? David, get up here, and let's clear this whole thing up and get a nice photo that will obviously be Lily's Christmas card." Well, wouldn't you know . . . he left by the time of my almost epic announcement.

David, I'm going to give you one more chance to save your fledgling career. Listen up. Where's my great movie role, Mr. I Love Casting Women Over Fifty? (He got Melissa Leo an Oscar for *The Fighter*, for Chrissakes, and Jacki Weaver a nomination for *Silver Linings Playbook*, and he gave Diane Ladd and Isabella Rossellini some of their best roles in years in *Joy*!) It's already unusual that a big-time Hollywood director even knows who I am, much less loves me, so let's just say, I'm ready to be your Mo'Nique in whatever you want, David, so get to writing my *Precious*—I'm ready for my close-up with Bradley Cooper and JLaw. David, you can cast me as a bipolar female boxer with a cleaning-product empire, and we'll call it *Joyfight*. Just get to work. But if you scream at me, I'm calling Lily.

———

RUSSELL, KURT
Great Actor, but also Fox News Pundit

In the interests of squeezing as much out of Oscar-winning Goldie Hawn as I could in order to agree to host her children's charity event, I added another clause to our negotiation. "I want dinner with you and Kurt. *Dinner*. Not whatever this was, with you looking like you just got off a treadmill. It's a dinner, with you and Kurt looking like movie stars."

She looked concerned. "Well, can we at least bring Marty Short?"

"Why?"

"Kurt's afraid of you," she revealed.

(Ah, Martin Short's their hedge against unpleasantness, their buffer.)

"Well, Kurt should be afraid of me," I said to Goldie. "Tell him to get his butt off Fox News and get his head on straight." (Kurt and Goldie are like the James Carville / Mary Matalin of Hollywood: deeply opposed about politics, but deeply committed to each other.)

She gasped. "Don't you think we have these fights every day? Your reaction is what I'm talking about. He's expressed . . . you know . . . nervousness."

I didn't mince words: "Well, you just said the worst thing you could say to me."

The night of the Love In For Kids arrived, and I chased Kurt all night long, like a frickin' bobbysoxer. I had my hands full hosting, but whenever I wasn't, I had my eyes on the prize, which was messing with Kurt. He was filming the western *The Hateful Eight* for Quentin Tarantino at the time, so his in-character grooming was on target. "Kurt! What's with the facial hair? Don't walk away from me, cowboy! Did you take Uber Horse here? What kind of 'stache is that? Where did you get it, at a Hollywood Boulevard magic shop? I love that you wore your wardrobe from the movie today, but you should put on your real suit now?!"

Whatever I said, Kurt's response was the same: "Heh heh heh . . ." and then backing away. At one point, he started dancing, and Goldie confided to me, "He *never* dances." That's me. I can get 'em to dance. At least Goldie was encouraging, saying, "Don't let him off the hook that easy."

Whatever I did, it was catching, because when it came time for Martin Short and Kurt and I to be onstage together, Marty let Kurt have it hilariously, announcing him as coming straight from his home on the range, and so on. It was a really fun evening, and it worked, too, because shortly after that night, I got word from Goldie's assistant, Iris, that Kurt and Goldie wanted to take me out to dinner. It hasn't happened yet, but I am due for my monthly call from Iris saying, "Goldie and Kurt really want to set up that dinner at Nobu in Malibu." Well, it's in this book now, so they can't ignore me.

SHAKUR, TUPAC
Big Reader, or . . . ?

Oh, you guys didn't know I spent the day with Tupac Shakur one time? You don't get me! I am #urban. I'm practically a "thot." I don't know how your day with Tupac went, but here's how mine went:

This little cat has had many lives. Believe it or not in this story, I'm the cat. One of my many jobs that I had on ill-fated television shows that I was completely convinced would catapult me into global fame was a six-episode sketch comedy show on Fox called *Saturday Night Special*. The show was executive produced by Roseanne Barr, while she was also starring in her wildly popular sitcom. I was cast as one of the sketch players along with my pal Jennifer Coolidge (Stifler's mom) and several other up-and-comers. It was 1996, and thanks to Roseanne's heat, the show snagged some really big guests, including Sharon Stone and Patti Smith, and hot up-and-comers like Green Day and D'Angelo. One of the most exciting things about being a cast member on this series was I honestly didn't know who was going to walk onto the soundstage as a performer or even a visitor. The energy on this set was extra exciting. Slash from Guns N' Roses and I did a sketch. Ice-T came in to do a sketch. In fact, on the day Ice-T came to set, he had a surprise for us. A surprise named Tupac Shakur. Not the hologram, kids. The real live Pac.

"Is it cool I brought Tupac?" Ice-T asked.

Roseanne, sensing an opportunity, said, "Yes! Let's throw Tupac into a sketch."

He ended up doing a sketch, his own performance, and . . . wait for it . . . a spoof, yet charming version of the Neil Diamond / Barbra Streisand classic duet "You Don't Bring Me Flowers." I have a pretty good eye and ear for a special moment, and this day was filled with them. Remember, Tupac was at the height of his "California Love" fame, and watching him goof around with Ice-T was not something I ever thought I'd see on a normal workday. I admit it. I just sort of followed them around all day like an observant puppy.

Let me just cut to the chase. I can't confirm this in any way, shape, or form, but it was my observation that Tupac was struggling with reading. I, myself, am wildly dyslexic. Watch this . . . lfaksdjfladjflk;ajds. See? Ice-T stayed close to Tupac, like a big brother. He appeared to be doing all of Tupac's reading for him, out loud: the contract, the script, anything. I recall Ice-T even filling out forms for him. I remember wondering that very day if Tupac Shakur, or frankly any global superstar, could reach that level of fame, be that talented, create an iconic and lasting legend, and still possibly have been illiterate??? Okay, I know that last sentence was a barn burner, but give me this much: 1) You never would have guessed that I would have met Tupac Shakur, 2) You can't blame me for thoughts that pop into my head as I'm falling asleep at night. Thoughts such as *I'm not sure Tupac could read.* Or . . . maybe Tupac was just so damn famous that he had a designated celebrity reader, in this case Ice-T, read for him. Now that's famous.

SHANDLING, GARRY
Television Comedy Pioneer, Former Fiancé (Kind Of)

I was fortunate enough to call him a friend, and if legendary Hollywood agent Sue Mengers had had her way, I might have called him my husband. She was set on me falling in love with him and marrying him. What she didn't know was that she did not have to sell me on falling in love with him. I was very much in love with him—in a platonic way.

One day, Sue yelled to me on the phone, "You need a strong, wealthy man who understands your world, and *you will marry Garry Shandling*!" Unfortunately for Sue, Garry and I were more like a brother and sister. As long as I knew Garry, he had preferred hot model types, and God bless him for it. Have you ever met a male stand-up comic? They have a type. Model types.

Sue's attempt at creating a comedically epic power couple for the ages was very touching to me. I was more than happy to break bread with my future husband at one of her famous dinners. As I was getting ready for this particular dinner in the fall of 2010, I could never have predicted how the evening would end. I took Megan Mullally as my date, and I went with no expectations on the matchmaking front—mostly I was excited to just be once again in the orbit of one of the funniest men on earth.

Garry was late, though, and Sue got mad, so I said, "You're right, Sue. Screw it! I'm calling off the engagement! Be honest, now. Tell everyone how you want to fix me up with Garry and that it's not going to happen, and now he's not even showing up because he doesn't want to go out with me." At which point, Garry walked in and sat down right next to me.

We were in plush chairs and sofas around Sue's coffee table—which she came to prefer for its intimacy over the formality of a dining room table—and Garry was so close I started to wonder, did Sue convince him this might work? He seemed really uncomfortable, which I attributed to the fix-up scenario. With Garry next to me, I found myself wanting to become even more emboldened by busting the balls of this big-time, well-dressed, handsome manager I hadn't seen in forever who was sitting right across from us. This dinner (like all of Sue's dinners) was a combination of famous people, titans of industry, award-winning novelists, and other distinguished influencers.

When I saw the manager dude in an expensive tailored suit, I just decided to make him my target for the evening in an Anderson Cooper–type of way. With Garry by my side, I seized the opportunity to live a dream: to have great comedic banter with this groundbreaking comedic force. Oh, how I loved sitting next to, and riffing with, the man who gave us all those nights sitting in for Johnny Carson, *It's Garry Shandling's Show,* and of course, *The Larry Sanders Show.*

Big-time manager dude was looking at his phone every few minutes. I thought that in and of itself was funny, considering this crowd. He told me his wife was sending him photos of runway couture clothing from God only knows what fashion show. He was clearly choosing not to engage with me, which fueled my fire even more. I admit, my real agenda was to make Garry laugh. Then Garry reached down and held my hand. What was going on here? Was he actually making a move? Was it time to pick out the china patterns? Would I have a future with him in which I could send him cell phone photos of couture clothing from a runway show?

Pretty soon, what might happen meant little, because Garry began chiming in with his witty brilliance, and soon he was on a roll with making everyone laugh. He was on fire that night, and at the end of the night in Sue's driveway, Megan and I rehashed the evening, saying repeatedly, "Is there anyone funnier than Garry Shandling?"

Though Garry and I parted ways after dinner, the next time I saw Garry, that night suddenly became a lot clearer.

"Do you know that I will always be grateful to you for that night?" he said.

"Oh, I know, you mean the discomfort of Sue trying to set us up?" I asked.

And he said, "No, no, no. Do you know that I was in one of the longest litigations in TV history with Brad Grey and that we *hate* each other?"

(Oh . . .)

"That I haven't seen him since then?"

(. . . My . . .)

"I walked in, and Brad is sitting there, and I sat next to you—"

(. . . God!)

"—and you were giving him so much shit. That's why I held your hand! I will never stop thanking you for getting me through what I'd always dreaded—running into Brad again."

Yes, that's right, the "well-dressed manager dude" I was making fun of was none other than Brad Grey. It had *completely* slipped my mind that Garry had sued his longtime manager/friend back in the 1990s for $100 million for improper leveraging of their relationship in order to benefit

Grey's business. (They settled the excruciating and public legal battle back in 1999.) What was even more embarrassing was that I didn't realize Grey wasn't even a manager anymore—he was the chairman and CEO of Paramount Pictures! (As Maggie rightly pointed out to me, "Why do you always have to make fun of the goddamn check signers! Jesus." Oops.)

Garry said to me, "You made that evening bearable, because you were—"

"Clueless??" I interrupted.

Garry, I was happy to unwittingly ease your discomfort, friend. I miss you so much. You were always generous with your support of me; you could make me laugh like nobody else, and oh, what a night we had!

SHATNER, WILLIAM
ACTOR, DAMN IT, ACTOR!

He really is my favorite red-faced, bloated space captain. I love how he's never had a downtime in his career. He's always been cool or anticool, hip or not hip, but always on the cultural radar.

Well, back in the 1990s, when I was on nobody's radar, I got to go to his house because he was auditioning people for a television pilot he was going to make. As you might imagine, I was excited. But I can't even remember the role or the script, because everything else about the audition was nuts. Are you surprised?

We were in his living room, and he sat across from me, very close, and when I said, "It's great to meet you, Mr. Shatner.

Would you like me to read?" he said, very intensely, "How do you *fee-e-e-e-l* about your *father*?"

Okay, not what I was expecting. I said, "Ummm . . . I like him?"

He shouted back, "GET IN THERE! How do ya *fee-e-e-e-l*? What PISSES YOU OFF?" Taken aback, and a little scared, I blurted out sheepishly, "When I'm really hungry?"

You'd have thought this was a hidden camera show, it was so bizarre. His veins were popping, his face was turning that deep crimson, he had his hands on his knees, and he was leaning in like a bad-cop detective ready to break me. The questions kept coming, and he wore me down. After twenty minutes I was telling him things I've never told anyone.

Shatner: "WHADDAYA WANT TO SAY TO YOUR FIRST GRADE SCHOOLTEACHER? GIVE IT TO HER! LET HER HAVE IT!"

Me: "SCREW YOU, SISTER MARY!! I'M SPECIAL!!"

It was insane. But I'd have gone back. Come on, an invite to Shatner's house? I got a "Good work" from him at the end, and yet nothing happened, and the pilot was never made.

When I see him now, it's the same every time. I lovingly blurt out, "Bill?!" And he slaps his knees and shouts, "Come here, honey!"

SHEEN, CHARLIE
Famous and Infamous

I met Charlie Sheen at a great time and in a great way. We were seated next to each other as judges of a charity event /

drag show benefitting Aid for AIDS. (This was years before he announced to the world that he was HIV-positive.) When one takes a seat next to Charlie Sheen, one does not know what one may be in for. Okay, you caught me. I'm "one."

Even in 2008, he had been in the tabloids for all kinds of behavior from antics on the set of his hit show, *Two and a Half Men*, to his divorce from Denise Richards. As if that isn't juicy enough, it was the time in his life when he was married to Brooke Mueller, whom he had a tumultuous relationship with, and, get this, she was pregnant at the time. Okay, it was before his "I'm winning" / tiger blood phase, but if you think I'd forgotten that I was sitting next to the Charlie Sheen that accidentally shot Kelly Preston, you are mistaken. My ears were pricked up like a newborn puppy. I love moments like this where I am up close and personal with a famous (and infamous) celebrity in a celebratory, yet somewhat formal, environment.

Obviously, Charlie and Brooke were going to be on their best behavior. The other judges at this event ranged from Charlie's father, the great Martin Sheen, to John C. Reilly to Julia Louis-Dreyfus to Melanie Griffith. I was saying things to Charlie that night like, "Now, you're okay with this, right? It's a bunch of dudes who dress up like chicks, and you're going to have to stand up and clap."

He said, "Sure, sure."

I've always heard from several pals that Charlie Sheen is very funny in real life, and he was. We were enjoying some fun, silly banter back and forth as the show was progressing. Keep in mind that we were in the front row, and this is one of those celebrity charity events where the celebrities are asked to stand and wave to the crowd. This is not a tale of Charlie Sheen going off on his pregnant wife or me. Sorry. No charges are going to be pressed during this story. Charlie did not lock a drag queen in a bathroom. Charlie did not throw a chair at fellow judge Molly Shannon. None of that. Yes, folks, here is the surprise. Charlie Sheen and his then pregnant wife Brooke Mueller were like the Bickersons! In fact, I would go so far as to say Brooke was really giving Charlie a run for his money in the bickering department. That is what caught me off guard. She argued with him about everything, from how much to donate to when they could leave to murmurs of things I couldn't hear or understand. The funny part was when Charlie would turn to me with, whether manufactured or genuine, kind of a henpecked husband series of gestures and comments. It was a lot of "What can I do? Heh heh heh..." and shrugging his shoulders as if to say, "She's normally nice!" It was weird and hilarious, like I was watching some old-timey marital sitcom.

At the point where Brooke wanted to leave early, he apologetically indicated to me that they were going to take off, with a look that I interpreted to mean, "Heh, heh, chicks, right? Whew! Right?" I couldn't resist this opportunity to say, "Charlie, this isn't one of those events where you can just leave in the middle." Nothing like stoking the fires.

He said something like, "I know, I know." He made a generous donation, and they exited early. As they were leaving, Charlie said, "So sorry. The show was awesome. Everything's good. Hey, you look great."

At least he didn't accidentally shoot me.

SHEINDLIN, JUDGE JUDY
Syndication Queen, Baller

Here's the power of Maggie Griffin. No matter how often I've asked Judge Judy to go out to lunch with me one-on-one, she'd prefer my mother—her biggest fan—to be there, too. (It hasn't happened yet, incidentally. Maggie's too busy.) Judy is as outspoken outside of her show as she is on it, dispensing common-sense TV justice to bitter, moronic litigants. Or comedians named Kathy Griffin. But what I didn't know until Joan Rivers spilled it was that Joan, Judy, Barbara Walters, and columnist Cindy Adams all had a secret pact they called the Alzheimer's Condo.

Joan asked me once what my plan was when I got really old. I said what anybody might say: "I'll get a caregiver and live as well as I can."

Joan said, "No, look. *I've* got a plan. It's called the Alzheimer's Condo. I've discussed it with Judy and Barbara and Cindy." This all happened, apparently, during a bed-and-breakfast trip Joan arranged for the four of them, in which they agreed that when dementia hit them all, they'd move into a place together. Of course, they argued over whose place. Judy pitched her apartment, and Joan countered with her fancy New York digs. But then they all realized Barbara won, because she has the Doris Duke apartment. (Also, Barbara doesn't lose.) Joan's rationale for becoming roomies? "We're all Jewish girls at heart: we still want to save money no matter what. We could share a dog walker." They'd also

all have the same caregiver, who would probably beat them and wind up the subject of a very special *Dateline*, but none of them would know because they'd be so out of it.

In any case, I found this all incredibly funny—dark, but funny—and I needed to know if it was true. I made it my mission to confirm it with each person. When the opportunity arose at a Beverly Hills dinner party to find out from Judy, I pulled her aside and said, "Okay, is it true? The Alzheimer's Condo? You're known for telling it like it is, lady, so is this pact the real deal? Joan Rivers told me."

She said, "I love Joan. I love her so much."

I couldn't take the suspense. "*Is it true*?!?"

"Of course it is!" she answered. "We decided at the bed-and-breakfast! Yes!" She was almost offended I might not believe such a brilliant idea.

Now that I knew she was a stone-cold truth teller, I wanted to confirm something else: about how rich she is. I'd recently read that she made more money in one year than LeBron

James. But I said to her, deliberately mixing it up to test her, "Hey, I wanted to congratulate you, I heard that you were second only to LeBron James—"

And she *immediately* corrected me, "I'VE MADE MORE MONEY THAN LEBRON JAMES."

No objection there, Your Honor.

SHRIVER, MARIA
Journalist, Kennedy, Brunette

Like a handful of names in this book, Maria is someone I will always love even though she does not love me. I mean, she's so smart and accomplished, and an Oprah bestie, and has had to deal with being married to the host of *The New Celebrity Apprentice.*

She really has had enough of my crap, too, to the extent that at a friend's birthday party, she said to me, as we were standing near the pool, "If I could throw you in this right now, I would." That's someone who's not a fan. And yet, when I saw her a couple of years later at a very fancy Beverly Hills shindig, I was excited. I went up to Maria and said, "Bummed there's no pool nearby?"

She shot back with, "I never said that! Stop telling people I said that!" (How quickly they forget.)

When it came time to sit down, I noticed the tables didn't have place cards, which always makes me happy because then I can sit where I want. But I needed to be careful, though, because there was a vague high school feeling to it all, and I worried I wouldn't be at the cool table. (That means Kathy Griffin doesn't sit down first. She waits for the right time. I will pace with a plate of food for an hour. I will wait these bitches out.) I saw Maria sit down and noticed an empty chair next to her. Perfect! I went up to her and said, "Look, Maria, here's the deal. I'm going to sit next to you, just because I know it'll drive you crazy." (I'm nothing if not honest about my intentions.)

She looked up at me and said, "Do you think, after everything I've been through, and all the people I've dealt with in my life, that I'm afraid of *you* and your *jokes*? SIDDOWN!"

Well, that to me was immensely charming. I absolutely loved how she put me in my place. We ended up having the best time, talking and laughing. I think a lot of celebrities could take a page from Maria: just let me sit down. You'll survive this. We might even bond. There may even be a pool party in our future.

SIA
Singer, Songwriter, Hider in Plain Sight

For a chanteuse who is known for only wanting to be visible as an incredible voice singing through a black-and-white wig with a bow on top, guess who ran up to me one time with plenty of photographers, saying, "I want to meet you! I want to meet you!" That's right. Sia. And just so you know, I not only asked for a picture with her, but she wanted one for herself, too. She's not always about keeping her face hidden from the spotlight—she's Instagrammed those photos with us—but her commitment to maintaining a semblance of privacy about how she looks is, in my opinion, edgy and interesting. We've

since become friends. I've gone to her house on Christmas Day. She threw me a huge solid favor when I asked her to sing "Titanium" when I was hosting a fund-raiser for the Trevor Project. That was pretty freaking cool. We've hung out and gossiped, and she even sent me a link for leather pants I should buy one year when I mentioned I get really cold doing CNN's *New Year's Eve Live* with Anderson Cooper.

What I love about her is that she'll burst into song at a moment's notice. A lot of singers won't and get weird about such requests, but I have no qualms going, "You know that Flo Rida song . . . ," and she ripped into: "Hey, I heard you were a wild one . . ." She wrote the Rihanna superhit, "Diamonds." I asked her if she sang the demo to Rihanna. Sia's response was to stand in her living room and sing the entire song to me a capella, PERFECTLY. I asked her what it was like to cowrite a song with Britney Spears, and she just started singing "Perfume." She's probably sung ten of her songs to me privately. Take that, Coachella!

There is one part of this Sia I just can't leave out. One night, Sia, Kelly Osbourne, and I randomly decided to take in a movie. Nothing unusual about that, right? Three chicks just having a night out at a movie. We had dinner before. What could go wrong? The film turned out to be a super artsy-fartsy movie called *Under the Skin*. It was very, very serious. Naturally, about twenty minutes in, the three of us started getting what I call the church giggles. That's when you are laughing at an inappropriate place and an inappropriate time and you can't stop. It is infectious.

Then we started getting shushed, and Kelly turned and said, "Don't make me punch you in the face!"

Sia said, "I'm Australian. I can take him!"

The usher kicked us out, and once in the lobby we all laughed for probably five minutes over the artsy-fartsy movie none of us understood. We all tweeted the photo with a caption something like, "The three worst people to see a serious movie with." Looking back, I should have just asked Sia to sing "Chandelier" to the usher.

SPEARS, BRITNEY
Singer, Snake Charmer, Patient

When I first met Britney, she was opening for *NSYNC, and I was already friendly with Lance Bass. Backstage at the preshow crew meal, she showed up in her " . . . Baby One More Time" getup. I blurted, "So you're the sexy cheerleader, huh?" and she said, "I know." She was in preshow mode and probably would have said "I know" to anything as she whisked past me with her backup dancers. When I hosted the Billboard

Awards with *NSYNC, she and Justin Timberlake were openly dating, and her stardom was so big, I was frankly shocked Justin was able to corral her for the skit we did. (Look it up, people. It's pretty damn cute.)

What I remember about the few minutes of rehearsal we got with Britney was that Justin kept calling her "baby." As in, "Baby! Baby! Baby! Focus, baby! You have a minute! Baby! Baby!"

I wanted to say, "Jesus, stop calling her that." But maybe he knew something we didn't. All I can say is that whole time was about the frenzy of being Britney.

Over a decade later, at the iHeartRadio concert in Las Vegas in 2012, I heard Britney was going to present. At the time, she was dating my former TV agent, Jason Trawick. I parked myself by the teleprompters, as I do, because I wasn't going to miss her before and after going onstage. Seacrest was there, and he asked if I was going on soon. I said, "No, I want to see how you handle Britney."

He looked quizzically at me. "Why?"

I said, "You know why."

They may as well have dollied her out Hannibal Lecter–style. It was a real pinwheel-eyes moment. Trawick handed her to Seacrest, with one arm holding her as if she were ninety. "Hi, Britney! It's Kath!" I yelled.

I got back a generic, "Hi, y'all." Then Seacrest escorted her onstage. Then it was back to the wings, and the handoff to Trawick. (When he was walking her out, I said to my former TV agent, "Come on, Trawick, get rid of Britney and represent a real star again for a change! You used to be my TV agent!" He chimed back with, "You're the reason I got out of the business!" I thought that was funny.)

Maybe the best story, though, is when my assistant, John, got the brilliant idea of getting me into her Vegas show for the "Freakshow" number—that's when an audience member, usually a man, gets the spanking/whipping treatment onstage. Her manager got the okay from Britney, then told me, "You know, she is afraid you're going to say something embarrassing while you're onstage with her."

To which I said, "As if the microphone's on." (When Jezebel.com reported that she was lip-synching the Vegas show, they called it "a shock to absolutely nobody.")

By the time my boyfriend and I got to the show, I was actually excited to see her do her thing, whatever shape she was in. It had been a while, and it was fun to see the spectacle and the dancing and hear all those hits. I knew she'd remember me. I've known her since she was sixteen! My boyfriend was skeptical. Then I got called onstage for my cameo appearance and what I have come to call my "This Is What It's Like to Be Britney Spears for Ninety Seconds" experience, which means the sexy male dancers—or backup gay angels, as I've named them—told me everything I had to do, which I assume is quite simply how Britney is handled 24-7. I didn't have to think for myself or remember anything! I was instructed: "Right arm up, left arm up, turn left, turn right, we're walking, walking, now stepping down, on your knees, all fours, hair whip, look at Britney, hug Britney, kiss Britney, good-bye." It was heaven, actually. At the end, she signed a T-shirt and gave it to me, which I found . . . odd. Then she said, "Give it up, y'all, for Miss Kathy," and I'd swear I heard one of her backup dancers say loudly in her ear, "It's Kathy [pause] . . . GRIFFIN." Looking back, it was one of our deepest conversations that I will always treasure.

STALLONE, SYLVESTER
Rocky, Rambo, Expendable

I ran into Sly in the run-up to the 2016 Oscars, when he was enjoying the awards circuit after getting nominated for playing Rocky Balboa in *Creed*. My in was his wife Jennifer Flavin, who was one of those smart businesswomen who took advantage of HSN early on and turned her hugely successful skin care line into an empire. I knew her from when she was a guest on *My Life on the D-List*, which, frankly, she wouldn't shut up about that night. (Flavin: "I was the best guest, and you never called me to be on again!" Me: "It wasn't a talk show.") Anyway, she's gorgeous and loaded, and I ribbed Sly on how she's got more money than he has. "You married up, and nobody knows that," I cracked, and he agreed, laughing. "That's not even a joke!" he said. So far so good.

I then complimented him on the nomination and said, "Tell me you're having the time of your life. You're having the year you were supposed to have with *Cop Land*." I was referencing an independent movie from 1997 in which he played a deaf, overweight cop, a role that was supposed to rescue him from action movies and showcase his drama chops. Although he was great in *Cop Land*, the love eluded him, and then almost twenty years later, playing an older, wiser, sadder Rocky Balboa in *Creed*, that love from Hollywood finally came out. Shows you how enduring that role was for him and what can happen to the legends if we—I mean, *they* (oops)—stick around long enough. Anyway, he loved that I referenced *Cop Land*, and so I made my move to get a picture with him. Of course, Flavin got in the middle, and I had no qualms telling her to scram. I'll say it to my boyfriend: "Randy, move aside, or you're gonna get cropped out." So Sly and I are posing, we're in close, he's on my left with his right arm around my waist, and with his left hand he keeps reaching over and grabbing my right forearm in the weirdest way. Finally, he just physically made me do what he wanted, which is stage the photo so my right hand is in a fist, just under his chin, like I'm going to punch him. Then he explained his polite grappling: "My whole career, no matter what picture I take with a famous person, this is the one that'll run. This is the one they want. Nobody wants anything else." Talk about a guy who knows how to turn being a punching bag—onscreen and off—into a lifelong turn in the spotlight. (By the way, the fist photo that ran was Sly with Jamie Foxx. Why didn't I take that Ray Charles role when they offered it to me?)

STEINEM, GLORIA

Feminist Icon, Founder of Ms. Magazine, Laugher

On my fiftieth birthday, I was a single woman determined to make the night special without the help of a MAN! I became bound and determined to meet the great Gloria Steinem, champion for women's rights and a stone-cold hero of mine. Among her many accomplishments, those of you who aren't up on the struggle and Gloria's place in it, is that she coined the phrase "reproductive freedom." What was funny about my sudden desire to meet her was that it was partly inspired by my having gone through a bad breakup. I was worried I was never going to find love again, and I thought about Steinem and how her life as an activist and target for antiwoman hatred probably made dating difficult for her, or even finding lasting relationships. Jane Fonda was kind enough to give me Steinem's e-mail, so I cold-e-mailed her and said I'd love to take her out to dinner on an upcoming trip to New York. I probably sounded a little desperate, but she wrote back with a yes, and I was thrilled.

We met at a fancy vegetarian restaurant, and I proceeded to ask her about her amazing life, the movement, and her range of experiences from going head-to-head on *Meet the Press* with a clearly sexist senator to marching in the streets with Angela Davis and Bella Abzug. Well, I was in heaven, and we were getting around to the state of feminism today. I felt silly asking this great feminist and intellectual about my boy problems. I shyly chimed in with, "I'm sad I'm not dating someone." As you might imagine, I sounded pathetic. I had suddenly turned into a fourteen-year-old crying, "I want a *boyfriend!*" Was I really complaining about this to Gloria Steinem?

But then she surprised me by saying, "Actually, I think relationships are important. I'm very much a romantic, and I believe in love. In fact, I'm a little bit of a matchmaker." I couldn't believe it. The great Gloria Steinem was going to help me!

"Let's think about this," she said. "What are you looking for?"

We spent the next hour laughing and going back and forth about essential and important qualities for the future Mr. Griffin. Does he have a fancy house? Not necessary; I have one. Is he smart? Necessary. Is he a feminist? Mandatory. Will he buy you trinkets, jewels, and a sports car? Never mind; I can do that myself.

After our meal, I remember walking out of the restaurant into the rain, and we were both still laughing as we said our good-byes. Such was the basis for a lasting friendship, one that to me proves how resolutely the great feminist icons care about laughing and the necessity of funny women.

It really irritates me when feminists get tarred with the no-sense-of-humor brush. Gloria is not only funny herself, but she knows how important and cathartic laughing is. In November 2014, she asked me to host a fund-raiser for one of her favorite organizations, Equality Now, where she was being honored along with Salma Hayek. Congresswoman Maxine Waters and Quincy Jones were also participating. Here I am yet again hosting a serious charity event in an A-list room with big-money donors. Steinem, how could you do this to me? You know I'm going to be too vulgar for these stiffs!

She was so sweet. She actually introduced me to basically let the audience know what they were in for. She gave me a great intro. She took the microphone, the audience hushed, and she brought me out to the following intro. "My friend Kathy is nervous to host this show because she's afraid she will be inappropriate, so I am here to tell you that it's okay to laugh!" The audience loved that. She continued with, "Laughter is the only truly free emotion. Even love can be compelled, if someone feels bound to someone else, practically captive. But no one can compel laughter. It's the ultimate proof of freedom. That's why we as women need to laugh and why we need to know that women can make us all laugh, men as well as women. Ladies and gentlemen, your host for the evening, Kathy Griffin."

STEPHANOPOULOS, GEORGE
ABC (Already Been Chewed) Anchor,
Council of Foreign Relations (Including Me)

Don't you hate it when one of your friends marries the White House communications director and you don't hear from her as much? Me, too. My old Groundlings pal Ali Wentworth got hitched to George Stephanopoulos in 2001, and I do not get to spend as much time with her as I would like. Whose fault is that? George's, of course. But I figured out a way to make him pay when I was asked to be a lead guest on *Good Morning America* to promote my 2015 performance at the iconic Carnegie Hall. Sometimes a good bit is fourteen years in the making.

I've been a fan of George's forever, and I respect him tremendously, but for a while there, I wasn't entirely sure if Ali was making up their relationship because I never hung out with them together.

I eventually had a super awkward experience with George in 2012 when I had plans to meet my friend Lara Spencer at the bar in New York's Mandarin Oriental hotel because I was doing a gay club appearance later in the evening (don't ask!) and she was coming from a taping of *Piers Morgan Live,* and there was an overlap window for a meet-up. Much to my surprise, the whole cast of *GMA* showed up to the restaurant. Maybe when Lara was planning a casual get-together with her old pal Kathy, it didn't occur to either one of us that it may appear as if I were crashing their intimate cast-only soirée to celebrate being number one in the ratings for the first time in years. Sensing her discomfort, yet knowing a comedy moment might be about to happen, I just looked at Lara and said, "Too bad!" I said, "I've got two hours, and I'm not leaving."

Robin Roberts and Sam Champion came up and said nice things to me, but I immediately had the impression that George was not overly comfortable with ending a very long workday, probably expecting a nice quiet recap with his workmates, only to be faced with this ME . . . and my boyfriend. I thought, *He'll survive! He survived the Clinton administration. He can survive me.*

Randy ordered some sliders, truffle cheese fries, and some charred brussels sprouts because we were both starving. When our order came, George started eating all of our food. I said, "You have to stop bogarting the food, because guess who's paying for it now? YOU, GEORGE." He laughed at that but quickly went back to looking like he was deep in the middle of planning his next interview with the secretary general of the UN or something. I get that a lot. Some ratings celebration, George! Not as exhilarating as taking the White House? Anyway, Randy and I settled our tab and left the *GMA* gang alone with their remaining appetizers and high ratings.

Anyway, back to my hilarious appearance ruling the couch on *GMA*. During the commercial break, I went to work on my friend Ali's spouse. "This isn't going to work, everyone, if George doesn't get me."

He said, in that even tone of his, "I get you."

I said, "Okay, but I feel like you're afraid of me, and I'm trying to be funny, and you're throwing me off my game, like the night you ate all my food at the Mandarin Oriental," and he had this "You remember that?" look. I had fun with him, and he took it like a champ, actually, so afterward, I said, "Hey, I e-mailed Ali, and it bounced back. I'm not sure if I have her current e-mail address, so will you put it in my phone?" So he takes my iPhone, and, because he's a techno-deficient fifty-something and nervous around Kathy Griffin, he struggled with this simple request. How do I know this? Because later on in the day as I was doing *Good Afternoon Manhattan* or something, I got an e-mail from George himself. Why? He had clearly accidentally put his own personal e-mail address in my phone, not Ali's. George has no idea he has unleashed the beast. The following is the actual e-mail correspondence between myself and George Stephanopoulos. Enjoy:

On Nov 11, 2015, at 8:36 AM, Stephanopoulos, George wrote:
Kathy says hi!

This is when I realized that George thought he was e-mailing his wife when he was actually e-mailing ME! I'm gonna have some fun here.

On Nov 11, 2015, at 9:16 AM, Kathy Griffin wrote:
Hello George
On Nov 11, 2015, at 9:17 AM, Stephanopoulos, George wrote: Hi.
Fun today!
On Nov 12, 2015, at 5:02 PM, Kathy Griffin wrote: Hello George
On Nov 12, 2015, at 5:48 PM, Stephanopoulos, George wrote: Hi
On Nov 20, 2015, at 3:06 PM, Kathy Griffin wrote: George. Yes,
I'm fine.
On Nov 20, 2015, at 7:12 PM, Stephanopoulos, George wrote: So
relieved!
On Dec 5, 2015, at 1:34 AM, Kathy Griffin wrote: I can't talk now.
On Dec 5, 2015, at 4:57 AM, Stephanopoulos, George wrote:
He's there?
On Jan 27, 2016, at 12:28 AM, Kathy Griffin wrote: I'm going to
Mexico until Sunday night. Cant talk. KG
On Jan 27, 2016, at 11:20 PM, Stephanopoulos, George wrote:
You're going to miss the debate?
On Feb 18, 2016, at 10:27 AM, Kathy Griffin wrote: SUBJECT: My
Day . . .
I'll probably go for a hike and do some light packing for my next
live dates. Why do you need to know? KG
On Feb 19, at 2:43 AM, Stephanopoulos, George wrote: Just
makes me smile.

It's a project that gives my life meaning, to the extent that I put it in my Carnegie Hall show. From the stage, I told of how the great political mind and broadcast journalist George Stephanopoulos doesn't even know how to use e-mail on a phone, at which point Ali—who was in the audience—stood up and shouted, "He's my husband, and *you're tearing my marriage apart!!*"

Thank you, Ali, for not only helping open up my lines of

communication with *GMA* and with your choice in men, but for also marrying someone who gave me material for my act! That's a true friend!

STREISAND, BARBRA
Singer, Actor, Director, Fierce

The first time I was ever near her, Brooke Shields and Andre Agassi were celebrating their engagement at David Foster's house in Malibu. The party was small—maybe forty people— and yet I had no contact with her. I could not act like we were BFFs. It was more like being in her orbit. It was a taste, but it wasn't enough.

Years later, I had a fun, brief encounter with her, and while I'm not trying to act as if we are besties, I will say even knowing her as little as I do, I felt oddly protective of her on this particular night. She was still beautiful, still endearingly had the Brooklyn "Hello, gorgeous" voice, and she was still Streisand. You get it (and if you don't . . . get the hell out of this book!).

I want to describe what happened at the STAPLES Center in downtown Los Angeles when Bette Midler was on her Divine Intervention tour. For shows like that, I don't want to be in a private celebrity skybox to the side with some angled view far from the action. I want to be in the seats, as close as possible. That night I took my seat, in the thick of the superfans. As I've often said in my act, do not ever underestimate the level of partying you will get from middle-aged gay men and Jewish ladies of a certain age. And they were there to par-tay. Take that, millennials! Oh, you're so badass at Coachella. Please. In other words, it was a perfect storm for what was to follow.

People began to notice me—"I want a pic-shuh! I want a pic-shuh!"—so I obliged with a series of selfies. I looked across the aisle from me, five or so rows up, and there was Billy Crystal. The woman behind me says, "Oh my GAWD, it's Billy Crystal!! Should we get a pic-shuh?!" I'd just taken a pic-shuh with her myself and was hoping she wouldn't bother Billy, who clearly didn't want to be noticed. But she went up anyway, stuck her iPad (not a cell phone or small camera, but a friggin' iPad) in his face and said, "Say something FUNNY!"

He said, "I don't know what you want me to say . . ."

You could feel the air molecules change, and thousands of people shifted their focus to Billy. I felt for him. But then, the room began to hum in a way that I can only describe as a low . . . gay . . . rumble. For those of you that watch too much Weather Channel, as I do, it was not dissimilar from how you would hear a midwestern tornado survivor describe the beginning of a massive twister. Something was happening behind me. It wasn't the show starting, because the house lights were still on. The rumble then became an oscillating wave of gay gasping as I saw HER walk down the aisle past me with HER husband James Brolin. Billy Crystal who?

What in the world was SHE doing in regular floor seats? Streisand does not move among the people! She wasn't in full movie-star hair and makeup, and where the hell was her diva lighting? Who's fallen on the job here? In a word: UNACCEPTABLE. There's nothing in Brolin's demeanor to suggest he was even worried about her. Well, he should have been, because people (in this case the people were, how shall I say,

Bette Midler's and Barbra Streisand's combined fan base) instantly lost all composure. The eye of the storm made land. It was a mêlée. And a gay-lée. Cell phones popping up by the hundreds. People rubbernecking more than any amount of Icy Hot could ever soothe. Bodies leaning forward, then back. Friends confirming that this was in fact a genuine Streisand sighting. The rumble got louder.

Meanwhile, my beloved fifty-five-year-old gay men and same-aged Jewish gals were standing on their chairs to take pic-shuhs, and some just ran in front of her to do it. Then the woman who had moved from me to Billy Crystal pivoted with her iPad in hand and started yelling, "BAWBRA! BAW-BRA! SING AH SOWNGGG!"

Even my boyfriend turned to me and said, "Should I go help her?"

And I said, "No, that might make it worse. You could get gay trampled."

The lights finally went down, and there were so many cell phones going that I heard Streisand say, "Look at all those rectangles." Classic. I get it; these fans have wanted to be up close and personal with La Streisand, but I have to admit, I was a little nervous for her. I'm just gonna say it: Jim Brolin needs to be on security duty a lot more. If they start showing up at Palm Springs street fairs together, you'll know I'm right.

STYLES, HARRY
Boy Oh Boy Band Member

When the Eagles brought their final LA shows to the Forum, I didn't know the seating gods would be smiling on me. I was seated next to Harry Styles of One Direction and up-and-coming model / reality star / professional Twitter scroller Candle Jenner. I think that's her name. Naturally, I stood up with open arms and said, "HARRY? Is that you?" Keep in mind I've never met Harry Styles. "CANDLE?" I shouted. She picked her head up from her phone long enough to sigh with the disdain of someone who was being forced to watch a bunch of old dudes sing songs from the last century. The one-fifth (Zayn, please come back to me) of One Direction, mean-

while, was wearing his beloved YSL double-breasted military-looking peacoat, and a headband, and if I could have given him a fife and a musket to complete the picture, I would have. And yet he also looked like he'd just stepped out of a One Direction concert. Did I mention that he

seemed not just like a Civil War reenactment character but—
and of course, I'm only alleging this here—he seemed like a
very, very wasted Harry Styles? I was also well aware of how
many times he was getting up and leaving, which seemed odd
considering he was in the company of a Jenner/Kardashian.
Each time he left, he wouldn't take his coat. Eventually, Candle, who must have been sick of being left behind, vacated
as well. Then Harry came back, handed his coat to Fergie of
the Black Eyed Peas, who was in the row ahead of us, and
took off. A little later, Fergie turned to me and said, "I have to
go home and take care of the kid, so will you watch Harry's
coat?" I said, "Yes. You are a very good judge of character,
Fergie." I heard her gorgeous and shallow husband Josh Du-
hamel laugh, so he knew what might happen. I then proceeded to "borrow" Harry's coat by wearing it, taking selfies in
it, and posting the pictures on social media. I knew it would
send ripples of fear/jealousy/giggles/bewilderment through
the Directioner world, and sure enough, my Twitter feed
blew up. I was ready to walk off with the coat when I heard
one of Harry's friends shouting, "Miss Griffin!" while snap-
ping his fingers and continuing, "Harry needs his coat back."
I couldn't convince him that I had gotten the coat at a sale
that day at Neiman Marcus, so I had to return it. Thank God
there's no such thing as Directioner jail. If there was, I would
be in it because of what happened moments later. After the
show, I took my backstage pass and was directed, no pun, into
a room to wait for the band. I was ushered into a small room.
My fellow backstage autograph-seeking fans included Jerry
Bruckheimer, Patriots owner Robert Kraft, Cindy Crawford,
Rande Gerber, Kris Jenner, and my old pals Rita Wilson and
Tom Hanks. I instinctively walked up to Tom first. I know I
can count on him to share an experience like this with. You

will see why in a moment. Okay, I don't remember what the hell I was talking about with Tom Hanks in that moment because in the next moment an allegedly very, very wasted Harry Styles walked into the room and made a beeline for Tom Hanks. I don't think Harry saw me at first, which can be essential for gathering celebrity material. It was as if I had taken my invisible pill and I was allowed to just observe and mentally log everything that these two titans of the arts would be talking about. Harry had a great opener:

Harry: Re-membah when you wuz savin' Private Ryan and had to bring 'im back to 'is mum? Re-membah?
Tom Hanks politely replies with caution: Yes.
Harry: Re-membah when you wuz in *Cappin Phillips*? And the other guy sez, "Oim' the capn' now"? 'Membah?
Tom, trying to figure this young man out: Yes, yes, I do remember.
Harry: Was that scaaarrry?
Even I wasn't expecting that question. I turned to Tom: Yeah, Tom, was that scary?
Tom, clearly trying to save Harry Styles from himself (in a way Candle Jenner never could): Harry, have you met my friend, the *comedian* Kathy Griffin? (Tom really hit the word *comedian* hard.)
Harry, eyeing me: Yeah . . . am I gonna be in one of your skits?

Ooh, he knows I'm a comedian now and apparently thinks I do "skits" reminiscent of the old *Benny Hill Show*. Maybe I should get a topless girl on a bicycle?

At this point, I had to shout out to Kris Jenner a few feet away and say, "Kris, tell young Harry here what a delight it is to be in my act!" Kris Jenner responded with a quick, "Oh, it'll be great. You can take our spot for a while." I turned back to Harry and simply said, "Congratulations, Harry, you've just walked into my act." Harry was unfazed and returned his attention to the great Tom Hanks again . . . with the questions. It was like he was doing a memory brain teaser.

> Harry: Re-membah when you wuz Forrest Gump?
>   'Membah? 'Membah?
> Tom, still indulging: I was, yes.
> Harry: You wuz always runnin'? 'Membah?

Yes, he was asking Tom Hanks if Tom *remembers* playing the role of Forrest Gump, for which he won the Academy Award. I can't point out here enough how Harry Styles seemed to think it was his mission to make sure Tom Hanks did not forget the names of any of his films or the fact that he had starred in these films.

> Harry: That was a good film.
> Tom: I do *remember*.

Without explanation, Harry Styles turned and pivoted away. Tom Hanks had been pretty much frozen in the same spot during this magical and epic exchange. Tom's answer was perfect and delivered very dryly:

> Tom: Sometimes, I just want to drive them to rehab myself.

———

SWIFT, TAYLOR
Singer, Songwriter, Cult Leader

She hates me. Pretty sure there's some bad blood.

We were at the same high-profile event in which the celebrities in the audience are actually called out by name. So when the host announced me, I had a funny little idea. You know me and my funny little ideas, the ones I implement before I've completely thought them out in my head. I stood up, looked right at Taylor, and gave her the two-finger "I'm watching you" gesture, while mouthing the words "I'm coming for you!" She looked bewildered and not happy. (What was I expecting? A blown kiss? Smiling, clapping, jumping up and down? Thank God, my idol Kathy Griffin noticed me! THINK, Kathy, THINK!) Well, a few minutes later, she and her infamous girl "squad"—Lorde, Cara Delevingne, and the band Haim (although in my twisted moments of selective memory loss I can't help thinking of them as the band Corey Haim; I can't explain why that just pops into my head)— walked past my seat on the way to the restroom. I stood up and started to say to her, "Swifty . . . I'm just effing with you!" They blew past me, and when I looked back at them, they'd gathered in a cluster—a very menacing cluster—and as if on cue, I realized I needed to use the bathroom, too. This lipstick isn't going to reapply itself. Now there was no way I could go to the ladies' room at that moment. She and her gang could have jumped my middle-aged ass without a second's thought. Touché, Taylor. Ever since, I've decided to save the

"I'm watching you" gesture until after I see the celebrity go and come back from the toilet. That's just smart strategic battle planning.

T, MR.
No Fool to Be Pitied, Surprise KG Tour Manager

When I was on *Suddenly Susan*, my profile was large enough that I began to book stand-up gigs at larger spaces than comedy clubs. I toured by myself then, which was not a completely thought-through decision, because unlike hitting clubs, where there are other comics on a bill to hang with, a solo tour where you're performing in music venues or theaters means you're just by yourself all the time. It was dumb that I didn't bring someone along to help me and keep me company. But it was certainly cool that I was selling too many tickets to do clubs.

Well, during this initial burst of larger-venue shows, I found myself in Chicago staying at the Ritz-Carlton, which is A-list all the way. It was getting close to showtime, so I went down to the hotel entrance to look for the venue's car at the appointed time, and it wasn't there! Minutes later, still not there. I'm starting to worry and getting ready to go in and look for a phone, when I see Mr. T walk out of the hotel. He's hard to miss, just ask Colonel Hannibal Smith or Lieutenant Templeton Peck. He's in the full Mr. T regalia, too: the Mohawk, the chains, the tank top, and if I remember correctly, balloon pants. He's got a small posse with him, and while I'm standing there staring at him, he looks at me and says, "Hey, funny lady."

I said, "Hi there. I didn't want to bother you, but it's a pleasure to meet you. How are you doing?"

He told me what he was doing in town—I think it was a charity benefit or something—and then asked me what I was up to.

I said, "Well, I'm actually headlining at a theater in twenty minutes, and I've been waiting for the car and it hasn't arrived. I'm kind of nervous."

Without hesitation, he pointed to his old-timey stretch limo and said, "Get in!"

I piled in with Mr. T and three of his buddies, and I got the sweetest ride to my gig. We had a great time chatting and laughing the whole way there, and when the limo pulled up to the theater, I said to him, "Will you do me a favor and just stay here for one second?" I flung open the door, hopped out, and yelled, "GAYS!" (I just want to acknowledge here that there was an assumption then on my part that the groups of men entering the theater were not heterosexual. I recognize the rashness of my outburst, but this was the '90s. It was a more innocent time.) Anyway, I said, "Stop whatever you're doing! I need witnesses! Look who drove me to my show: Mr. T! Wave, Mr. T!" And Mr. T popped his head out of the limo roof and gave a friendly wave. Maybe ten people saw this, but they clapped excitedly. The limo peeled out, and I had the first ten minutes of my act.

So "if you have a problem," are late for a stand-up show, "if no one else can help, and if you can find them, maybe you can hire . . . the A-Team."

———

TATUM, CHANNING
Stepper, Stripper, Chubby

I've known Tatum for a while. I've known his wife, Jenna, through the Lance Bass game-night party circuit, even longer. I can tease Tatum pretty easily. Don't act like you wouldn't have been a little bit excited to see *Step Up*'s Tyler Gage walk past you in first class to take his seat in coach on a rather long flight to Toronto. He was wearing a hoodie as if I wasn't going to recognize him. As I sat in my comfortable first-class seat, I may have raised my voice a hair as he passed me and said, "Tatum! Economy class? Really?? You announce you were once a male stripper, sorry . . . I meant dancer, and suddenly you're kicked out of first class?" He laughed and said, "Hi, Kathy."

In 2014, I did a Fox television show that was a celebration of rescue dogs, which was a pretty celebrity-packed affair. After I said hi to Jenna in the backstage area, I went up to Tatum, no longer my pal from Lance Bass's kitchen potlucks but now a global movie star, and said, "What have you been up to, Tatum, anything?"

In his sweet, gentle way, he said, "Oh, hi, Kathy."

I said, "Jesus, you've been gone awhile. It was *Step Up* and then nothing. Are things that bad?"

Without any irony, as if he really thought I didn't know that he'd become the biggest star in Hollywood, he said, "Oh, I just wrapped *Mike 2*."

I made a disappointed face and did the slow clap and

proudly announced to the rest of the awaiting celebrities in the backstage dressing room, "Tatum, what's happened to you? Are you so insider you talk about your movies like everyone's the key grip and hip to crew lingo? I believe the title is *Magic Mike XXL*. Ladies and gentlemen, Channing Tatum from the upcoming *Mike 2*, whatever that is. Sounds like something you yell during an audio check."

He always gives me the good-sport smile. I'm almost positive he knows that it's best just to answer any question of mine with simple facts in the hopes that I'll get bored and leave. Smart move. If you ask me, Tarantino got it wrong; he should have put him in *The Loveable Eight*.

THURMAN, UMA
Actress, Mother, Killed Bill

Quentin Tarantino's sense of humor is such that when he invited me to his nontelevised friar's roast in 2010, he purposely seated me next to Uma, because he knew I made fun of her affectations in my act. (The changing accent makes her sound like she's from some nebulous continental country, one I call Europia.) God, I love him for that.

I was excited, of course. So excited that before the show, I banged on her dressing room door: "Uma! Uma! It's Kathy Griffin! My dressing room doesn't have a bathroom"—big lie—"and I have to use yours!" She let me in; I used her bathroom, then came out and said, "Whew! What's going on? Lot of pressure out there. Sam Jackson, Harvey Keitel—this thing's big-time! You ready? Know what you're saying?"

I just wanted to ramp her up. It was fun! She was sitting at a vanity a little bit slumped over, checking her BlackBerry. Maybe I had gotten her to cry already? Damn. I don't want to shoot my load this early. Not with Thurman.

Then, when we were seated next to each other at the long table that flanks the podium and faces the audience, and she realized she was stuck with me for a few hours, she mentioned a few times how nervous she was that she wouldn't be funny when she spoke. So I said, "You are going to be HI-LARIOUS. You're known for your rock-solid one-liners! Just get up there and be you!"

She eyed me suspiciously and stated the obvious: "I know you're making fun of me."

"What are you talking about? When I think funny, I think *Thurman*. Just give them the chunk you do on Leno or at the clubs, about airplane food or dirty diapers or whatever, and you will rock it!"

Mostly, though, she kept checking her BlackBerry. Keep in mind here we were all on a dais and visible to the large ballroom audience.

"Uma. Uma! The whole audience can see you, you know. It's not about you today. It's about Quentin." I turned to movie mogul Harvey Weinstein, who was on my other side, and said, "Harvey, take care of your star. She's doing a little something called stealing focus. Ever hear of it? Get her off her BlackBerry."

"It's the kids," she said. Everyone's excuse.

"Are they dead?" I asked.

"Oh, that's *horrible*!"

"Exactly. So get off the phone."

Of course, when her turn came, she very wisely was just charming and beautiful and spoke of how much she loved

Quentin. Although her why-do-I-have-to-sit-next-to-Kathy-Griffin material would have killed, probably.

Oh, hell, I have to tell you something else. While I have had a lot of fun recapping my Uma Thurman experience, I must, in the spirit of full disclosure, admit to you that when it was my turn to take the podium and deliver a hilarious roast to Quentin, I . . . BOMBED. Badly. When interviewers, or anyone, say things like, "Oh, I don't believe that you ever bomb anymore; that must have been your early days of stand-up," I have to admit that if you ever uncovered a tape of this roast from 2010, you will see otherwise. Yep, it still happens, and that is why every single day I try to get better, funnier, and sharper—whatever it takes. So in this case, I can freely admit to you that I totally tanked my performance but that I had a *very funny* banter with Uma Thurman. When I think back on that day, I don't know why I choked when it was time for me to take the podium. It happens. I wanted to share this story with you because sometimes the funniest bits are behind the scenes.

TOMLIN, LILY
Chameleon, Genius, Loves Cock

After I stalked the great Lily Tomlin to be on *My Life on the D-List*, we became pals. I courted her properly, too: we were performing at the same casino in Canada on different nights, so I flew up early to see her show, then met her afterward. We instantly clicked. We filmed a scene for my show where the two of us sat on her bed in her hotel room gossiping. She

was even kind enough to stay in Canada an extra day to film an extra scene where we sat in a restaurant and prank called celebrities.

As a performer, she's unparalleled. If you haven't seen her one-woman masterpiece, *The Search for Signs of Intelligent Life in the Universe*, or any of her incredible movie roles, from *Nashville* to *Grandma*, you've got homework.

As long as she's been doing this, too, her timing is still as edgy as ever, and even when we just talk now, I always feel that anything could happen at any moment with her. She's got this wry, naughty sense of humor that pops up when you least expect it. Yet she always acts like I'm the one shocking her. It's as if we're trying to adjust our shock-ometers so that the other one is surprised. Just when I'm dialing mine down from ten to seven, she's jacking hers up, and vice versa. She knows what she's doing. And I love it.

I asked her once if, during the filming of *Grandma*, in which she plays a vibrant, radical lesbian who once had an affair with Sam Elliott's character, there was maybe one moment during filming in which she wanted to screw Sam Elliott.

I said, "Come on, Lily. I know you lesbians say your mind's made up, but wasn't there maybe one minute where you thought . . ."

And she said, "NO! No, not for a minute! I wasn't attracted to him!"

Pause.

"I'm kidding. I'd screw the shit out of him."

She's such great fun to talk to, and any time she lets me see her impish side, I'm in heaven.

My favorite story of hers is what she told me about the year she was nominated for an Oscar for *Nashville*. She said she always regretted something about that ceremony. It was the pre–Joan Rivers era when the red carpet wasn't covered the way it is now or considered that important. "In those days, we just went to a department store and pulled something off the rack! The idea that anyone would ask what you were wearing . . . I mean, come on!" What she wishes she'd done, however, is shown up as either her five-and-a-half-year-old character, Edith Ann, or—preferably—her hilariously arrogant switchboard operator, Ernestine. "You don't know how much I wanted to show up like that," Lily told me. "I wanted to go in full head-to-toe costume and stay in character for the red carpet."

I remember thinking, *That would have been a lot of hours holding that pinched face.*

She's talked often about how physically painful it was to do Ernestine for long periods of time. Of course, I love the other regret she had about that night. "When I lost, I wish I would have been dressed in character and could have flipped the bird to the camera."

And I thought I invented that bit.

TOP, CARROT

Propmaster General, Maligned Comic

You realize he's insanely rich, right? He may be a punch line to a lot of comedians, but he couldn't be nicer, he couldn't be harder working, and he always kills when he performs. When I first met him (real name: Scott Thompson), he had mastered the college circuit, and let me say, if the kids love you, you're golden. So while everyone else made fun of him, he raked it in. I appreciate that ability to tune out the hate and do your thing. But when I look at Carrot Top, there's something I can't help but see. It's not what you think.

Back in the late '90s, I had a small role in a movie called *Intern*, which was filming in New York. (Not to be confused with *The Intern*, starring Robert De Niro, although I would have liked to have been in that one, too.)

One day, the girl who was doing my hair and makeup said, "You're a comedian. Do you know Carrot Top?"

"Sure, I know Scott."

"You want to know the craziest thing? I went out with him a couple of times."

"You're not the first girl I've met who's dated him. Carrot Top gets laid all the time."

"I know," she said, "but I have to say, not only was he amazing in bed, but he has a giant, giant dick. So when I hear people say stuff about Carrot Top and how he needs props to be funny, I think, well, he didn't need a prop when I fucked him. He was amazing, and he had a huge dick."

Rich and well endowed, haters. Chew on that. Now when I see him, I just look at his crotch.

TRAINOR, MEGHAN
Bass NOT Treble, Millennial, Singer

What would I do without my assistant, John? Whenever I'm in a celebrity-rich environment, I'm looking for legends, and he's smartly, rightly, shrewdly steering me to get photographed with anyone under eighty.

At a Jingle Ball concert in Los Angeles, John pushed me toward Meghan Trainor and said, "Get a selfie with her! That's going to help you!" So I went up to her and told her about how I'd seen her perform live, and in an era of lip-synching pop stars, I appreciated that her voice was amazing and congratulated her on having actual good ole-fashioned talent. I said, "You blew me away when you sang 'Like I'm Gonna Lose You' with John Legend." Trainor corrected me slightly and showed she had a sassy sense of humor. She told me that it was her song that she *let* John Legend be featured on. I love a sassy gal.

Have I mentioned that on that night she was wearing an adorable but ridiculous Mrs. Claus–like Christmas outfit that lit up? I want to reiterate here her outfit actually had battery-powered bulbs on it that lit up. Look it up.

iHeartRadio had her doing "Hey, you having fun tonight?" interviews with the various acts, like One Direction and Joe Jonas. So obviously, she was both star and employee that night, but we ended up hanging out a lot, partly because she

had a female relative in tow who was obsessed with me. God, I love when that happens with the young kids. So I designated myself as Meghan Trainor's fun and naughty Aunt Kathy. As the evening wore on, bulbs kept going out on her getup, but she had this great "whatever" attitude and may have had a drinkie or two. We made her dressing room "party central" and had the best time, taking what seemed like a thousand selfies over the course of the night.

It meant that when I ran into her again not long after that, at a *Hollywood Reporter*–sponsored breakfast celebrating powerful Hollywood women at which we were coincidentally seated at the same table, she came up and said, "Dude! I'm so glad to be next to you!"

I now know that "dude" is a millennial endearment, so I said, "Me, too, bro."

We had fun then, too, with me pointing out the legends she didn't know. I teased her with my descriptions: "There's a lady over there named Barbra Streisand, and she's been singing songs for a lonnng time."

Trainor giggled at that one. "Dude, I know who that dude is!"

It was cute, because a lot of people wanted to take pictures with her. I was starting to feel like a pop culture mentor for young Ms. Trainor.

It all culminated in her big Grammy win in 2016. She was very emotional during her acceptance speech, which was directed at her father in the audience. I immediately texted her with "Congratulations, but stop crying you're embarrassing me."

She immediately hit me back with "HAHAHAHAHA fuck u Kathy HAHAHAHAH I love u." So when she sings her famous "Like I'm Gonna Lose You," she certainly can't be talking about me. I have proof she loves me.

TRUMP, THE DONALD
President or Loser (Pick One, This Book Went to Press Before the Election)

My relationship with the Donald spans two decades, and it is completely shame based.

Here's the deal: when you've been in the game this long, you just kind of end up rubbing elbows with everybody. I met the Donald when he was still married to Marla Maples. I sat next to the Donald for hours at a Larry King birthday tribute celebration. I begrudgingly spent time with him on the set of *Celebrity Apprentice* when I happily supported my pal Joan Rivers in one of her challenges, and she went on to win the entire competition. Many innocent run-ins. The reason I say *innocent* is because I honestly didn't know his character was that which we have come to know. I simply saw him as an over-the-top, fame-hungry, harmless blowhard. I kind of saw him as an orange '80s/'90s version of one of the dudes on *Million Dollar Listing*. Never in my wildest dreams did I think he would be the Republican nominee. So have I got a jaw-dropper for you.

First of all, he wants you to call him "the Donald," which is "the weird." He also is one of those guys who when he is asking a favor of you acts like he is doing you a favor. Let me give you an example. Now this is my story and my story alone. Whether you are a fan or on either side of the aisle, you cannot deny that you are a little bit intrigued about the time I spent in a golf cart with Donald Trump and . . . Liza Minnelli.

His "the team" called me and asked if I would participate in a final challenge on a season of *The Apprentice*, which took place at Trump National Golf Club Westchester in Briarcliff, New York. Hmmm, does it sound like the Donald was maybe using this as an opportunity to do a charitable deed while mostly promoting the Trump National Golf Club Westchester in Briarcliff, New York? I think so, too. Oh, how I wish I could tell you I put the Donald in his the place and told him to shove his nonpaying offer that would only benefit his high-paying television show and shove it up his ass. Well, I can't. When I found out that I would be the host and that the headliner would be the one and only "Liza with a Z," I just blacked out and found myself sitting on a plane to New York. It's Liza, damn it.

When the three of us were finally all together, he started right in. Oh, he laid it on thick. "It's gonna be terrific" and "It'll be dynamite" and "This will be huuuge for you two." Okay, I'm just me, but I'm pretty sure this isn't going to be the appearance that puts Liza over the top. You know since she's already an EGOT and Sally Bowles and everything. I don't know what he was thinking, but the Donald decided to hop in the driver's seat of his golf cart and put the Liza and the Kathy in the backseat for a whirlwind tour of his dumb, boring golf course. Boy, he really knows two golf fans when he sees them. Liza, who looked terrified, held on to the railing of the golf cart for dear life and was saying things like, "Honey, he's going too fast. I'm getting the spins." The Donald, oblivious as always, was touting the design features of the green or whatever and waving to other rich golf dudes as if Liza and I care.

The Donald is accidentally funny. I admit it cracked me up that he kept repeating that he would love to have Liza and me come back as his guests and stay at the resort for several days and play eighteen holes every day. You could not find two people less interested in playing even one hole of golf unless all the caddies were the chorus boys from *Cats*. Liza was looking queasy. I distinctly remember yelling at the Donald to let us off this damn golf cart because Liza is about to sing "New York, New York" as a giant favor, and by the way, you shouldn't be driving her around in a golf cart when she's wearing her sequined Halston jumpsuit. Some guys just don't get it.

Hours later, when it was time for the actual performance, the Donald, the Liza, and I were alone in a curtained-off de facto dressing room. This was my chance to see if the Donald had any, what we call, "room awareness." One of the things I look for as a comic when I'm deciding whom to put in my act is someone who is extremely well known, like the Donald. Check. And someone who lacks a sense of humor about themselves or even has the ability to share a laugh during a fun moment. Check and check.

At one point, I saw Liza sitting in a folding chair and doing her own hair and makeup on a shoddy little table using one of those cheap fold-up drugstore mirrors with a light ring around it.

I said to Trump, "Jesus, the Donald, how cheap can you be not to get a living legend like Liza a fancy Manhattan hair and makeup team? Why is she doing this herself?"

He gave me a vapid stare as if to say, "Hey, it ain't my problem."

Oh, for God's sake, the Donald.

Liza jumped in with, "Oh, honey, it helps me get in the zone. I'm more comfortable doing it myself."

I had written off the Donald at this point because it was fun just to watch the Liza do her hair and makeup. Clearly, she had been doing it herself for years, and if it helped her get in the zone, then I was just happy to watch. In a small, curtained room of three people, no amazing moment should go unnoticed by any party. Least of all, one who would like to be elected to notice just about everything, everywhere.

Get ready. Here it comes.

Liza finished doing her own hair and makeup in a way that suggested to me that she had been doing this in backstages all around the world. Her final step was the moment I will never forget. She casually reached for a black Sharpie marker, pulled the cap off, and used it to put on her famous mole. WAHHHH? I foolishly thought that witnessing this moment together would in some way bond the Donald and me.

I whispered to him with a glint in my eye, "The Donald, did you see that? The Liza used a Sharpie to put her famous mole on. And we were here to see it! That is a gift from God to witness. Right, buddy?"

Nothing. No reaction. I don't think he saw it. I don't think he noticed it.

And that reason alone is why I would never vote for him for president. That's enough! If you don't get Liza, you certainly don't get to be in the Oval Office.

ULLMAN, TRACEY
Comedy Goddess, Dame Somebody, Surprise Roommate

I actually had to Google "British phrases" and "British puns," so get ready! If you don't already worship Tracey Ullman . . . then off with your head!

Let's review for you kids who only know Tracey from *Robin Hood: Men in Tights*, shall we?

The Tracey Ullman Show on Fox debuted and exposed to the world a little animated short you may have heard of called *The Simpsons*.

Tracey Takes On . . . was on HBO for four seasons, and she had a top-ten hit—"They Don't Know"—in which Sir Paul McCartney was in the music video.

She had a breakout dramatic role in the Academy Award–nominated film *Plenty*.

Oh, there are so many credits and accomplishments that if you don't get it by now, I'm going to get very femi-furious.

Before I get to the main event, I must say for some reason one particular run-in makes me giggle. We ran into each other at the BAFTA Awards in Beverly Hills. The BAFTA Awards are the British version of the Oscars and the Emmys, and they have events all over the world. I innocently asked her if she was living in Los Angeles full-time now or splitting her time between the UK and America. Trying to make small talk but also leading up to a possible lunch. She had a mini-outburst that I must be clear with you was adorable and not hostile, but for some reason it tickles me.

"I have lived in America for decades, but no matter where I go, people ask me if I live here or in England. I live in Los Angeles!"

Fine, I thought, *I'll rent out the damn Hollywood Bowl so we can have lunch at a very Los Angeles location where no one will ever ask you where you live again.* PS: Tracey has a new series called *Tracey Ullman's Show*, which currently is on in the UK. I don't know where she tapes it! Probably on Capitol Hill in Washington, D.C.

Back to the main event. I saw her somewhat recently at a sit-down party, and as usual, I was fangirling out a bit. As we were sharing the same table, I couldn't resist confirming a juicy tidbit I had heard about her from one of her former staff writers.

I blurted out, "Is it true that when Meryl Streep comes to Los Angeles, she stays with you and your family at your home?"

Unlikely duo, you're thinking? Apparently, the two have been friends since they costarred in the 1985 movie *Plenty*. I wanted to find out from Tracey herself if this was true, and she confirmed! God, I love when that happens! I just loved the idea that super prestigious, Oscar-winning Meryl Streep, out of all the big movie people she knows, connected most with the groundbreaking chick comic and that when Meryl goes to LA, it's not about staying at the Four Seasons, the Five Seasons, or even the Six Seasons. I'm picturing Tracey, who has hilariously depicted everyone from Dame Judi Dench to Dame Maggie Smith, fluffing the pillows of her guest-house in preparation for the arrival of Dame Meryl Streep. They're both so rich they have to have their own pads all over the world, but I love imagining these two genius gals sitting around, shooting the shit, probably breaking out hi-larious impressions of people they know, and trading stories about being powerful women in a not-so-kind-to-us industry. Wouldn't you want to be a fly on the wall in that living room when the wine's flowing and the husbands aren't around? How cool is that??

Where's my Streepy?? How can I get Jimmy Carter to be my Meryl Streep? And then years later, some young co-median comes up to me and says, "Is it true that President Jimmy Carter always stayed at your house?"

And I'd say, "You mean Uncle Jimmy?!?"

USHER
R&B (Great!), Bieber Discoverer (Bad!)

I met the R&B superstar when he was a teenager and just coming into his own as a triple threat: singing, acting, and dancing. Remember, this guy could do all the Michael Jackson moves when he was earning his chops, and he later became friends with his idol. I remember watching him rehearse at an awards show and being super dazzled by his professionalism and talent. He also laughed when I once introduced him by saying, "Ladies and gentlemen, USHER . . .

me down the aisle."

When I see him now, my favorite thing to do is completely assault him for unleashing Justin Bieber on the civilized world. In the way the Kardashians can be blamed on Ryan Seacrest, Bieber is Usher's doing, because it was Team Usher who saw the YouTube videos and gave that precocious pipsqueak his big break. Bieber is his crime, and I'll attest to that in a court of law when Usher goes on trial for it. Sure, it may happen in the deep recesses of a Canadian small-claims court, but damn it, I'll be there.

I just can't resist this kind of loving confrontation whenever I run into Usher: "You owe the country some sort of apology. It's not too late. A statement, a press conference, Oprah confession, whatever. Cash will do, too."

I love also that ever since Bieber has gone off the rails—including some not-so-generous words about his mentor—Usher has done the careful distancing act. That'll happen when one's protégé assaults people, commits acts of vandalism, and writes about Beliebers in the guest book at the Anne Frank house. So it's only natural that I would say to Usher in public, "Hey, how's your big protégé? Pissed in any buckets lately?"

His response is always a professional "Ha ha ha ha ha," and then boom, he's gone. It's as if he's always in a state of dancing away from me. And he knows by now, if he spots me coming, my opening line is not going to be, "Hey, so when's your new album dropping?" It's going to be, "Sooooo . . . Bieber!" POOF! Seriously, every time I see him, it's as if he's airborne. Or he's FloJo in the bottom position, and when he sees me, he hears a gun go off, and he's gone. I'm that member of the press with the microphone who says, "Bieber . . . nice work . . . any comment?" I'm a constant for him that way.

He'll always be incredibly talented and wonderful and loving and great and an inspiration to all. But nobody is perfect. Ford made the Edsel. Steve Jobs started NeXT. And luckily, Usher can always scream, "Yeah!" (featuring Lil Jon and Ludacris).

————

VALDERRAMA, WILMER

Actor, Relationship Saint, #1 Lovatic

I've run into the handsome actor over the years since he hit it big on *That '70s Show*, but in the years since he started dating Debbie Lovato and I've been dealing with the Lovatics, we've mostly steered clear of each other. But at one event that was being hosted by Emilio Estefan, I couldn't resist. He didn't say a word to me, but I routinely teased him. He was gentlemanly about it and chuckled, but it's not as if he wanted to hang. That was obvious. Finally, I told Emilio that I was going to steal Wilmer's gift bag just to piss off his girlfriend.

While holding Wilmer's gift bag in my hand, Emilio said to me, "Why do you do stuff like that?"

"Why?" I said, "I like to see what happens. I love science!"

So I took Wilmer's gift bag, removed the chocolates for myself, and put in a cocktail napkin from the event on which I wrote, "Dear Wilmer, now you know what it's like to have spent the evening with a REAL star. Love, Kathy Griffin."

I handed it back to him and said, "Look, I'm going to come clean. I stole your gift bag. I'm keeping the chocolates, but give the cocktail napkin note to your girlfriend, Debbie."

I'm realistic. If I know Wilmer—and his girlfriend—he would have scoured that bag, found my note, and smartly not followed through on my request. I hope he did follow through, though. #Confident

VAN DYKE, DICK
Sitcom Legend, Rubber Band Man

I could really name this book *Six Degrees of Suzanne Somers or Lance Bass*. I've met so many people through them. Somers is how I met the illustrious Dick Van Dyke, everyone's favorite chimney sweep and ottoman-tripping dad.

Somers had a dinner party and had hired a jazz trio to perform since she knew Dick liked jazz. You could tell he was having the time of his life with that music filling up the room. He seemed incredibly youthful, and we made small talk about comedy and music. I referenced *The Dick Van Dyke Show* being honored somewhere, and he said very quietly, "Yeah, they always want to go down memory lane." Hmmm. It struck me that Dick's one of the legends who doesn't want to be seen as a walking monument to nostalgia. He certainly doesn't act like someone who isn't vital. He's got the young wife, and he's cheated death a few times, having been rescued by a pod of porpoises that nudged him to shore after he fell asleep on his surfboard and surviving a car fire in his sporty Jag. That kind of thing sounds like what happens to reckless teens. Dick was in his eighties both times.

He's a bundle of energy, and that was never more evident than when I hosted a star-filled award show in 2016, where Dick was asked by Bryan Cranston to give him his Best Actor award for *Trumbo*. (Their mutual appreciation society goes back to when Bryan appeared on Dick's show *Diagnosis: Murder*.) I was backstage with Dick, who was getting ready for his appearance, and while we were talking, Thelma Houston had gone onstage to sing "Don't Leave Me This Way."

Dick, who couldn't sit still, said, "I can't help it. I gotta disco dance!"

And let me tell you, even though he had just turned ninety, he was still made of rubber. Everyone around us—my gay assistant, the hair and makeup people, the producers, the stage manager, oh, and Bette Midler, who was also backstage rehearsing her presentation—were all so charmed by Dick's force-of-nature vivacity. I would bet every one of us was thinking, *I'm going to be like that when I'm ninety.*

When Thelma finished her song, there must have been a snafu somewhere, because suddenly, the stage manager turned to me and said, "VAMP!" which means I needed to go out and entertain the crowd until the problem was fixed. In a panic, I said, "Dick!!" (He's deaf as a post, incidentally.) "DICK!" He looked up, I crooked my finger in the come-here gesture, and—this is why I love the legends—he shuffled right on over and walked out with me. Believe me, I would never even attempt that with Taylor Swift or any of the seconds from 5 Seconds of Summer. They'll probably just ignore me, or their posses might just glare. But the legends, they know not to keep an audience waiting. Now, Dick did think it was his time to present, but the point is, when I needed him, he didn't flinch. There was no team to check with, no "I didn't get my water" or "I have to do my exercises" or "Who's bothering me?"

I screamed at the producers to cue the Thelma Houston track, and I dragged Dick Van Dyke onstage to dance with me to kill time, which resulted in one of the most adorable moments of the evening. Immediately, a sea of cell phone cameras popped up as this room erupted in applause and appreciation. Everyone was commenting later on how sprightly Dick still looked and how game he was. It was inspiring and touching. Later, he went out to present to Bryan Cranston, and the way he lauded Bryan, you'd have thought Bryan was the legend and Dick was the admiring younger fan.

I just love how strolling down memory lane isn't nearly as exciting to Dick Van Dyke as proclaiming, "I can't help it. I gotta disco dance!" Well, I'm not going to stop him. Although maybe someone needs to take the car keys away. Just a thought.

VANDERBILT, GLORIA
My Other Mom, Legit Pedigree

Anderson handed his phone to me one New Year's Eve and said, "It's my mom. She wants to say hi." That was a shocker. Suddenly, I was talking to the one and only Gloria Vanderbilt: famous heiress, fashion maven, artist, author, and onetime lover of Marlon Brando and Frank Sinatra. That deep, mon-eyed voice was like gold in my ear:

"Kathy, it's *Glor*-ria. I think you and *An*-derson are *hilarious*. I mean, the things you *say*. They're just *out there*. I just a-*dore* you and would *love* to meet you one day."

I said, "Wednesday?" (I don't dick around.)

That's what started our friendship, and I have to say, it's a genuine bond that doesn't include Anderson, because he is, frankly, traumatized by her. I like to think that Glo and I are the only two women who can get him curled up into a ball and pulling on his hair like he does when he's anxious. Anytime I bring up his mom around Anderson, he usually responds with a low "Auughh," muttered like an embarrassed twelve-year-old, followed with an exasperated, "She's so inappropriate."

He loves to tell the story about how he had to proofread his mother's romance memoir and balked at her description of one gentleman suitor as being "the Nijinsky of cunnilingus." Well, who wouldn't want their mom saying that?

She's invited me to countless dinner parties with authors and artists and thrown two in my honor, and they're glorious affairs, which I leave at the end of the night firmly believing the art of conversation isn't dead. (Anderson doesn't go to them, though. "Ugh, my dinner parties with my mother are long over, trust me!" Whatever, gurrl!)

The first time I visited her at her apartment, I said, "So where are the jeans?"

She said, "What are you talking about?"

I said, "I'm sure you have the jeans, at least one in every color."

She had to think about it and then said, "No, I don't think I do."

How about that? She doesn't live in the past, that Glo. And yet my bucket list includes buying a pair on eBay and sending them to her so she can make a dream box. Let me explain, you pervert. Gloria puts together a plexiglass work of art that can be either a wall-mounted piece or a freestanding structure. She puts together various items that bring together a theme inside these boxes. When she created one for me, she asked me to send her all of my mementos (hand-printed menu, dinner plate, invite, etc.) from my evenings with the royals and Joan Rivers in England.

I knew we were going to be close the first time I went to one of her dinners. I was nervous about not being up enough on literature and art for the other guests, and though I tried to do my homework, I felt a little like I was barely keeping my head above water. But then Glo turned to me and said in that erotically husky way of hers, "*Kathy*, what is going *on* with the *Lo*-hans?" Now that's a host: giving each of her guests a chance to shine with his or her particular specialty. (Even *New York Times* theater critic Ben Brantley got giddy at the topic, adding, "What do you really think of Dina?")

She's the epitome of unforced elegance in her blunt-cut bangs and casual chic. You look at a choker she'll be wearing and think, *I bet Lagerfeld gave her that*. She's always been incredibly gracious whenever she's given me her time, and she's given me invaluable advice. Asked the secret of youth, she answered, "Curiosity. If you're always curious, that's the fountain of youth. You will never feel old." Another time, we'd been talking about the benchmarks of her life, from the sculpting and painting to her fashion line to the novels and memoirs and all those men—she had a wild sexual encounter with Brando in a cloakroom and had an affair with Howard Hughes!—and I said something like, "How do you keep going?" She said, "Well, there's *ALWAYS* more, and you're *NEVER* done." She said it almost as if I'd asked a silly question. I loved that. And I try to live it.

And by the way, she slept with hot Brando, not fat Brando.

WALTERS, BARBARA
Newswoman, Groundbreaker, Killer Shark

I have two versions of Barbara Walters in my mind. You get to decide which one is real and which one is fantasy because God knows I can't tell anymore.

I have a genuine and warm fondness for her. My favorite quote of hers is when one time I complimented her on her hair, and she said to me, "Female newscasters don't get older, they get blonder."

I have spent a lot of time around her. I love to try to make her laugh. She's a tough cookie because she's had to be. In fact, in her final couple of years on *The View*, you may recall, she wouldn't be on the panel every day, so I would tell the producers that I would only be on the show if it was a "Barbara day." In fact, I am such a scholar of Barbara's that even in this entry of this book, I am clearly buttering all of you up—including you, Barbara—before I go in for the kill.

I always assumed that when Diane Sawyer got her big TV interview with Caitlyn Jenner, Barbara Walters was holed up in the dark in her Doris Duke apartment with a feather boa eye mask, eating a gallon of ice cream. That's because Barbara still has the eye of the tiger when it comes to competitiveness in the news business. She broke all the barriers. It's ingrained in her. I'll always love her for that, even though she hates me.

I can hear her now. Whenever I greet her with "Remember me? You've loathed me for years as I have loved you every

moment!" she replies, in that cool broadcaster tone of hers, "Why do you do this evwy time, Kathy? You have this powtwayal of me as if we don't get along! I think you're a-dow-able. I always have. Is this Wandy?"

Oh yes, she flirts with Randy, and she'll go so far as to take his hand in both of hers, which I assume is some old-school girl's way of slipping a boy her number. (I make "Wandy" empty his pockets every time, because I'm pretty sure she slipped him a little note with her secured landline phone number on it.) She also brings her voice down to a supple coo when her eye is on *my* tiger: "Where did you get that wondawful suit, Wandy? You know you have the build fow a suit like that." I've said to her on more than one occasion, "Back off, bitch. He's not Mort Zuckerman. Don't make me pop off!" She ignores me and keeps going. That's our current shtick.

I've known Barbara a long time now, and teasing her never gets old. She hates it when I follow her into the bathroom at *The View*, which is a series of stalls open to everyone. One time, she was leaving early when we still had one more show to tape. She said it was for an Oscar de la Renta fashion show, but I accused her of trying to get away from me. I banged on her stall: "I'm still here! Why are you leaving!" You could see her dress around her ankles.

She yelled back, "It's Oscuh's show! I have to go!"

I said, "I don't believe you! You think this is my first merry-go-round with you, lady? I'm checking online later to see if you were really there!"

She said, "Go ahead! You will see me! In the fwont wow! He's an owld fwend!"

Based on the fact that one of the high-level producers rushed into the ladies' room to rescue Barbara, I can almost imagine several staffers were standing in the hall outside sure that they were listening to an old-timey catfight. When I replay this scene in my head, it's eerily similar to the bathroom scene in *Valley of the Dolls*. (I admit I do go back and forth on which of us gets to be Neely O'Hara and Helen Lawson. Please submit your answers to www.KathyGriffin.com.)

WILLIAMS, BILLY DEE
Malt Liquor Lovah, Actor, Secret Tailor

Who knew that there is a fabric store in Los Angeles called International Silks & Woolens (and no, I'm not a paid spokesperson) where one can happen upon a coterie of celebrities on any given day?

I was in the store filming a scene for *The D-List* in early 2010 with Lauren Conrad, and the gag revolved around *The Hills* star showing me how to build a clothing empire. My director, Blake Webster, had seen someone who clearly brought out his heterosexual geek boy when he squealed in delight,

"Holy shit, you're not going to believe this, but Lando Calrissian is here!"

"Who?"

"Billy Dee Williams!"

"You mean Brian Walker from *Mahogany*? The man who gave Tracy Chambers, beautifully played by MISS Diana Ross, a run for her money until she realized her money was no good without the true love that only Brian Walker could give her? That Billy Dee Williams?? Oh, and *Dynasty*???" (Sorry, space nerds, my references are better.)

Of course, LC didn't know who he was. But he walked over, and honestly, it was like a wondrous vision of old-school dapper: perfectly coiffed, wavy hair, sporting a casual suit, and anchored by a full-on lamé scarf, very sparkly and with fringe, wrapped around his neck. If he'd had a can of Colt 45 in his hand, I might have been forgiven for thinking I'd stepped inside a television set circa 1977. If he'd been wearing a cape, too—and he's rocked capes before—I might have fainted right then and there. LC probably thought some older gentleman had followed me in the store, but I knew better: this was suave, smooth, sex royalty of the "they don't make 'em like that anymore" variety.

Then Billy Dee opened his mouth, and that champagne baritone turned a fabric shop into a seduction chamber: "Well, hell-ooooo, young lady. What a treat it is to see such a humorous woman in person. May I have the pleasure of shaking your hand?"

I looked around for the velvet-flocked wallpaper and round bed. Were the lights dimming? Is that Barry White song just in my head? Of course, then Blake had to come up to me and say Billy Dee wouldn't sign a release to be in the episode. Win some, lose some. I guess I didn't win this charmer over this time.

Once we all caught our breaths, we were ready to get back to work, and then, wait for it, Helen "Academy Award Winner" Mirren strode in! Yes, I know Helen Mirren. In fact, I met her in a quite fabulous way. She approached me at the primetime Emmy Awards and volunteered that she thought *My Life on the D-List* was hilarious. How 'bout that?

"Hey, Kathy!"

"Hi, Helen!"

She had on a skirt and blouse and was scanning the aisles like she knew the place. (I'll bet she sews her own clothes and they're fabulous.) Helen asked how my mother was.

"I find her so amusing," she said—and I said, "Great. We're filming *The D-List* today."

"You know, I love that show."

Okay, then. Maybe Helen will be on it! I asked her to sign a release so we could put her in the episode, and she said, "I'm so sorry, dear. I don't have any makeup on, or my hair done. But it was great to see you!"

"Hey, guess who's here, two aisles over? Billy Dee Williams!"

"Noooo! Realllly?"

"Yes! It's like some crazy celebrity food court!"

After our exchange, I went over to LC.

She said, "I know that old lady."

I felt like I was staring at a blank page before me. The rest is still unwritten.

XTINA (AGUILERA, CHRISTINA)

Dirrrty Burlesque, Genie Voice Singer

With certain divas, time is also a powerful decongestant.

When I met the enormously talented Christina, who was in her first flush of "Genie in a Bottle" stardom, I was hosting the Billboard Awards at the MGM Grand in Las Vegas, and she was, frankly, young and ridiculous. At a primetime awards show like the Billboards back in the day, there were so many stars, backup dancers, and posses that shuttles were needed to ferry everyone between the MGM Grand and their hotels, so no matter how big you were—and I was the damn host—at some point you were probably on that shuttle and sitting next to a Backstreet Boy or a Lisa Loeb. Well, one time, I was on that bus when Christina boarded. She'd just finished her sound check, and I'll never forget her charging the entire length of that shuttle down the center aisle like it was an effing Naomi Campbell catwalk. Nobody said a word, so I couldn't resist an opportunity to try to get the people around me to crack up. So I shouted, "It's a *bus*, honey!" She just looked at me with a withering sneer that said, "Ugh, is it *talking*?" She probably had no idea who I was. That's fine. I thought it was funny.

Over ten years later, we had a similarly funny exchange that indicated how much she'd grown. One was at a Grammy nomination announcement event. CBS turns these into full-on televised concerts with a red carpet and everything, so fans can see their favorite singers perform and also find out who got nominated. I was doing the red carpet, and knowing I would run into Christina—who I'd seen off and on over the years—I did my homework and filed away in my brain that her son's name was Max. When we had our exchange, there was none of that artifice from when she was a teenager. She was a working-stiff pop icon, a star, a diva, but with a much more mellow "been there done that" vibe.

I said, "Hi, Christina. Good to see you."

"Hi, Kathy. Good to see you, too."

I said, "I'm really hoping I get nominated for Best Comedy Album. Fingers crossed."

"Oh, I hope you do! I'm pulling for you."

"How's Max?"

"Good."

Pause.

She said, "You don't really care about my kid, do you?"

"No," I said. "I just looked it up before I got here."

And she . . . laughed! The look on her face was priceless. That bus sneer had transformed over the years into a knowing, between-us smirk. And it was really sort of touching. She realized that now that she's a mom and a household name and a music fixture, she can laugh at the funny redhead because she's got nothing to lose. I think when you're young and going places, you must believe you have to keep the act up every second. The real stars know how to turn that diva thing into a talent that excites the atmosphere rather than poisons it or makes it absurd.

My shtick with her now when I see her at a dinner party or nonperformance event is to say, "Here's the thing. I don't want you to sing. No one here does. But if you feel like you have to trot out 'Genie in a Bottle,' I'll give you a pity clap," and she just laughs.

XXX ADULT STAR JEREMY, RON

Human Plow, Dear, Dear Friend

I first met porn legend Ron Jeremy in the '90s on a public access show called *Colin's Sleazy Friends*, which featured a comedian (Colin Malone) interviewing porn stars, with the occasional comedian guest on hand, too. (Margaret Cho and Janeane Garofalo appeared on it.) During my appearance, I tried to change Ron's mind about his entire industry—which I refuse to believe is an "elective" one for the women involved— and it obviously didn't work. Ron probably had a shoot later that day, for all I know. I was tough on him. Tougher than any vagina had ever been.

I said things like, "So, how many times have you had to stop filming because one of your female costars, who is probably an incest survivor with a tragic childhood beyond anything you can imagine, you filthy pig, has broken down into tears and couldn't stop crying? A lot, I'll bet. I'll bet that happens a lot, doesn't it, Ron? But you don't think about that part. These young women are human beings. You will never convince me that these women have won in life in any way or that they make more than their male counterparts and therefore they are the ones in charge." Once again, I was behaving perfectly appropriately for a comically driven public-access talk show.

I noticed Ron had to catch his breath in that "we've got a live one here" way. But the way he bit back at my criticism told me that Ron is at heart a frustrated comedian, even if he tells the hokiest, Henny Youngman–like one-liners and does his own rim shots. Trust me, Ron has at least twenty of these rim shot jokes he can insert here. Oh God, he probably has twenty more "insert" jokes as well.

The point is he loves the funny, he's very nice, and because of that, believe it or not, we hit it off. We've hung out many times since and have appeared in a Foo Fighters video together, and I've always enjoyed his company. And let me just add, while it's hard to believe any woman ever let him and his penis near her, Ron remains maybe the most recognized celebrity I've ever appeared with in public. *Everybody* knows him.

Except my dad.

One year, I put out the word to friends that I was hosting an orphan Thanksgiving, and Ron said he'd love to come over. He brought one of his lady friends from "work," who sported emo makeup, a biker jacket, and a vibe that told me voting was a very recently acquired right. He also brought Dennis Hof, the bald bordello mogul from HBO's *Cathouse*. (He's the one who recently had to deal with Lamar Odom in a way Khloé Kardashian never has.) It was a real mix of civilians and celebrities, which I like, even if Ron was pushing it with his plus ones.

At a certain point, the gregarious John Griffin was carving off a piece of turkey when I said, "Dad, this is my friend Ron."

My father innocently said, "Ron, what line of work are you in?"

Ron said, "I do films."

Dad replied, "That's terrific. How long have you been doing films?"

Ron said, "As a matter of fact, I've done over two thousand films."

My dad gave back a "Good for you. That's quite an impressive body of work in a very competitive industry. Have you ever attended one of those large film festivals such as Cannes or Sundance?"

Ron really knew how to play this game. "Oh yes, Mr. Griffin. I have attended several film festivals."

And then I pivoted and just turned to another guest, and 'til the day my father died, he thought Ron was my friend in the film industry, which, by the way, is true.

YANKOVIC, "WEIRD AL"
Parodist, Accordionist, Great Perm

I have great respect for guys who not only stay in their lane, but also keep rolling strikes. Weird Al is kinda like that. I'm not limiting him; I'm trying to say he has carved out a very successful niche for himself in the worlds of comedy and music. The look's mostly the same (save the missing mustache and glasses from the '80s days), the parodies keep coming, and then he puts out an album in 2014 that becomes the first comedy album to hit #1 on the Billboard charts since the 1960s. Then he wins a Grammy for it. (He has four, and he's been nominated countless times over the years.) That's somebody who's built a brand and maintained it with care. I find it especially funny that he's outlasted some of the artists he's parodied. I'm looking at you: Gerardo, Tiffany, and El DeBarge.

He's also incredibly nice. We were once both Grammy-nominated the same year, and at the ceremony, he told me, "I swear, I want you to win. I've already won." Nobody ever says that. He's also one of those funny guys who exudes sweetness and isn't secretly tortured inside, and believe me, he's been through some heavy stuff. One thing that always stuck with me was something you may not be aware of.

This man has suffered real tragedy. In 2004, his parents were found dead in their home, the victims of accidental carbon monoxide poisoning from their fireplace. Several hours after his wife notified him of his parents' death, Yankovic went on with his concert in Appleton, Wisconsin, saying that "since my music had helped many of my fans through tough times, maybe it would work for me as well" and that it would "at least . . . give me a break from sobbing all the time."

Some of you may know that I, too, took to the stage very soon after my father's passing for the very same reason. A lot of comics probably look at him with a sense that what he's doing is in some specialized corner that isn't really connected to them, but when I think about the time and effort it takes to pick the right songs to parody, then get the permission from the artist—he doesn't have to under "fair use" laws, but he does, to maintain good relationships in the music world—and then find the right tone in riffing on it, I think he's got to be one of the smartest entertainers out there. His family Christmas cards are so classically silly and yet somehow heartfelt that they put the easiest smile on my face (i.e., an oversized photo of his dog looking at a tiny snow globe with the Yankovics floating around merrily. C'mon, you fucking cynics, admit it—that's adorable!).

Maybe I feel a kinship with him because our humor involves what celebrities do—in his case, their art; and in my case, their behavioral patterns. When a Michael Jackson or a Madonna claims they find the parody funny—Lady Gaga called it a "rite of passage" to be spoofed by Weird Al when he did "Perform This Way"—it's probably as gratifying for him as when the people I make fun of turn out to be good sports about it. To me, comedy needs the Weird Als to help us all remember that everyone needs to lighten up. I use profanity, he uses polka, but we're in the same racket.

ZELLWEGER, RENÉE
Academy Award Winner, a Friendship Evolution, Bridget Jones

Lay off my pal Renée Zellweger! You heard me. Okay, you may know that in the past, I may have referred to her as a sweaty, puffy coke whore, and after that, she sent me flowers with a card that simply said, "Best Wishes." But that doesn't mean we aren't friends now, you weirdo. Enough time has passed so that she actually laughs at my jokes, we talk on the phone, and she even lets me call her Bridget, even though I think her actual name is still Renée. Don't you get it yet, people? In my act, I'm a celebrity flip-flopper. One day I'm making fun of the best and brightest, then I change my mind. This happens all the time.

I've always been a fan of Renée's work, and when I saw a paparazzi photo of her sitting in an airport reading a Jimmy Carter book, I thought maybe I could fall in love with her. Another time she was on Oprah, blushing over a story Hugh Grant was telling about her and Jack White, and then a weird feeling in me emerged. Was I developing . . . *protective feelings* . . . for Zellweger?

Then, a few years ago, I was scheduled to participate in a children's charity event in San Francisco—a great group

called the Painted Turtle—and they told me, "You're sharing a dressing room with Annette Bening, Amber Riley, and Renée Zellweger."

I gulped back, "Um, what was that last name?"

I had ample time to prepare for our dressing room hello, and yet I was a little intrigued, since this was weeks after a super unflattering photo of Zellweger had gotten out that appeared to show a changed face. As someone who's a bit of an expert at "changed faces," I wanted to take a good, hard look at her. Well, the moment arrived, I walked in, looked right at her and thought, *She's gorgeous.* In fact, she did not resemble that unflattering photo that had been making the rounds online at all. She didn't just look beautiful (and you know I wouldn't say this lightly), she actually looked like she hadn't had any work done at all. Go figure.

After spending the day with her, I quickly realized she's super smart and a great laugher, and she seemed to understand I'm just a comic doing my job. That was probably helped when I told her, "Look, I'm not guaranteeing you'll ever be out of my act because we're buds now, but you have to take it because I'm just a comic doing my job!" (Sometimes you have to be very literal with these A-listers.)

We've become texting buddies and talk on the phone occasionally. I'm proud of this because it's rare that someone I have given a hard time to in my act gets beyond it. I was especially excited one night when in the middle of a live performance I happened to bring my real phone onstage with me for a bit, and during the show, I got a voice mail from my new bestie, Academy Award winner Renée Zellweger! Without even screening it, I put it on speaker, held the phone up to the microphone, and told the audience we should all listen to this voice mail from Bridget Jones together. This was my moment to prove to thousands of audience members that I am such a pro that I am able to walk the high wire to furiously make fun of whomever I like and yet still garner the love and friendship of those very people. God love Renée. Not only was her message to me hilarious but—and this is why she has awards—she even delivered it in a Meryl Streep–level thick Russian accent. The audience roared with laughter when they heard Renée playing a character saying, "Hello? Um . . . I know who are you. You keep text meee an then I theenk you got wronk number. PLEEZE don't call diz number 'gain an don't text me pleeze. Okay? Thank you, and God bless you. Bye." Is she a riot or what? I must have played this voice mail for at least my next seven live shows in a row before I finally had a chance to get her on the phone and thank her.

Days later, my assistant, John, handed me his work phone and told me Renée was on the line. I congratulated her on figuring out a new and exciting way to get into my act without me making fun of her at all. She was giggling. I told her that was no small feat. I asked her what it felt like to be in my act, knowing that voice mail gets uproarious laughter show after show, and yet I don't have to say one single negative thing about her. She laughed again. She then informed me that the voice mail was NOT from her.

Um, what?

This whole time I thought I had been texting and leaving messages for my new friend Bridget. It turns out my assistant had her proper number, and they had been communicating while I had been reaching out to some poor woman who probably just escaped the oppression of an Eastern Bloc dictatorship. I'm not kidding; I did my hilarious in-character voice mail from the supposedly real live Bridget Jones bit for thousands of people. Maybe tens of thousands. Naturally, I immediately blamed Zellweger. She laughed so hard I knew deep down inside she had realized there was a little karmic payback at work.

"I wish I was that committed, to come up with a character and call you like that," she said. "But I think you should keep playing it, and I'll even play along. I love it." And so you should, Bridget.

ZEVON, WARREN
Musician, Werewolf of London, Excitable Boy

In 1999, singer/songwriter Warren Zevon was a guest star on *Suddenly Susan* for an episode, playing himself, alongside fellow guest star Rick Springfield, and it was weird and wonderful and inspiring. (By the way, my beloved millennial assistant, John, admitted he didn't know who Warren Zevon was, so if you need a sec to Google him, go ahead, I'll wait.) This was three years before he was diagnosed with the cancer that very quickly took his life, and his diagnosis led to a special hour-long David Letterman show on which he was the only guest, which made for a shattering public good-bye to everyone.

What I remember from his time on *Susan* was that he was one of the rare musical icons who was naturally funny. He brought his guitar to the set every day. I remember during a break in rehearsal, watching him sitting on one of the sofas singing, "Lawyers, Guns and Money." His sense of humor was incredibly wry, and I thought, *I want to hang in this guy's orbit as long as I possibly can.* I think he just took the gig for fun, because he didn't seem to know Brooke Shields (or Rick Springfield, for that matter), and it wasn't as if he was some professed fan of workplace sitcoms starring Calvin Klein models. He might have thought it was a new experience worth checking out. I also wondered if this was one of those situations where four other more well-known musicians turned down the gig, and then we luckily ended up with somebody truly great, instead of somebody just famous. It did lend a strangeness to his scenes, because his humor was delightfully dry, and though he delivered his lines with professionalism and superb timing, I also detected in his respectfulness a belief that he was in a comedic environment not entirely in his wheelhouse. During the tapings, he joked around with the audience between takes, which I'm sure for the 10 percent of them that knew who he was and loved him, it was an experience they'll remember for the rest of their lives.

A lot of musicians don't bring the guitar, don't want to sing the song, don't want to be bothered, but he was really the perfect guest—did the work, made friends, wasn't demanding, made us laugh—and it taught me a lesson. On *Suddenly Susan*, I was incredibly happy to have that job, and yet I knew that on Saturday night, I could go to a theater somewhere and really say what I wanted to say completely uncensored. I felt as if Warren Zevon was in that frame of mind. Instead of acting like he had better things to do or complaining that nobody got him, his vibe was, "Life's short. Let's do something really off the grid and be silly and have fun." Considering the incredible grace and dignity and artistry he brought to living the last year of his life, it's a memory I'll always cherish. Keep him in your heart for a while.

Afterword

Now that I've walked you through my various and sundry celebrity run-ins, I would like to give you some handy and helpful tips on how to deal with a celebrity run-in of your own. At some point in your life, no matter who you are, you will run into a Kardashian.

That's just science. Let's use their family and extended family—children, husbands, lovers, men who may or may not have the Kardashian curse, someone who is Kim-like or Khloé-ish, whoever is Scott Disick–esque in your world—as an example. The following are guidelines for such an encounter.

CONSIDER YOUR SURROUNDINGS

You see Kourtney, but she's eating. Which she doesn't, so that's not a good example. Let's go with Rob. He's almost certainly going to be eating. I know that when I'm midbite, and somebody approaches with "I never do this . . . ," it's picture time. But Rob should be allowed to finish eating, because otherwise you might lose a good finger. Nevertheless, it's trickier to have a quality encounter when the celebrity is eating. A Kardashian walking down the street is a better scenario because it's public, and you're probably the tenth person who's approached them that day, anyway. If you see Kourtney shopping, just know you're bothering her doing what she considers her full-time job, so be considerate.

DON'T STARE

You'll be tempted. It's a Kardashian, or somebody Kardashian-adjacent. They're beautiful. You're going to want to look them right in the face, or faces, as seems to be the case with young Kylie. We may reach a point in surgical technology where their faces or at least their lips start to morph right in front of you. But try to avoid this. I have a look-and-blink-away system. Or should that be Look-and-Blink-Away System, since I plan on trademarking it. It involves a quick glance and then a blink with a head pivot to the left, as if you have something more important to look at, even though you have nothing more important to look at. This move should be quick and decisive. Practice it at home with one of your pets, although your pet may think you've gone mad.

PICTURE VERSUS MENTAL PICTURE?

We live in a world where the phone is already out, and mental capabilities are way, way down. We live in a camera-first, communication-second society. No coven exemplifies this more than the United Church of Kardashian. Luckily for you, one of them will be Snapchatting before you even approach them. In fact, Kim will have already Snapchatted Candle to tell her that a stranger is approaching and that all smartphones should be on a high-filter alert. (Although for the Kardashians, the compound word *smartphone* might be a contradiction. They probably call them *fame devices*.) So they'll be ready for you, and you may not even have to ask for a photo. Look for a Kardashian to already be posing: duck face, skin-case light bar on, heavenward glance. That's the sign to get the photo.

DO I SAY ANYTHING?

It's happened. There they are, Northwest and Saint, right in front of you. You'll want to gush. They have been on your bucket list for days. And here they are, trippin' in Daddy's clown-sized Yeezys, rockin' Auntie Kylie's matte liquid lipstick and lip liner, and Rob's Fuck Off socks. (No, seriously, he sells socks that say FUCK on one, and OFF on the other.) What do you do? You'll want to gush. Or you'll see Blac Chyna and want to yell, "Blac! Chyna!" which will sound racist. Now is not the time to panic. In fact, I've never met a celebrity who does not respond to the opening line, "Congratulations." Try it. It takes four seconds for them to come up with the reason they're being congratulated, and they're instantly in a good mood. Saint will be smiling because he's just made his first doody in a toilet, and Northwest will have just shot her first *Forbes* cover. If it's Khloé, she'll assume you mean the solid ratings for her new children's show, *Khloé Kan't Kount*, or as the kids call it, *KKK*. So keep that in your pocket, saying, "Congratulations." They'll instinctively say, "Thank you," and pow, you're in the middle of a typical showbiz conversation.

EXIT STRATEGY

The last thing you want is for your hero Caitlyn to think you're a weirdo, so how you end the encounter is extremely important. Don't goose them. (Caitlyn will pick you up and throw you like a javelin.) Don't pretend you're suddenly best friends and invite them to lunch (especially Rob). The best thing to do, after you've secured your photo or hug or post-"Congratulations" thank-you, is to smile and walk away.

Maybe a passing "I love your new line, Mason." With that simple blind affirmation, you will be able to exit this encounter smoothly, knowing in your heart that you've successfully nourished their egos and given them a reason to live.

There's really only one rule to any celebrity run-in you have: don't follow my example. Have you learned nothing from this book? I screwed up most of the time. My mistakes are there to educate you as you go about your lives, knowing that statistics dictate you'll run into 2.73 Kardashians a year. (That number will grow.) Do as I say, not as I do. Celebrities everywhere will thank you.

AUTHOR QUESTIONNAIRE

Q: Where does the word *celebrity* come from?
A: It comes from the Roman word *celebritas*, which first appeared in the ancient text *MaximUS Weekly*.

Q: You describe these experiences as run-ins. Have you ever literally run into a celebrity?
A: I've never actually collided physically with Justin Bieber, but he knows I'm interested in sitting on his face.

Q: Is there a celebrity you haven't met yet that you'd like to?
A: Former president Jimmy Carter. I think he's afraid I'm going to ask to sit on his face, which I would never do because I love and worship him.

Q: If you could be any celebrity for a day, who would it be?
A: Justin Bieber, the day Kathy Griffin sits on his face, which is admittedly a way of saying I want to have sex with myself. Actually, I've always wondered what it would have been like to be Ryan Seacrest before he passed away tragically at the hands of Oprah Winfrey. If he's still alive as of publication, then I rescind this.

Q: The encounters in this book come with names attached. Tell us a celebrity run-in where you're afraid to name who it is.

A: I'm almost positive a certain beloved daytime talk show host once had me kicked out of the backstage dressing room at the Emmy Awards. I can't prove it, but this person, who has short blond hair, has a mean streak that all of Hollywood knows about.

Q: Most of the arts are covered here, plus news, sports, and politics. You don't have any names from religion, though. Are you just not meeting enough priests?
A: I'm sure not. I will certainly troll some Catholic day care centers for the sequel to this book. That's where the priests are.

Q: Will people be surprised to learn that you slept with O. J. Simpson?
A: Um, we cut that story, remember?

Q: Oh yeah. Sorry. Whose run-in was just too boring to be included in this book?
A: I met that dude from *Hamilton*, Lin Carmen Miranda or whatever. What's the big fuss? I saw the play, by the way, and it turns out Hamilton isn't even alive anymore.

Q: Lauren Bacall once said, "Stardom isn't a profession; it's an accident." Do you agree?
A: The only accident I'm aware of is the one my beloved mother might have in her diaper after she reads this book. I may be strapping on a diaper myself soon.

Q: When somebody famous becomes even more famous after you meet him or her, do you see a connection?
A: Clearly. Thank God somebody finally brought that up. Let's face it, Aaron Paul is one, if you bothered to read this book. But

also, I'm willing to take credit for Facebook. When I met Mark Zuckerberg, he was four hours old. I was visiting a friend in the hospital and peeked through the glass where they keep the newborns, our eyes locked, and I whispered, "Facebook." I'm still waiting for my check.

Q: What about if they die after you meet them?
A: Talk to my lawyer.

Q: What would a world without celebrities look like?
A: Your family.

Q: Why isn't your dog Larry in this book?
A: He's a little overweight, and as you've learned from this book, in the celebrity world, that gets you exiled faster than a DUI, a domestic, or first-degree murder, which no forward-thinking celebrity would ever do anyway.

Q: Did the A-to-Z format prove difficult? What letters did you struggle with?
A: All I can say is, thank God Christina Aguilera has also been called Xtina. *X* was a bitch. So was Xtina early on, but you'll have to read the entry to find out why. *Q* was tough, until I realized Richard Quest has many, how shall I say this, layers?

Q: Do you own a selfie stick?
A: There are four in my gift closet right now. I learn martial arts with them, because I see it as a self-defense weapon. If I see that self-righteous, übergloomy Lorde running at me with her smoky eyes and dark aura, I can fight her off with it. And then, of course, get a picture.

Q: Oscar Wilde famously said there was only one thing worse than being talked about, and that was not being talked about. Is that one way the people you write about should think about this book?

A: First off, I thought Olivia Wilde said that. (I just love her fashion sense.) But yes, celebrities in this book who might be upset should get a grip and realize that the minute they aren't the subject of other people's stories, they should worry. Are you sure it wasn't acclaimed child thespian and *H. R. Pufnstuf* star Jack Wild who said that?

Q: If Oprah had a celebrity run-ins book, would you make the cut?

A: The only celebrity Oprah runs into has a name that rhymes with Dayle Ding. And where Oprah runs is into her arms. I don't judge.

Q: Which entry was the hardest to write about?

A: In all seriousness, I've never told my Night Stalker story before. He is not a celebrity in any positive way, but that case was so well known, and my participation in it is something that has been nothing but an embarrassment up till now. When I say I was glad to get out of that one alive, I mean it.

Q: Who didn't make the cut who should be grateful?

A: Neil Patrick Harris.

Q: Is it better to run into a celebrity at a swanky gala event or out and about during the day?

A: Swanky gala, for sure. Because they have nowhere to run. The women will be in high heels and uncomfortable dresses. Not optimal escape attire. As for the men, even if they have bodyguards, it's unbecoming to openly tackle a five-foot-three, 110-pound redhead who is gesticulating wildly and is drop-dead gorgeous.

Q: Have you ever met Kathy Griffin? I mean, really, really met Kathy Griffin?
A: You know what? I've been to paradise, but I've never been to me.

• AN OPEN APOLOGY FROM KATHY GRIFFIN •

Dear Reader:

I'm afraid this section is not for you.

Love and best wishes,
Kathy Griffin

Dear Celebrities Who Are Pissed Off They Are Not in This Book but Won't Admit It:

It's a brutal business. It's not that I don't love you. It's that I'm no longer IN love with you. I still want to be friends. We loved your reading but decided to go with someone younger and thinner, or crazier. Maybe you're not in this book because you're famous but a little boring. Have you ever thought about that? You might want to up your game. I'll be taking meetings for the follow-up over the next few months. Please schedule with my office. Know that my entire staff is LGBTQIA2. (And let's be honest, the 2s can be moody. Take that into consideration.)

I'll need a cover letter, portfolio, and sperm sample. I expect you to be off book and wait for "Action." Nudity is accepted.

Men, a word about the casting couch: this simple and time-tried audition process has really gotten a bad rap. Not if but when Drake begs to be considered for the sequel to this book, I suggest he make his best pitch wearing only a carefully placed sock.

Ladies, good news: I can be bought lock, stock, and barrel. Again, not if but when Rihanna pleads to be in the next installment, I think a G6 to the Bahamas for some gal time and R&R should do the trick. By R&R, I mean "Rihanna Rewards."

You'll notice this wasn't an apology. I don't do that. Suck it up, people. That's why you love me, remember?

Love and best wishes,
Kathy Griffin

ALTERNATE TITLES FOR THIS BOOK THE PUBLISHER THOUGHT WERE INAPPROPRIATE

Kathy Griffin's Celebrity Fuckfest
Official Book Club Erection
Kathy Griffin's Pulitzer Prize–Winning Book
What Are You Lookin' At?
I Know You Are, But What Am I?
The Bible
Killing Bill O'Reilly
The Girl Pulling the Train
A Queef History of Time
The Fart of the Deal
Poop: Gwyneth Paltrow's Goop Made Easy

All these suggestions were far too cerebral for the editors at Flatiron Books, their parent company, Macmillan, and all that they represent.

Acknowledgments

First and foremost, I would like to thank the good lord Jesus Christ almighty. From what I hear, she is all powerful, and I felt her presence throughout this journey. You too, Allah, Joseph Smith, Brigham Young, Buddha, Vishnu, Xenu, David, and probably Deepak Chopra.

Okay, now that I've secured a spot for myself in heaven I can move on to the real acknowledgments.

It's time to thank the people I lovingly call the counsel. I make no major decisions regarding my career and life without consulting one, some, or all of them. They are (in no particular order): my beloved longtime attorney Bill Sobel, my tireless stand-up agent and friend Steve Levine, my William Morris team: Nancy Josephson, Justin Ongert, Richard Weitz, Ari Emmanuel, Ivo Fischer, and Mel Berger, my business manager and gurrl/confidant Barbara Karrol, my juggernaut publicist Cindi Berger, who gets me every time she yells the following statement at me: "YOU ARE A STALLION AND I AM GOING TO MAKE SURE THE ENTIRE INDUSTRY LETS YOU RUN LIKE THE CHAMPION YOU ARE," and, of course, Suze Orman, who to this day lets me know if I am approved or denied for any major financial decision.

My friend and collaborator Robert Abele helped me tremendously with this book.

For Randy, the Jay-Z to my Beyoncé. And if you've seen him in person, the resemblance is uncanny. Thank you for asking me out five years ago at "Burgers and Beer Night" at the LA Times: The Taste food festival.

To my beloved assistant, John Oliveira, who by the way gave his notice two days before I wrote this, so he is going under the bus right now. Yes, John has been a Team Griffin member for five years but noooooooooooo, apparently working for me isn't gay or fabulous enough so like every gay man that I have loved he is choosing to abandon me even though I am the recipient of HRC's Ally for Equality, GLAAD's Vanguard award, The Trevor Project's Life Award, a commemorative sword from the GAYVN Gay Porn Awards, and a White Party ICON Award. By the way, those last two aren't easy to get; ask Kim Zolciak.

I would like to thank my two Emmys and my Grammy: Emmy, Emily, and Sammi. Yes, they have names.

My therapy dogs, Larry and Pom Pom. They are therapy dogs because they are too old to do anything but lie at my feet and love me.

A special thanks to my editor, Amy Einhorn, and the rest of my Flatiron Books publishing team. While Amy gave me nothing but helpful and specific guidance, I cannot resist this opportunity to revive an e-mail I got from Amy's team before I started writing the book that makes me laugh to this day. In the initial stages when we were trying to agree upon who would make the cut as the lucky, lucky celebrities that would be featured in this book, I received suggestions from helpers deep in the bowels of the literary world for which celebrities I should include. They included: Spencer Tracy (I was six when he died), Judy Garland (died when I was eight), *Pretty Little Liars* girls, the Pope, Dwayne Reed, Eva Mendex, and Lindsay Logan. This gives me life.

I must thank every celebrity that I've had a run-in with, whether they are in this book or the next one.

If you're reading this because you purchased this book, I want to thank you most of all.

And finally, to the woman who taught me the art of the run-in from a very early age. In fact, I ran out of her womb and will run to get her a box of wine whenever she wants it— my mom and best friend, Maggie Griffin. Although she did remind me this week that, for reasons only known to her, she would prefer to be known as Deidre.

Index

Page numbers in *italics* refer to photographs.

DIAZ, CAMERON

Actress, Giraffe, "Fuck" in Any Game of Fuck Marry Kill

We both appeared on *The Graham Norton Show*, which is a popular British talk show, and before going onstage, we shared pleasantries. Cameron Diaz looks like a beautiful human giraffe. She happened to be dressed as one that day as well. She was wearing a skintight animal-print dress with a hemline that showed off all four of her legs. There was a pause in our conversation, and I thought, *Oh shit. She's been in the act. Here's where she lays into me.* But instead of defending herself, she said, "I just want you to know, all those things you say about my friend Gwyneth are not true! She's a really good friend of mine, and she's a really amazing mom, she's an amazing person, and I know you make fun of her, but I think you should know that I can say for a fact that she really is that amazing!"

Now, in my head I thought there were at least five ways this could go. Reader, can you guess which one I did?

A) Escalated the situation ("Oh yeah? Well, not only that, Paltrow's a sour pill on a good day!")

B) Lie ("I've never mentioned her once in my act!")

C) Cry and crumble

D) The non-denial pivot ("Oh, I just say those because I'm jealous and I wish I was her!")

E) The funny backpedal ("How can I make it up to her? Lifelong subscription to GOOP?")

Since we were about to go on the air, the only real option was D. As I stood next to this tall, leggy, blond model-turned-movie star, I admit I adjusted my approach. Cameron Diaz seemed like a perfectly nice person who was clearly just sticking up for her friend. After I told Cameron I was simply jealous and wished I could be Gwyneth Paltrow, she paused and said, "Okay, that's fair!"

PROBST, JEFF
Island Tyrant, Host / KG Victim / Friend

The guy has four Emmys for keeping those *Survivor* contestants in line, and they're well-deserved awards. He's a super nice guy, although when I first met him, I got a little bit of a cocky vibe. Cute, courteous, but cocky. This was probably the first season of *Survivor*—being on a hit show will puff your chest out, surely—and we were both doing a charity gig in Las Vegas. For some reason, I was obsessed with getting a better room than he had, all the time thinking, *Who is this guy? What does he really do? He lights a torch. He reads out rules. Well, tonight, that stops.*

We were on the same Southwest flight, and I said to him, "So where are you staying?"

He looked puzzled. "Aren't they just putting us up at Caesars?"

"I don't know. Where are they putting YOU?"

"I think Caesars."

I said, "Okay, then me, too. What kind of suite do you have?"

"I don't know," he answered.

I was like, "Really? You don't know what kind of suite you have? Don't you care?"

"I'm sure we'll find out when we get there."

When we checked in, I said, "I have to get a bigger suite than you."

"Why?"

I shot back, "I just do!" And I did. I mean, I'm such an ass-hole that I actually said to the poor front desk worker at Caesars, "Whatever it takes, I have to have a better suite than that CBS darling Jeff Probst!" Look, I can't explain these moments either. The entire front desk staff, as well as Probsty (as I call him), clearly thought I was crazy.

Years later, after we became friends, he and his wife Lisa came over for dinner, and we were laughing about that Vegas incident and telling old war stories. I was making fun of him and his multiple Emmys, and I said, "Do you want to see if mine is heavier because it was actually awarded to me based on talent?" He laughed, but then he picked up one of my precious two Emmys, and sure enough, the ball that the winged figure holds fell off! (The ball is supposed to represent an atom.) Everyone gasped, and I screamed, *"You broke my Emmy! You broke my Emmy!"* He was stricken. I immediately grabbed my phone and took pictures of him holding my busted award, which I immediately tweeted out with something like, "Dear world, @jeffprobst just broke my Emmy." Then I had to confess: I'd broken it long before that, and obviously, the glue hadn't completely mended it. But I enjoyed making him feel horrible for an hour or so. It's called being the perfect friend. He was even going to call the Television Academy for me and get it replaced. Oh, and of course I made him pose for a photo with my broken Emmy. The tribe has spoken.

WELCH, RAQUEL

Stunner, Actress, Doe-Skin Bikini Babe

Let me tell you a little story about my friend Rocky. Yeah, I call her Rocky. This one has all the bells and whistles, so buckle up.

Jane Fonda and her boyfriend Richard took me as their third wheel to a very fancy-schmancy black tie event in Beverly Hills. Take that part in for a second. It gets better.

After the event, Jane tells me we're going to the famed Polo Lounge for a drink. At our booth were Jane and Richard, Nigel Lythgoe, Alana Stewart, Raquel Welch, Raquel's date (whose name I do not recall), and myself. This is some Hollywood legend action going on here and I was never so happy to be a third wheel.

We settled in to our booth, and Nigel was teasing everybody with references to the old days. "Anybody have any coke?" he said. "Oh right, I forgot, we don't do that anymore." Everyone: "Ha ha ha ha ha . . ." It was that kind of rapport. I was the newbie, so I just sat back and listened for once. It was soon apparent that this was a cozy gang of longtime chums. Rocky looked absolutely ravishing in an eggplant-colored gown that magnificently showed off those famous curves. I probably teased her about the wig, though, because she's beautiful and I can. Also, she's made a fortune from her wig line and you know I respect a gal who knows how to make a buck. She's got a great sense of humor—she adored Joan Rivers, who probably made fun of her hot-hot-hotness repeatedly. A good time was being had by all. This was clearly a situation where these longtime pals wanted to come down after a high-profile event and chill out in a quiet setting. Everyone seemed relaxed, or so I thought.

An inebriated, middle-aged random dude aggressively approached the table. He looked like an extra from *Goodfellas*. This fan was saying things like, "I gotta tell yous, seeing yous all here is somethin'. I nevah thawght wud see here in Hollyweird (chuckle, chuckle)!" Obviously, these legends, in particular Jane and Raquel, have had a lot of experience dealing with this situation. I, for one, did not see trouble coming. You could sense he was overstaying his welcome, but I certainly wasn't going to be the one to say anything. Jane was gracious, saying, "Well, thank you very much," and Rocky offered a soft-spoken "Thank you, nice to meet you." Big deal, a fan is excited to see some celebrities and he's a little tipsy. Raquel Welch's boyfriend, however, had a reaction that caught everyone off guard. He decided this was the time to pick a fight . . . at the Polo Lounge . . . with classy gang. He raised his voice and said to the fan something like, "All right, buddy, that's enough." Uh oh, I thought. Here we are at one of the city's more prominent celebrity hangouts—with a legacy table of A-listers, including one producer (Nigel Lythgoe) who could buy and sell everyone there. Rocky's date seemed to think he could pull an alpha male move and save the day. If there's one thing celebrities don't want, it's unwanted attention *on top* of unwanted attention. The women said, "No, no, we're good." Good?! Actually things were just beginning to erupt. Raquel's date wouldn't let up. The fan wouldn't let up. It escalated to the point where the fan got louder because he was already tipsy, then Raquel's date got louder, and then the manager of the Polo Lounge himself came over. I panicked inside, convinced this would end up on the celebrity blogosphere (and not in a good way). The paparazzi were out in force that night. I caught a nervous look in Jane's eyes. As the restaurant staff ushered the loud fan out, he blurted, "Hey, you know what? SAURRY! I just wanted to say HELLOS!" Well, yous did.